THE FACTS ON FILE
ASIAN
POLITICAL
ALMANAC

THE FACTS ON FILE
ASIAN
POLITICAL
ALMANAC

Compiled by
Chris Cook

☑ Facts On File®

AN INFOBASE HOLDINGS COMPANY

THE FACTS ON FILE ASIAN POLITICAL ALMANAC

Facts On File, Inc.
460 Park Avenue South
New York NY 10016

Library of Congress Cataloging-in-Publication Data

Cook, Chris, 1945–
    The Facts on File Asian political almanac / compiled by Chris Cook.
        p. cm.
    Includes bibliographical references and index.
    ISBN 0-8160-2585-1
    1. Asia—Politics and government—1945– I. Facts on File, Inc.
    II. Title.   III. Title: Asian political almanac.
    DS35.2.C69   1994
    950.4′2—dc20   93-26319

Facts On File books are available at special discounts when purchased in
bulk quantities for businesses, associations, institutions or sales
promotions. Please call our Special Sales Department in New York at
212/683-2244 or 800/322-8755.

Text design by Ron Monteleone
Jacket design by F. C. Pusterla Design
Printed in the United States of America

KA MP 10 9 8 7 6 5 4 3 2 1

This book is printed on acid-free paper.

PREFACE AND ACKNOWLEDGMENTS

The primary aim of the *Asian Political Almanac* has been to assemble, within a single one-volume work of reference, as many of the key facts and figures as possible on the major political developments in Asia from 1945 to the present day. It is hoped that the information presented here on such topics as heads of state, constitutions, diplomacy and warfare, as well as elections and political parties, will provide the user with a rich quarry of material. This information, much of it presented in readily accessible tabular or statistical form, has been supplemented by biographical details of leading politicians and statesmen, a glossary of political terms, and convenient chronologies of key events.

Inevitably, no work of reference of this size can ever attempt to be comprehensive. Rather, the aim has been to concentrate on those countries and events for which the reader is most likely to require information.

Even as this book has been in preparation, Asia has seen enormous changes. It has been the aim of the *Asian Political Almanac* to attempt to record these changes in a continent likely to play an increasing role in the world of the 21st century. (For the purposes of this work, we have excluded the nations of the Middle East and the Persian Gulf and the former Soviet republics in the Caucasus and central Asia.)

The compilation of this volume was considerably facilitated by the generous assistance provided by a variety of friends and colleagues. For their help with research I am particularly indebted to Harry Harmer and James Robinson.

It is hoped that future editions of this book will update and expand the material presented here. Both author and publishers would welcome suggestions for new sections to be included in the second edition.

Finally, my grateful thanks are due to Susan Schwartz and Drew Silver of Facts On File for their encouragement of this new work of reference and for their hospitality in New York and London.

CONTENTS

CHAPTER 1

THE NATIONS OF ASIA: BASIC DATA

AFGHANISTAN

Name of State	Republic of Afghanistan
National Name	Jamhouri Afghanistan
Area	647,500 sq. km.
Current Population	16,600,000 (est. 1991)
Infant Mortality/1,000	182
Capital	Kabul
Monetary Unit	Afghani
Languages	Pushtu, Dari Persian
Religions	Islam (Sunni 74%, Shi'ite 25%)
Literacy Rate	12%
GDP	$3 billion
GDP per capita	$200

BANGLADESH

Name of State	People's Republic of Bangladesh
Area	143,998 sq. km.
Current Population	116,600,000 (est. 1991)
Infant Mortality/1,000	120
Capital	Dhaka
Monetary Unit	Taka
Languages	Bangla, English
Religions	Islam 83%, Hinduism 16%
Literacy Rate	29%
GDP	$20.6 billion
GDP per capita	$180

BHUTAN

Name of State	Kingdom of Bhutan
National Name	Druk-yul
Area	46,620 sq. km.
Current Population	700,000
Infant Mortality/1,000	142
Capital	Thimphu
Monetary Unit	Ngultrum
Language	Dzongkha
Religions	Buddhism 75%, Hinduism 25%
Literacy Rate	15%
GDP	$273 million
GDP per capita	$199

BRUNEI

Name of State	State of Brunei Darussalam
Area	5,765 sq. km.
Current Population	300,000
Infant Mortality/1,000	7
Capital	Bandar Seri Begawan
Monetary Unit	Brunei Dollar
Languages	Malay (official), Chinese, English
Religions	Islam (official, 60%), Christianity 8%, Buddhism 32%
Literacy Rate	45%
GDP	$3.3 billion
GDP per capita	$9,600

CAMBODIA

Name of State	Cambodia
Area	181,000 sq. km.
Current Population	7,100,000 (est. 1991)
Infant Mortality/1,000	125
Capital	Phnom Penh
Monetary Unit	Riel
Languages	Khmer (official), French
Religions	Theravada Buddhism
Literacy Rate	48%
GDP	$890 million
GDP per capita	$130

CHINA

Name of State	People's Republic of China
National Name	Zhongua Renmin Gongheguo
Area	9,561,000 sq. km.
Current Population	1,800,000,000 (1993)
Infant Mortality/1,000	33
Capital	Beijing
Monetary Unit	Yuan
Languages	Chinese (Mandarin and other local dialects)
Religions	Atheism officially proclaimed
Literacy Rate	76%
GDP	$350 billion
GDP per capita	$320

INDIA

Name of State	Republic of India
National Name	Bharat
Area	3,185,019 sq. km.
Current Population	859,200,000 (1991)
Infant Mortality/1,000	91
Capital	New Delhi
Monetary Unit	Rupee
Languages	Hindi and English (official), Bengali, Gujarati, Tamil, Telugu, Urdu; a total of 18 major languages and numerous minor languages and dialects
Religions	Hinduism 83%, Islam 12%, Christianity 2%, Sikhism 2%
Literacy Rate	36%
GDP	$333 billion
GDP per capita	$400

INDONESIA

Name of State	Republic of Indonesia
National Name	Republik Indonesia
Area	1,904,344 sq. km.
Current Population	181,400,000 (1991)
Infant Mortality/1,000	73
Capital	Jakarta

Monetary Unit	Rupiah
Languages	Bahasa Indonesia (official), Dutch, English, over 60 regional
Religions	Islam 88%, Christianity 9%, Hinduism 2%
Literacy Rate	62%
GDP	$80 billion
GDP per capita	$430

JAPAN

Name of State	Japan
National Name	Nippon
Area	377,815 sq. km.
Current Population	123,800,000 (est. 1991)
Infant Mortality/1,000	4.5
Capital	Tokyo
Monetary Unit	Yen
Languages	Japanese
Religions	Shintoism, Buddhism
Literacy Rate	99%
GDP	$2.92 trillion
GDP per capita	$23,730

LAOS

Name of State	Lao People's Democratic Republic
Area	236,800 sq. km.
Current Population	4,100,000 (est. 1991)
Infant Mortality/1,000	124
Capital	Vientiane
Monetary Unit	Kip
Languages	Lao (official), French, English
Religions	Buddhism 85%, animism and others
Literacy Rate	85%
GDP	$585 million
GDP per capita	$150

MALAYSIA

Name of State	Malaysia
Area	332,370 sq. km.
Current Population	18,300,000 (1991)

Infant Mortality/1,000   29
Capital   Kuala Lumpur
Monetary Unit   Ringgit
Languages   Malay (official), Chinese, Tamil, English
Religions   Islam, Buddhism (mainly Chinese), Hinduism
Literacy Rate   65%
GDP $37.9 billion
GDP per capita $2,270

MONGOLIA

Name of State   Mongolian People's Republic
National Name   Bugd Nairamdakh Mongol Ard Uls
Area   1,565,000 sq. km.
Current Population   2,200,000
Infant Mortality/1,000   64
Capital   Ulan Bator
Monetary Unit   Tugrik
Languages   Mongolian
Religions   Tibetan Buddhism; Islam 4%
Literacy Rate   90%
GDP $1.06 billion
GDP per capita $532

MYANMAR (BURMA)

Name of State   Union of Myanmar
National Name   Pyidaungsu Myanmar Naingngandau
Area   676,552 sq. km.
Current Population   42,112,082 (1991)
Infant Mortality/1,000   95
Capital   Yangon (Rangoon)
Monetary Unit   Kyat
Languages   Burmese (and minority languages)
Religions   Buddhism 85%, Islam, Christianity, and others
Literacy Rate   78%
GDP $11 billion
GDP per capita $280

NEPAL

Name of State   Kingdom of Nepal
Area   141,059 sq. km.

Current Population	19,600,000 (1991)
Infant Mortality/1,000	42
Capital	Katmandu
Monetary Unit	Nepalese Rupee
Languages	Nepali (official), Newari, Bhutia, Maithali
Religions	Hinduism 90%, Buddhism 5%, Islam 3%
Literacy Rate	20%
GDP	$2.9 billion
GDP per capita	$158

NORTH KOREA

Name of State	Democratic People's Republic of Korea
National Name	Choson Minjujuui Inmin Konghwaguk
Area	121,129 sq. km.
Current Population	21,800,000 (1991)
Infant Mortality/1,000	30
Capital	Pyongyang
Monetary Unit	Won
Languages	Korean
Religions	Atheism 68%, others 32%
Literacy Rate	95%
GDP	$28 billion
GDP per capita	$1,240

PAKISTAN

Name of State	Islamic Republic of Pakistan
Area	803,936 sq. km.
Current Population	117,500,000 (1991)
Infant Mortality/1,000	112
Capital	Islamabad
Monetary Unit	Pakistan Rupee
Languages	Urdu (national), English (official), Punjabi, Sindhi, Pashtu, Baluchi
Religions	Islam 97%
Literacy Rate	26%
GDP	$43.2 billion
GDP per capita	$409

PHILIPPINES

Name of State	Republic of the Philippines
National Name	Pilipinas
Area	300,000 sq. km.
Current Population	62,300,000 (1991)
Infant Mortality/1,000	54
Capital	Manila
Monetary Unit	Peso
Languages	Filipino (Tagalog), English, regional languages
Religions	Roman Catholicism 83%, Protestant Christianity 9%, Islam 3%, others 5%
Literacy Rate	88%
GDP	$40.5 billion
GDP per capita	$625

SINGAPORE

Name of State	Republic of Singapore
Area	570 sq. km.
Current Population	2,800,000 (1991)
Infant Mortality/1,000	6.6
Capital	Singapore
Monetary Unit	Singapore Dollar
Languages	Malay, Chinese (Mandarin), Tamil, English
Religions	Islam, Christianity, Buddhism, Hinduism
Literacy Rate	90%
GDP	$27.5 billion
GDP per capita	$10,300

SOUTH KOREA

Name of State	Republic of Korea
National Name	Taehan Min'guk
Area	98,500 sq. km.
Current Population	43,200,000 (1991)
Infant Mortality/1,000	23
Capital	Seoul
Monetary Unit	Won
Languages	Korean
Religions	Confucianism, Christianity 28%, Buddhism
Literacy Rate	91%

GDP	$200 billion
GDP per capita	$4,600

SRI LANKA

Name of State	Democratic Socialist Republic of Sri Lanka
Area	65,610 sq.km.
Current Population	17,400,000 (1991)
Infant Mortality/1,000	19.4
Capital	Sri Jayawardenepura Kotte (Colombo)
Monetary Unit	Sri Lanka Rupee
Languages	Sinhala, Tamil, English
Religions	Buddhism 69%, Hinduism 15%, Islam 8%, Christianity 8%
Literacy Rate	87%
GDP	$7 billion
GDP per capita	$416

TAIWAN

Name of State	Republic of China
Area	35,988 sq. km.
Current Population	20,500,000 (1991)
Infant Mortality/1,000	6.2
Capital	Taipei
Monetary Unit	New Taiwan Dollar
Languages	Chinese (Mandarin), Taiwanese, and other dialects
Religions	Buddhism, Confucianism, Taoism
Literacy Rate	94%
GDP	$161.7 billion
GDP per capita	$7,332

THAILAND

Name of State	Kingdom of Thailand
Area	514,000 sq. km.
Current Population	58,800,000 (1991)
Infant Mortality/1,000	39
Capital	Bangkok
Monetary Unit	Baht
Languages	Thai, Chinese, English

Religions	Buddhism 96%, Islam 4%
Literacy Rate	82%
GDP	$64.5 billion
GDP per capita	$1,160

VIETNAM

Name of State	Socialist Republic of Vietnam
National Name	Cộng Hoa Xa Hoi Chu Nghia Viet Nam
Area	329,566 sq. km.
Current Population	67,600,000 (1991)
Infant Mortality/1,000	44
Capital	Hanoi
Monetary Unit	Dong
Languages	Vietnamese (official), French, English, Khmer, Chinese
Religions	Buddism, Roman Catholicism, Islam, and others
Literacy Rate	78%
GDP	$14.2 billion
GDP per capita	$215

CHAPTER 2

CHRONOLOGY OF CONTEMPORARY ASIA SINCE 1945

1945

India
New Labor government in Britain announces that it seeks "an early realization of self-government in India." In Indian elections, Muslim League strengthens its hold on Muslim areas.

Indochina
Japanese disarm French forces and an "independent" Vietnam with Bao Dai as emperor is proclaimed (March). Japan surrenders (15 Aug); demonstrations in Hanoi spread throughout the country. Communist-dominated Viet Minh seize power; Ho Chi Minh declares Vietnam independent and founds Democratic Republic of Vietnam (2 Sept). French troops return to Vietnam and clash with Communist forces; Nationalist Chinese occupy Vietnam north of 16th Parallel (Sept).

Indonesia
Unilateral declaration of independence by Republic of Indonesia (17 Aug); Sukarno becomes president (13 Nov).

Japan
Atomic bombing of Hiroshima (6 Aug) and Nagasaki (9 Aug). Japan accepts terms of surrender (14 Aug). Authority passes to General Douglas MacArthur as Supreme Commander of the Allied Powers (SCAP).

Philippines
Liberation of the Philippines from Japanese occupation (5 July).

1946

Ceylon	Soulbury Constitution proposed. Sinhalese and Tamil to replace English as official language.
China	Civil war resumes between the Kuomintang and the Communists after a failed American attempt to mediate the conflict.
India	British offer full independence to India. Negotiations between British Cabinet Mission and Indian leaders fail to agree on a plan acceptable to both Congress and Muslim League. Muslim League declares "direct action" to achieve separate state of Pakistan. "Direct Action Day" (16 Aug) provokes massive communal rioting in Calcutta, leaving over 4,000 dead; spreads to Bengal, Dacca and Bihar. Lord Wavell succeeds in drawing Congress and League representatives into an interim government but fails to bring Congress and the League into a Constituent Assembly to create a constitution for a united India.
Indochina	Franco-Chinese accord allows French to reoccupy northern half of Vietnam (Feb). France recognizes the Democratic Republic of Vietnam as a "free state" within the French Union (6 March). Breakdown of March accord, French bombard Haiphong, and Ho Chi Minh calls for resistance to the French; beginning of Indochinese war with surprise attack on French bases (Dec).
Indonesia	Linggadjati agreement between Dutch and Indonesian Republic, agreeing to Republic's control of Java, Madura and Sumatra as part of a federal United States of Indonesia in a Netherlands-Indonesian Union (17 Nov).
Japan	Emperor Hirohito makes the "Human Being Declaration" (Jan). New Japanese constitution is promulgated (Nov); women obtain the vote. War crimes trials begin.
Malaya	Malayan Union established (April); Sarawak and North Borneo ceded to Britain (May–July).
Philippines	Philippines gain independence from United States. Roxas inaugurated as first president; Quirino as vice president.

Thailand   King Ananda Mahidol assassinated; succeeded by Bhumibol Adulyade (June).

1947

Ceylon   Formation of United National Party (UNP).
                    Senanayake leads UNP to victory in general election.
India/Pakistan   India and Pakistan become independent states (15
                    Aug); Nehru and Ali Khan lead their respective cabinets. Up to 250,000 people die in rioting and massacres that accompany the partition process.
                    Mass exodus of refugees across new borders between India and Pakistan in the west, smaller flow and less violence in the east between India and East Pakistan. Hindu ruler of Kashmir "accedes" his largely Muslim state to India. Sikh Punjab is scene of some of the most serious violence; two million Sikhs flee across border into India, where they demand greater autonomy or independence for Sikh Punjab.
Indonesia   Formal signature of Linggadjati agreement (March), but breakdown leads to "police action" by Dutch (July).
Japan   MacArthur bans general strike of government employees (1 Feb). New constitution comes into effect (3 May). Socialist Katayama Tetsu becomes prime minister (24 May).
Korea   United States brings Korea question before UN.
Philippines   United States signs 99-year lease for air and naval bases (March).

1948

Burma   Burma becomes independent (Jan).
Ceylon   Ceylon becomes independent dominion (Feb).
China   Lin Biao begins the offensive against the remaining Nationalist strongholds in Manchuria (Jan). CCP announces the creation of the North China People's Government (Sept).
India/Pakistan   Assassination of Mahatma Gandhi in Delhi (30 Jan).
                    Mohammed Ali Jinnah dies.
                    UN truce line established in Kashmir, leaving a third of the state in Pakistan and two-thirds in India.

	Pakistan demands implementation of UN-sponsored plebiscite on future of Kashmir.
	India sets up Atomic Energy Commission.
Indochina	French create "State of Vietnam" with Bao Dai as head of state (June).
Indonesia	Dutch and Indonesian truce agreement (Jan), but Communist rebellion leads to renewed fighting (Nov–Dec).
Japan	Tojo, Hirota and five others are executed for war crimes (Dec).
Korea	General election held in South Korea (May). Syngman Rhee becomes president (July). North Korean state established (Sept).
Malaysia	Malayan Union becomes Federation of Malaya (Feb); beginning of Communist insurgency (May).
Philippines	Hukbalahap movement outlawed by Roxas (6 Mar). Death of Roxas (15 April), succeeded by Quirino. Amnesty granted to Hukbalahap, but negotiations with Huk leader Luis Taruc break down.

1949

Ceylon	Federal Party (FP) formed by Chelvanayakam. Tamils of Indian origin deprived of franchise.
China	Chinese People's Republic proclaimed (Sept). A People's Political Consultative Conference passes Organic Laws and a Common Program setting up a multinational communist state with chairman of the republic as head of state. Mao Zedong first chairman (Oct). Chinese Nationalist forces take refuge on Formosa (Taiwan) and garrison islands of Quemoy, Matsu and Tachen.
Indochina	Laos recognized as an independent state linked to France (July).
	Cambodia recognized as an independent state linked to France (Nov).
Indonesia	Peace Conference at the Hague opens (Aug); transfer of sovereignty to United States of Indonesia agreed (Nov) and formal independence granted (Dec).

Japan	MacArthur fixes exchange rate of 360 yen to the dollar (12 May).
South Korea	Communist Party outlawed (Oct).

1950

China	Outbreak of Korean War (June). Chinese troops intervene to repulse United Nations counteroffensive into North Korea (Oct); 250,000 Chinese troops cross the Yalu River and force retreat of UN forces. Chinese invasion of Tibet (Oct). Agrarian Law dispossesses landlords and gives land to peasants, who are grouped together into collectives.
India	Constitution of Indian Union promulgated. India becomes a republic within British Commonwealth.
Indochina	Communist China and the Soviet Union recognize the Democratic Republic of Vietnam led by Ho Chi Minh (Jan). United States announces military and economic aid for the French in Indochina (May).
Japan	The "Red Purge" of suspected Communist sympathizers in office begins (Feb). The Japanese create the National Police Reserve (Oct).
Korea	Outbreak of Korean War (June). North Korean Communists launch invasion across 38th parallel. UN forces (primarily American) dispatched. UN counteroffensive begins with Inchon landing (Sept). Pyongyang recaptured (Oct).

1951

Ceylon	S.W.R.D. Bandaranaike founds Sri Lanka Freedom Party.
China	UN condemns Chinese aggression in Korea (Feb); further Chinese offensives held off by UN troops (Feb–May). Tibet signs agreement giving China control of Tibet's affairs (May); Chinese troops enter Lhasa (Sept).
India/Pakistan	Liaquat Ali Khan assassinated. First national general election in India confirms Congress Party dominance (1951–52).
Indochina	Communist offensive takes most of northern Vietnam.

Japan   Japanese peace treaty with Allies is signed in San Fran-
                     cisco.
                     Japan signs the Mutual Security Agreement with
                     United States (Sept).
Korea   Truce negotiations begin at Kaesong (July).

1952

Ceylon   D. S. Senanayake dies; Dudley Senanayake becomes
                     prime minister. UNP returned to power in general
                     election.
Japan   Occupation of Japan ends. Agreement signed on US
                     bases in Japan (28 Feb). Anti-American riots in To-
                     kyo (1 May). Soviet Union vetoes Japanese admis-
                     sion to the UN (18 Sept). National Police Reserve
                     reorganized as National Security Force.
Korea   Talks begin on normalization of relations with Japan.

1953

Ceylon   The Hartal (general strike). Senanayake resigns. Sir
                     John Kotelawela becomes prime minister.
China   First Five-Year Plan nationalizes most industry.
Japan   Hatoyama Ichiro forms separate Liberal Party (18
                     March).
Korea   Cease-fire in Korea (July); Korea–U.S. Mutual Defense
                     Treaty signed (Oct).
Philippines   Quirino defeated by Magsaysay in presidential elec-
                     tions (Nov).

1954

China   Permanent constitution established; guarantees domi-
                     nant place of the Communist Party.
India   India–China treaty.
Indochina   Battle of Dien Bien Phu (March–May) ends in French
                     defeat.
                     Ngo Dinh Diem appointed premier in South Viet-
                     nam by Bao Dai (July).
                     Geneva Agreements on Vietnam, temporarily parti-
                     tioning Vietnam along 17th parallel (July). Peace
                     agreement provides for a referendum in 1956 to de-
                     termine government of united Vietnam (Aug); agree-

ment is not signed by the United States or South Vietnam.

Southeast Asia Treaty Organization (SEATO) set up in Manila to combat Communist expansion (8 Sept). Viet Minh assume formal control of North Vietnam (Oct).

Japan	National Security Force reorganized as Self-Defense Force (1 July).
Philippines	Huk leader Taruc surrenders to Filipino government (May).

1955

China	U.S. Navy evacuates 42,000 Nationalist troops and civilians from Tachen Islands following artillery bombardment.
India	Bulganin and Khrushchev visit India.
Indochina	United States begins direct aid to government of South Vietnam (Jan); U.S. instructors requested (May). Cambodia becomes an independent state (Sept). Diem deposes Bao Dai and proclaims the "Republic of Vietnam" (Oct).
Japan	Liberals and Democrats in Japan merge to form the Liberal Democratic Party.

1956

Cambodia	Prince Sihanouk renounces SEATO protection (Feb).
China	Mao encourages criticism of regime, declaring "Let a hundred flowers bloom."
India	States Reorganization Act. India begins Second Five-Year Plan and builds several steel plants.
Japan	Japan is admitted to the United Nations (Dec). Ishibashi becomes prime minister (23 Dec).
Laos	Communists share power (Aug).
Pakistan	New constitution declares Pakistan an Islamic state.

1957

Indonesia	Sukarno introduces authoritarian rule as "guided democracy."
Japan	Kishi Nobusuke becomes prime minister (25 Feb).

	Treaty of Commerce with Soviet Union signed (6 Dec).
Laos	Communist Pathet Lao attempt to seize power (May).
Malaysia	Malay states become independent as Federation of Malaya (Aug).
Philippines	Magsaysay dies in plane crash; Carlos García sworn in as president (18 Mar).

1958

Ceylon	Anti-Tamil riots (May); emergency declared (continues until March 1959).
China	Shelling of Quemoy leads to U.S. military buildup. Mao Zedong inaugurates Second Five-Year Plan and "Great Leap Forward" to increase industrial production by 100% and agricultural output by 35%. Collective farms to be grouped in communes and industrial production based on them.
Indonesia	Revolt in Sumatra and Sulawesi.
Pakistan	Ayub Khan becomes president of Pakistan.
Vietnam	Communist guerrillas involved in attacks in South Vietnam.

1959

Ceylon	Assassination of Bandaranaike; Dahanayake becomes prime minister.
China/Tibet	Great Leap Forward yields disappointing results following huge dislocation of production; major famine in parts of China. Uprising in Tibet put down and Dalai Lama forced to flee to India (March).
India	Treaty signed between India and Pakistan over Indus waters.
Japan	Marriage of Crown Prince Akihito to Miss Shoda Michiko, a commoner.
Laos	Communist Pathet Lao seek to gain control over northern Laos.
Vietnam	Communist Party Central Committee in South Vietnam sanctions greater reliance on military activity; Communist underground activity increases; Diem government steps up repressive measures.

1960

China — Quarrel with Russia over "revisionism" leads to withdrawal of Russian advisers and technical support.

India — Union of Kashmir with India.

Japan — Demonstrations occur when the Mutual Security Agreement with United States is ratified (May). Prime Minister Ikeda announces the "Income Doubling Plan" (Sept).

Malaya — Official end to "emergency" (July).

South Korea — Syngman Rhee reelected president in rigged elections.

Vietnam — National Liberation Front of South Vietnam formed (Dec).
U.S. "advisers" to the South Vietnamese government forces number 900.

1961

Korea — Military coup led by Major General Park Chung-hee.

Laos — Pro-Western government formed in Laos; North Vietnam and Soviet Union send aid to Communist insurgents.

Philippines — Macapagal defeats García (14 Dec). Inaugurates "era of the common man."

South Vietnam — President Kennedy decides to increase military aid and advisers in South Vietnam (Nov); U.S. personnel number more than 3,000 by end of year.

1962

Burma — Military coup led by General Ne Win (March); Revolutionary Council set up and publishes program, "Burmese Way to Socialism." Burma Socialist Program Party set up and all others abolished (July).

China — War with India in Himalayas.

India — Indian and Chinese forces fight in the Himalayas; cease-fire agreed to.

Japan — Narita becomes secretary general of Socialist Party (29 Nov).

South Vietnam — "Strategic hamlet" program begun (Feb).
Australian military forces arrive in Vietnam (Aug); U.S. forces reach 11,000 (Dec).

1963

Japan
First visit of a British foreign secretary (28 March); followed by French Foreign Minister Couve de Murville (12 April). Japan invited to join OECD (18 July).

Malaysia/
Indonesia
Federation of Malaysia established (Sept); beginning of "confrontation" with Indonesia.

South Vietnam
Buddhist riots in Hué against government repression; seven monks commit suicide by fire as part of protests; martial law introduced (May–Aug). U.S.-backed coup overthrows Diem (1–2 Nov); General Duong Van Minh takes over (6 Nov).

1964

China
China explodes first atomic bomb.

India
Nehru dies; Lal Bahadur Shastri becomes prime minister.

Japan
Olympic Games held in Tokyo (Oct).

South Vietnam
Military coup led by Major General Nguyen Khanh replaces Minh government (Jan).

U.S. destroyers allegedly attacked in Gulf of Tonkin (2–4 Aug); U.S. aircraft retaliate against targets in North Vietnam (4 Aug); Congress passes Gulf of Tonkin resolution authorizing use of U.S. forces in Southeast Asia "to prevent further aggression" (7 Aug).

Number of U.S. forces in South Vietnam reaches 23,000 by end of year.

1965

Cambodia
Sihanouk breaks relations with United States (May).

India
Indo–Pakistan War.

Tamil riots against Hindi language; English confirmed as official language of India.

Indonesia
Following abortive coup, Communist Party banned; thousands of political dissidents and ethnic Chinese massacred.

Korea/Japan
Korea–Japan Basic Treaty signed in Tokyo (June).

Philippines
Ferdinand E. Marcos elected president (Nov).

Singapore
Singapore becomes independent from Malaysia (Aug).

South Vietnam
Sustained aerial bombardment of North Vietnam, "Op-

eration Rolling Thunder," begins (March).
U.S. Marines arrive at Da Nang (March); United States announces its troops will now be used routinely in combat (June). Period of political turmoil ends with Air Vice-Marshal Nguyen Cao Ky as head of South Vietnamese government (June).
U.S. military strength reaches 181,000 by end of year; widespread antiwar demonstrations in the United States.

1966

China	Beginning of Cultural Revolution, attempt to introduce Maoist principles in all aspects of life. Red Guards inaugurate attacks on all hierarchic and traditional features of society. Intellectuals and others forced to undergo "self-criticism."
India	Shastri dies; Indira Gandhi becomes prime minister. Indian government redraws boundary of Punjab state to give it a majority of Sikhs, and attempts to appease Sikh separatist agitation.
Indonesia	General Suharto assumes emergency powers (March).
Malaysia	Agreement signed ending "confrontation" with Indonesia (June).
Philippines	Agreement with United States to reduce leases on bases from 99 to 25 years; $45 million aid package agreed on.
South Vietnam	U.S. air attacks on North Vietnam resume after 37-day pause (31 Jan). B-52 bombers first used (April). Buddhist and student protests against the war in Hué, Da Nang and Saigon put down by South Vietnamese troops (March–June). American strength reaches 385,000 by end of year.

1967

China	Schools and educational institutions closed by Red Guards (continues into 1968).
Indonesia	President Sukarno hands over power to Suharto (Feb).
Japan	Demonstrations against Japan's support for U.S. involvement in Vietnam War (Oct).

South Vietnam	"Operation Cedar Falls" against Communist-held "Iron Triangle" north of Saigon (Jan).
	"Operation Junction City," biggest land offensive of the war, along Cambodian border (Feb).
	General Nguyen Van Thieu elected president; Ky becomes vice-president (Sept).

1968

Indonesia	General Suharto elected president (March) and introduces "New Order."
Japan	Students occupy Tokyo University campus (June 1968– Jan 1969).
Philippines	New Communist Party of the Philippines founded, pledges to follow principles of Mao Zedong (26 Dec).
South Vietnam	Communist Tet offensive against major cities of South Vietnam (30–31 Jan); intense fighting in Hué and Saigon.
	My Lai massacre (March).
	President Johnson announces he is withdrawing from presidential race, will seek negotiations (31 March).
	Paris Peace Conference opens (31 May).
	Bombing of North Vietnam halted (31 Oct).
	Nixon elected U.S. president, promises gradual troop withdrawal (Nov).

1969

China	Chairman of Republic, Liu Shaoqi, disgraced. Border clash with Soviet Union.
Laos	Laotian government requests U.S. aid to resist Communist pressure (Oct).
North Vietnam	Ho Chi Minh dies (3 Sept).
Pakistan	Yahya Khan becomes president of Pakistan.
Philippines	Marcos becomes first president to be reelected.
South Vietnam	Number of U.S. troops reaches peak of 541,500 (31 Jan).
	U.S. raids against North Vietnam resume (5 June); Nixon announces first troop withdrawal—25,000 combat troops (8 June).

1970

Cambodia/ South Vietnam	U.S.-backed General Lon Nol ousts Sihanouk in Cambodia (March); Khmer Republic set up. American and South Vietnamese forces invade Cambodia (March–April). Antiwar demonstrations in U.S. universities; six students shot at Kent State (4 May). U.S. ground troops withdraw from Cambodia (June). U.S. forces in Vietnam down to 335,800 (Dec).
Japan	Mutual Security Agreement with US renewed (June). Mishima Yukio attempts a coup and then commits suicide (Nov).
Philippines	Anti-American "patriot youth" riots (5 April), followed by general strike protesting increased oil and transport costs (7 April). Assassination attempt on Pope Paul VI in Manila (27 Nov).

1971

Ceylon	State of emergency declared following disclosure of plot to overthrow government by ultra-left JVP. Over 1,000 killed and 4,000 arrested. JVP insurrection; emergency declared that lasts for six years; draft republican constitution prepared.
China	Deputy Prime Minister Lin Biao disgraced, killed in air crash.
India	Growing clashes with Pakistan (Nov). War with Pakistan (Dec), invasion of East Pakistan. Pakistan accepts cease-fire and recognizes new state of Bangladesh. Adjustment of border between India and Pakistan in Kashmir agreed on at Simla Conference. Zulfikar Ali Bhutto becomes president of Pakistan.
Japan	United States agrees to return Okinawa to Japan (June).
Laos	South Vietnamese forces invade Laos to attack Ho Chi Minh Trail (Feb–March).
Pakistan	Revolt in East Pakistan, which secedes from Pakistan to form state of Bangladesh (March). Revolt crushed (May), but guerrilla war continues.
Philippines	Marcos invokes martial law to "liquidate Communist apparatus" (a blatant exaggeration of a very remote threat).

South Vietnam   Nixon announces withdrawal of 100,000 U.S. troops
                   by end of year (7 April); 500,000 antiwar demonstra-
                   tors march on Washington (24 April).
                   Australia and New Zealand announce withdrawal of
                   troops from South Vietnam (Aug).
                   Nguyen Van Thieu confirmed as president in one-
                   man "election" (3 Oct).

1972

Burma   Ne Win and 20 army commanders "retire" and be-
                   come civilian members of government.
Ceylon/   Ceylon adopts new constitution and becomes Republic
Sri Lanka   of Sri Lanka. Tamil United Front formed (May).
Pakistan   Pakistan leaves the British Commonwealth.
Philippines   Marcos declares martial law and arrests leading opposi-
                   tion figure Benigno Aquino along with several hun-
                   dred Aquino supporters (Sept).
South Vietnam   Nixon announces reduction of U.S. forces to 69,000 by
                   1 May (13 Jan).
                   North Vietnamese forces invade South Vietnam (30
                   March); renewed bombing of north authorized
                   (April); mining of ports ordered (May).
                   Last American ground combat troops leave Vietnam
                   (Aug). Peace negotiator Henry Kissinger reports sub-
                   stantial agreement on nine-point plan with North
                   Vietnam (26 Oct); United States suspends talks (13
                   Dec); bombing of North Vietnam resumed (18 Dec);
                   bombing halted after North Vietnam agrees to a
                   truce (30 Dec).

1973

Burma   New constitution adopted by referendum (Dec).
China   Deng Xiaoping, disgraced in Cultural Revolution, be-
                   comes deputy prime minister.
Laos   Cease-fire in Laos (21 Feb).
Pakistan   Bhutto becomes prime minister of Pakistan under new
                   constitution.
Philippines   Marcos lifts curfew, eases restrictions on free speech
                   (23 July). National referendum renews his "man-
                   date" (31 Dec).
Thailand   Civilian power returns to Thailand after resignation of

	military rulers following killing of 400 student protesters (Oct).
Vietnam	Kissinger and Le Duc Tho sign peace agreement "ending" the war (27 Jan); last U.S. military personnel leave (29 March).

1974

Burma	Military rule formally ended and Revolutionary Council dissolved; Ne Win becomes first president of Burma as a one-party Socialist Republic (March).
Cambodia/ South Vietnam	War in South Vietnam resumes (Jan). Communist insurgents advance on capital of Cambodia (July). President Nixon resigns (Aug); Congress puts ceiling on military aid to South Vietnam.

1975

Bangladesh	Sheikh Mujib ur-Rahman, ruler of Bangladesh, deposed and killed in military coup; Khandakar Mushtaq Ahmed is sworn in as president.
Cambodia	Capital, Phnom Penh, falls to Communist Khmer Rouge insurgents (17 April).
China	New constitution replaces single head of state with a collective, the Standing Committee of the National Peoples' Congress.
India	State of emergency declared in India because of growing strikes and unrest; opposition leaders arrested.
Indonesia	Invades East Timor (7 Dec).
Japan	Investigation into "Lockheed affair" begins (April).
Laos	Pathet Lao consolidate Communist takeover of Laos; Laos becomes a communist state (3 Dec).
South Vietnam	North Vietnamese forces launch offensive; the north and central highlands fall to Communists, and South Vietnamese forces are forced into headlong retreat (March). President Thieu resigns and flees to Taiwan (21 April); North Vietnamese troops enter Saigon (29 April); unconditional surrender announced by President Van Minh (30 April).

1976

Burma	Attempted coup by young officers fails (July).
Cambodia	Democratic Kampuchea established under Pol Pot, who inaugurates program of revolutionary terror (Jan).
China	Death of Mao Zedong (Sept); Hua Guofeng becomes chairman and prime minister. Begins action against "Gang of Four" and Mao's widow, Jiang Qing.
Indonesia	Formally annexes East Timor (17 July).
Sri Lanka	Formation of Tamil United Liberation Front, pledged to establish separate Tamil state (Tamil Eelam).
Thailand	Army seizes power after violent clashes between police and students (Oct).

1977

China	Deng Xiaoping reinstated. Jiang Qing expelled from party and sentenced to death, commuted to life imprisonment. More pragmatic economic policy adopted.
India	Morarji Desai leads Janata Party to victory over Indira Gandhi in general election. First defeat of Congress Party since independence.
Pakistan	Bhutto overthrown after allegations of ballot-rigging; constitution suspended.
Philippines	Marcos eases martial law, retaining power to rule by decree (22 Aug). Aquino sentenced to death by military tribunal (25 Nov). Marcos reopens trial after worldwide outrage.
Sri Lanka	Serious rioting in Tamil areas of Sri Lanka. Constitution amended to strengthen president.

1978

Afghanistan	Communist People's Democratic Party overthrows government in violent coup, abolishes constitution, outlaws other parties (27 April).
China	New constitution modifies constitution of 1975. China opens formal diplomatic relations with the United States.

Japan	Treaty of Peace and Friendship between China and Japan signed (Aug).
Pakistan	General Zia ul-Haq becomes president of Pakistan.
Philippines	Marcos becomes prime minister as well as president (12 June).
Sri Lanka	New presidential system of government adopted. Jayewardene becomes president. "Liberation Tigers" (Tamils) proscribed.

1979

Afghanistan	Amid continuing rebellion, the Soviet Union invades in support of unstable Communist government (27 Dec).
Cambodia	Vietnamese invasion of Cambodia deposes Pol Pot and installs Heng Samrin as head of People's Republic of Kampuchea. Khmer Rouge and Pol Pot take up guerrilla war.
China	Chinese invasion of Vietnam.
	Demonstrations for greater freedom in Beijing. Cultural Revolution denounced as a disaster.
Pakistan	Ex-Prime Minister Bhutto executed.
Sri Lanka	Prevention of Terrorism Act passed. Emergency declared in Tamil areas with military occupation of Jaffna district.

1980

China	Zhao Ziyang becomes prime minister, succeeding Hua Guofeng.
India	Indira Gandhi wins election victory for Congress Party and returns to power.
Japan	Prime Minister Masayoshi Ohira dies (23 June). Zenko Suzuki forms government (July).
Philippines	Opposition leader Benigno Aquino allowed to leave for United States (May).
Thailand	General Prem Tinsulanonda sets up civilian–military government.

1981

Burma	General San Yu becomes new president.
China	Hu Yaobang succeeds Hua Kuofeng as chairman of party until post abolished in 1982.

Philippines	Martial law lifted (Jan). Marcos reelected to a further six-year term (16 June).
Sri Lanka	State of emergency declared because of attacks by Tamil Tigers.
Thailand	Unsuccessful coup attempt in Bangkok (April).

1982

Cambodia	Forces opposed to Heng Samrin regime form a coalition including Khmer Rouge, Prince Sihanouk and Son Sann (June).
China	New constitution approved for Communist Party, abolishing posts of chairman and vice-chairman. New constitution for China approved, increasing powers of prime minister.
Japan	Nakasone forms government (Nov).

1983

Bangladesh	General Ershad assumes presidency of Bangladesh.
China	National People's Congress elects Li Xiannian to revived post of president; Deng Xiaoping chosen chairman of new State Military Commission. "Rectification" campaign conducted against corrupt officials.
India	Emergency rule invoked in Punjab to suppress Sikh terrorism.
Japan	Ex-prime minister Tanaka found guilty on charges arising from the Lockheed affair.
Philippines	Benigno Aquino assassinated at Manila airport on his return from the United States (21 Aug); nearly two million join funeral procession.
Sri Lanka	Serious violence breaks out between Sinhalese and Tamils.

1984

Cambodia	Vietnamese launch major offensive on guerrilla bases on Thai border; UN calls on Vietnam to withdraw from Cambodia/Kampuchea (Oct).
China	Modernization drive reverses emphasis on collective agriculture; central quotas and price controls relaxed; factories given greater autonomy. Agreement

	reached with Great Britain on future of Hong Kong (Sept).
India	Indian troops storm Golden Temple in Amritsar, center of Sikh separatists (June). Indira Gandhi assassinated by Sikh members of her bodyguard, and her son, Rajiv Gandhi, becomes prime minister; Hindu attacks on Sikhs kill an estimated 2,000 people. Fighting between Indian and Pakistani troops on the Siachen Glacier in Kashmir.
Indonesia	Muslim riots in Jakarta suppressed by troops (Sept).
Pakistan	General Zia confirmed as president by referendum.
Sri Lanka	Talks between Tamils and President Jayawardene of Sri Lanka break down; conflict escalates in Tamil areas.

1985

China	Five-Year Plan announces slowdown in pace of economic reform; fewer cities open to foreign investment, and party control reasserted.
India	Further heavy fighting in Kashmir.
Pakistan	President Zia confirmed in office for five-year period.

1986

China	Campaign for greater democracy suggested by leadership; student demonstrations in Shanghai and Beijing (Dec).
Japan	Nakasone wins outright victory in general election after period of dependence on minority parties (July).
Pakistan	Benazir Bhutto returns to Pakistan and demands end to martial law and free elections.
Philippines	Corazon Aquino, widow of Benigno Aquino, elected president of Philippines; Marcos goes into exile (Feb); coup attempts in July and November suppressed. New constitution proposed (Nov).
Sri Lanka	Tamils kill Sinhalese in further terror raids.

1987

Cambodia	Talks between Prince Sihanouk and Vietnamese-backed Prime Minister Hun Sen in Paris on Cambodian settlement.

China	Backlash against reform; Hu Yaobang forced to resign, succeeded by Zhao Ziyang. Agreement with Portugal on return in 1999 of Macao to China. Thirteenth Party Congress (Oct) leads to retirement of eight senior politicians and promotion of younger technocrats. Li Peng becomes prime minister in place of Zhao Ziyang, who is confirmed as general secretary.
India	Emergency rule imposed in Punjab.
Indonesia	Official Golkar Party wins landslide victory in general elections (April).
Japan	Takeshita chosen to succeed Nakasone (Oct).
Philippines	New constitution approved (Feb); coup suppressed (Aug).
Sri Lanka	Indian Prime Minister Rajiv Gandhi and President Jayawardene sign an accord (July) offering more autonomy to Tamil areas; Indian peacekeeping force invited into Sri Lanka to supervise. Attacks on Indian army lead to assault on Tamil strongholds in Jaffna peninsula.

1988

Afghanistan	Soviet Union begins pullout of troops (15 May).
Burma	Student demonstrations against Ne Win's government suppressed by the army (March–July); Ne Win resigns as party chairman and San Yu as president (July). Brigadier General Sein Lwin becomes president and party chairman and imposes martial law, but resigns after riots (Aug).
	General Saw Maung takes power but declares commitment to elections; BSPP becomes National Unity Party.
Cambodia	Vietnam announces it will remove all troops by Dec 1990 (May); Jakarta talks on peace settlement (June); resumed in Beijing (Aug) and Jakarta (Feb 1989), fail to reach earlier date for withdrawal.
China	Demand for greater speed in reform by Zhao Ziyang (March), but inflation and industrial unrest lead to freeze on price reforms for two years (Sept).
Pakistan	President Zia of Pakistan killed in air crash (Aug); Benazir Bhutto's party wins largest number of seats in general election (Nov) and she becomes prime minister.

Philippines   Interim agreement with United States on U.S. bases in
                   Philippines; United States to pay $481 million for
                   two years (17 Oct). Grand jury in New York indicts
                   Ferdinand and Imelda Marcos for fraud and embez-
                   zlement.

1989

Afghanistan   Soviet Union completes pullout of troops (15 Feb).
Burma   Military government announces that elections will take
                   place in May 1990 (Feb).
Cambodia   Vietnamese forces begin withdrawal (Sept).
China   Death of Hu Yaobang (April) leads to demands for his
                   rehabilitation; student-led sit-ins and demonstrations
                   held in several cities.
                   Over 100,000 students march through Beijing (27
                   April). Students occupy Tiananmen Square (4 May).
                   Hunger strike among students (13 May); million-
                   strong pro-democracy march through Beijing (17
                   May); Li Peng announces martial law (20 May). Chi-
                   nese troops disperse students in Tiananmen Square,
                   causing over 1,000 deaths, and similar protests
                   quelled in other Chinese cities (4 June). Chinese gov-
                   ernment arrests thousands of democracy supporters
                   in spite of world outrage at events of 4 June.
Japan   Emperor Hirohito dies (7 Jan); succeeded by Crown
                   Prince Akihito.
                   Takeshita forced to resign over "Recruit" scandal
                   (April). Foreign Secretary Uno succeeds, but forced
                   to resign over sexual allegations (July). Toshiki Kaifu
                   becomes prime minister (9 Aug).
Pakistan   Pakistan rejoins the British Commonwealth.
Sri Lanka   Amid continuing violence, Indian forces agree to with-
                   draw.

1990

China   National People's Congress approves the Basic Law,
                   the constitution for Hong Kong after 1997.
India   Vote of no confidence results in resignation of Prime
                   Minister Singh (Nov).
Japan   Coronation of Emperor Akihito (Nov).

Korea	Meeting of prime ministers of North and South Korea (Sept).
Nepal	New reform government formed, led by Krishna Prasad Bhattarai.
Pakistan	President Khan dismisses Premier Benazir Bhutto (Aug); Bhutto's Pakistan People's Party defeated in national and provincial elections (Oct).

1991

Afghanistan	Cease-fire announced by President Najibullah and the Mujaheddin to permit UN peace plan to be put into effect.
Bangladesh	Election of Abdur Rahman Biswas as president.
Cambodia	All parties finally sign the Paris Accords (Oct), agreeing on a UN mandate to prepare and supervise elections by May 1993. Prince Sihanouk returns as interim head of state.
China/Vietnam	Peace accord announced (Nov); diplomatic relations to be reestablished.
Hong Kong	Great Britain and Vietnam announce agreement for forcible repatriation of Vietnamese "boat people" from Hong Kong; Liberal Democratic candidates win sweeping success in first direct elections to Hong Kong parliament (15 Sept).
India	Rajiv Gandhi, former prime minister, assassinated (May); general election caused by resignation of Prime Minister Shekhar in March is postponed.
Laos	New constitution (with elected executive president) adopted by Supreme People's Assembly (13–15 Aug).
Mongolia	New draft constitution published (June).
Nepal	First multiparty general elections since 1959 won by Nepali Congress (12 May).
Philippines	Agreement on future of U.S. bases formally signed (Aug); Philippine senate refuses to ratify naval base treaty (Sept) but compromise formula agreed on (Oct).
South Korea	Opposition parties merge to form New Democratic Union under leadership of Kim Dae Jung (April); terms of nonaggression pact for Korean peninsula agreed on with North Korea (Dec).
Taiwan	National Assembly elections won by ruling KMT (Kuomintang) (Dec).

Thailand   Military coup in February ends three years of democ-
                  racy; martial law imposed (lifted in May).

1992

Afghanistan   Fall of President Najibullah (April) as Mujaheddin re-
                  bels encircle Kabul. End of Communist rule, but no
                  real political stability.
Cambodia   Heng Samrin replaced as head of state by Chea Sim
                  (April).
China   Diplomatic relations with South Korea established
                  (Aug); tension with Great Britain over Patten's pro-
                  posals for greater democracy in Hong Kong (Nov–
                  Dec); Party Congress endorses continued economic
                  reform program.
India   Hindu extremists seize control of Ayodyha; mosque de-
                  stroyed. Communal rioting precipitates political cri-
                  sis.
Myanmar   General Than Shwe becomes chairman of the Law and
                  Order Restoration Council and also prime minister.
Philippines   Fidel Ramos elected president to succeed Aquino
                  (May); 1957 law banning membership in the Com-
                  munist Party repealed (Sept).
South Korea   North and South Korea agree on pact to ban nuclear
                  weapons from the Korean peninsula (Jan); National
                  Assembly elections held in South Korea (March);
                  Democratic Liberals still largest party but lose over-
                  all parliamentary majority. Hot line between North
                  and South Korea established (Sept). Kim Young Sam
                  elected first civilian president for 32 years (Dec).
Thailand   Massacre of antigovernment protesters in May. Fall of
                  General Suchinda.
Vietnam   New constitution approved by National Assembly
                  (April).

1993

Afghanistan   Burhanuddin Rabbani becomes head of state (1 Jan).
Cambodia   Elections held under UN supervision. Prince Sihanouk
                  returns as head of state.
China   Jiang Zemin becomes state president (27 March). New
                  constitution adopted.

India   Terrorist bombs rock Bombay; over 225 dead, 1,100 in-
                  jured. Further bombs in Calcutta (March).
Indonesia   President Suharto reelected for five-year term.
Japan   Liberal Democrats lose majority in general election (18
                  July); widespread gains made by reformist breakaway
                  parties (the Japan New Party, the Renewal Party of
                  Hata, and the Harbinger Party); Kiichi Miyazawa re-
                  signs; Hosokawa new prime minister.
Malaysia   Hereditary ruler's immunity from prosecution ended
                  by constitutional amendment (Jan).
Pakistan   Benazir Bhutto returns to power in October elections.
Singapore   First-ever elections for post of president (Aug). Ong
                  Teng Cheong defeats Chua Kim Yeow.
Sri Lanka   President Premadasa assassinated by suicide bomber (1
                  May).

CHAPTER 3

HEADS OF STATE AND GOVERNMENT

AFGHANISTAN

Heads of State

King

Mohammed Zahir Shah	Nov 1933–July 1973

President

Sardar Mohammed Daoud	July 1973–April 1978
Nur Mohammed Taraki	April 1978–Oct 1979
Hafizullah Amin	Oct 1979*–Dec 1979
Babrak Karmal	Dec 1979–Dec 1986
Mohammed Najibullah	Dec 1986**–April 1992[†]
Sibghattolah Majaddedi	April 1992–June 1992
Burhanuddin Rabbani	June 1992–

Heads of Government

Prime Minister

Sidar Hashim Khan	Nov 1929–Mar 1946
Shad Mahmud Khan	Mar 1946–Sept 1953
Sardar Mohammed Daoud	Sept 1953–Mar 1963

---

* Amin replaced Taraki as secretary general (SG) of the People's Democratic Party of Afghanistan (PDPA) in Sept 1979 but did not officially become president until Oct 1979.

** Najibullah replaced Karmal as SG of the PDPA in May 1986 but did not officially become president until Dec 1986.

[†] Abdul Rahim Ratif was briefly acting president in April 1992 after the fall of Najibullah. Majaddedi then became acting president for three months before handing over the post to Rabbani.

Mohammed Yusa	Mar 1963–Nov 1965
Mohammed Maiwandwal	Nov 1965–Oct 1967
Abdullah Yakta (acting)	Oct 1967–Nov 1967
Nar Etemadi	Nov 1967–June 1971
Abdul Zahir	June 1971–Dec 1972
Mohammed Shafeq	Dec 1972–July 1973
Sardar Mohammed Daoud	July 1973–April 1978
Nur Mohammed Taraki	April 1978–Mar 1979
Hafizullah Amin	Mar 1979–Dec 1979
Babrak Karmal	Dec 1979–June 1981
Soltan Ali Keshtmand	June 1981–May 1988
Mohammed Hasan Sharq*	May 1988–Feb 1989
Fazal Haq Khaliqyar	May 1990–April 1992
Abdul Sabur Fareed	April 1992–Mar 1993
Gulbuddin Hekmatyar	Mar 1993–

BANGLADESH

Heads of State

President

Syed Nazrul Islam (acting)	Dec 1971–Jan 1972
Mujib ur-Rahman	Jan 1972
Abu Syed Chowdhury	Jan 1972–Dec 1973
Mohammed Ullah	Dec 1973–Jan 1975
Mujib ur-Rahman	Jan 1975–Dec 1975
Khandakar Mushtaq Ahmed (deposed)	Aug 1975–Nov 1975
Abusadat Mohammed Sayem	Nov 1975–April 1977
Zia ur-Rahman	April 1977–May 1981
Abdus Sattar	May 1981–Mar 1982**
Ahsanuddin Chowdhury	Mar 1982–Dec 1983
Hussain Ershad	Dec 1983–Dec 1990
Shehabuddin Ahmed (acting)	Dec 1990–Oct 1991
Abdur Rahman Biswas	Oct 1991–

Heads of Government

Prime Minister

Tajuddin Ahmed	Dec 1971–Jan 1972
Mujib ur-Rahman	Jan 1972–Jan 1975

---

* Replaced by 20-man Supreme Council.

** Acting president May 1981–Nov 1981

M. Mansoor Ali   Jan 1975–Aug 1975
(Aug 1975–March 1979 post abolished)
Azizur Rahman   Mar 1979–Mar 1982
(March 1982–March 1984 post abolished)
Ataur Rahman Khan   Mar 1984–1988
Moudud Ahmed   1988–Aug 1989
Kazi Zafar Ahmed   Aug 1989–Dec 1990
Khaleda Zia   Mar 1991–

BHUTAN

Heads of State

King (hereditary since 1907 in the Wangchuk family)
Jigme Wangchuk   Aug 1926–Mar 1952
Jigme Dorji Wangchuk   Mar 1952–July 1972
Jigme Singhi Wangchuk   July 1972–

Heads of Government

Prime Minister
Jigme Dorji   1952–April 1964
(post vacant until July 1964)
Lendup Dorji   July 1964–Nov 1964
(post abolished from Nov 1964)

BRUNEI

Heads of State

Sultan
Ahmad Tajuddin   1924–1950
Omar Ali Saifuddin   1950–1967
Hassan al-Bolkiah   1967–

CAMBODIA

Heads of State

King (until 1960)
Norodom Sihanouk   April 1941–Mar 1955
Norodom Suramarit   Mar 1955–April 1960

(From April to June 1960 there was a regency council under Prince Monireth)

Head of State

Norodom Sihanouk (for second time)	June 1960–Mar 1970
Cheng Heng	Mar 1970–Mar 1972
Lon Nol	Mar 1972–April 1975

(During April 1975 Saukham Khoy was acting head of state before being deposed)

Norodom Sihanouk (for third time)	April 1975–April 1976
Khieu Samphan	April 1976–Jan 1979
Heng Samrin	Jan 1979–Nov 1991

In November 1991 Prince Sihanouk became titular president. In September 1993, the monarchy was re-established with Sihanouk as king.

Heads of Government (since independence, 9 Nov 1953)

Chan Nak	Nov 1953–Mar 1954
Norodom Sihanouk	Mar 1954–April 1954
Samdech Penn Nouth	April 1954–Jan 1955
Leng Ngeth	Jan 1955–Sept 1955
Norodom Sihanouk	Sept 1955–Jan 1956
Oum Chheang Sun	Jan 1956–Mar 1956
Norodom Sihanouk	Mar 1956–Mar 1956
Khim Tit	April 1956–Sept 1956
Norodom Sihanouk	Sept 1956–Oct 1956
San Yun	Oct 1956–April 1957
Norodom Sihanouk	April 1957–June 1957
Sim Var	June 1957–Jan 1958
Ek Yi Oun	Jan 1958–Jan 1958
Samdech Penn Nouth	Jan 1958–April 1958
Sim Var	April 1958–July 1958
Norodom Sihanouk	July 1958–April 1960
Pho Proeung	April 1960–Jan 1961
Samdech Penn Nouth	Jan 1961–Oct 1962
Norodom Kantol	Oct 1962–Oct 1966
Lon Nol	Oct 1966–May 1967
Son Sann	May 1967–Dec 1967
Samdech Penn Nouth	Jan 1968–Aug 1969
Lon Nol	Aug 1969–Mar 1972
Sirik Matak	Mar 1972–Mar 1972
Son Ngoc Thanh	Mar 1972–Oct 1972
Hang Thun Hak	Oct 1972–April 1973

In Tam	May 1973–Dec 1973
Long Boret	Dec 1973–April 1975
Penn Nouth	April 1975–April 1976
Pol Pot	April 1976–Sept 1976
Nuon Chea (acting)	Sept 1976–Dec 1976
Pol Pot	Dec 1976–Jan 1979
(From January 1979 to June 1981 the post was abolished)	
Pen Sovan	June 1981–Dec 1981
Chan Si	Dec 1981–Dec 1984
Hun Sen	Dec 1984–

Considerable instability followed the election of May 1993. However, effective power remained with Sihanouk as head of state, with Hun Sen and Prince Norodom Ranariddh as co-premiers until October 1993 when the latter took sole office.

CHINA

Heads of State (since the proclamation of the People's Republic)

Chairman of the Republic

Mao Zedong (Mao Tse-tung)	Oct 1949–Dec 1958
Zhu De	Dec 1958–April 1959
Liu Shaoqi	April 1959–Oct 1968
Deng Piwu (Acting)	Oct 1968–Jan 1975

Chairman of Communist Party

Mao Zedong (Mao Tse-tung)	Oct 1949–Sept 1976
Hua Guofeng (Hua Kuo-feng)	Oct 1976–June 1981
Hu Yaobang (Hu Yao-pang)	June 1981

Prime Minister

Zhou Enlai (Chou En-lai)	Oct 1949–Jan 1976
Hua Guofeng (Hua Kuo-feng)	Jan 1976–Sept 1980
Zhao Ziyang (Chiao Tzu-yang)	Sept 1980–Oct 1987
Li Peng	Oct 1987–

Chairman, Military Affairs Committee
(effective leader)

Deng Xiaoping (Teng Hsiao-ping)	June 1981–

President

Jiang Kaishek (Chiang Kai-shek)	May 1943–Jan 1949
Li Tsung-jen (acting, deposed)	Jan 1949–Sept 1949

Mao Zedong (Mao Tse-tung)	Oct 1949–April 1959
Liu Shaoqi	April 1959–Oct 1968
Deng Piwu	Oct 1968–Jan 1975
Chu Teh	Jan 1975–July 1976
Soong Ching-ling (acting) (widow of Sun Yat-sen)	July 1976–Mar 1978
Ye Jianying (Yeh Chien-ying)	Mar 1978–June 1983
Li Xiannian (Li Hsien-nien)	June 1983–Mar 1988
Yang Shangkun	Mar 1988–Mar 1993
Jiang Zemin*	Mar 1993–

EAST TIMOR (former independent state)

In November 1975 the former Portuguese colony of East Timor declared itself independent, but in December 1975 it was occupied by Indonesia and in July 1976 incorporated into Indonesia as the province of Loro Sae.

President

Francisco do Amaral	Nov–Dec 1975

Prime Minister

Nicolau Lobato	Nov–Dec 1975
Arnaldo Araujo	Dec 1975–July 1976

HONG KONG (British colony until 1997)

Governor (since liberation from Japanese occupation in 1945)

Sir Mark Young	Sept 1941–July 1947
Sir Alexander Grantham	July 1947–Jan 1958
Sir Robert Black	Jan 1958–April 1964
Sir David Trench	April 1964–Nov 1971
Lord MacLehose (Sir Crawford Murray MacLehose)	Nov 1971–May 1982
Sir Edward Youde	May 1982–April 1987
Sir David Wilson	April 1987–July 1992
Christopher Patten	July 1992–

---

* Under the present constitution, Jiang Zemin was appointed president in 1993.

INDIA

Heads of State

Governor-General
Louis, 1st Earl Mountbatten	Aug 1947–June 1948
Chakravarti Rajagolpalachari	June 1948–Jan 1949

President
Rajendra Prasad	Jan 1949–May 1962
Sarvepalli Radhakrishnan	May 1962–May 1967
Zahir Hussain	May 1967–May 1969
Varahgiri Venkata Giri (acting)	May 1969–Aug 1969
Varahgiri Venkata Giri	Aug 1969–Aug 1974
Fakhruddin Ali Ahmed	Aug 1974–Feb 1977
Basappa Danappa Jatti	Feb 1977–July 1977
Neelam Sanjiva Reddy	July 1977–July 1982
Giani Zail Sing	July 1982–July 1987
Ramaswamy Venkataraman	July 1987–July 1992
Shankar Dayal Sharma	July 1992–

Heads of Government

Prime Minister
Jawaharlal Nehru	Jan 1949–May 1964
Gulzarilal Nanda (acting)	May 1964–June 1964
Lal Bahadur Shastri	June 1964–Jan 1966
Gulzarilal Nanda (acting)	Jan 1966
Indira Gandhi	Jan 1966–Mar 1977
Shri Morarji Ranchodji Desai	Mar 1977–July 1979
Charan Singh	July 1979–Jan 1980
Indira Gandhi	Jan 1980–Oct 1984
Rajiv Gandhi	Oct 1984–Nov 1989
Vishwanath Pratap Singh	Nov 1989–Nov 1990
Chandra Shekhar	Nov 1990–June 1991
P. V. Narasimha Rao	June 1991–

INDONESIA

Heads of State

President
Ahmed Sukarno	Aug 1945–Feb 1967
Raden Suharto	Feb 1967–

Heads of Government

Prime Minister

Sutan Sjahrir	Nov 1945–June 1947
Amir Sjarifuddin	July 1947–Jan 1948
Mohammed Hatta	Jan 1948–Dec 1948
Sjarifuddin Prawiraranegara	Dec 1948–May 1949
Susanto Tirtoprodjo	May 1949–July 1949
Mohammed Hatta	July 1949–Jan 1950
Halim	Jan 1950–Aug 1950
Mohammed Natsir	Sept 1950–Mar 1951
Wirjosandjojo Sukiman	April 1951–Feb 1952
Wilopo	April 1952–June 1953
Ali Sastroamidjoyo	July 1953–June 1955
Burhanuddin Harahap	Aug 1955–Mar 1956
Ali Sastroamidjoyo	Mar 1956–Mar 1957
Djuanda Kartawidjaja	April 1957–Nov 1963
Ahmed Sukarno	Nov 1963–Mar 1966
Suharto	Mar 1966–Feb 1967*

JAPAN

Heads of State

Emperor

Hirohito	Dec 1926–Jan 1989
Akihito	Jan 1989–

Heads of Government

Prime Minister**

Kantaro Suzuki	April 1945–Aug 1945
Prince Naruhiko Higashikuni	Aug 1945–Oct 1945
Kijuro Shidehara	Oct 1945–May 1946
Shigeru Yoshida	May 1946–May 1947
Tetsu Katayama	May 1947–Feb 1948
Hitoshi Ashida	Feb 1948–Oct 1948
Shigeru Yoshida	Oct 1948–Dec 1954
Ichiro Hatoyama	Dec 1954–Dec 1956
Tanzan Ishibashi	Dec 1956–Feb 1957

---

*   Post abolished Feb 1967.

**   Names are given in English order, i.e., surnames follow given names.

Nobusuke Kishi	Feb 1957–July 1960
Hayato Ikeda	July 1960–Nov 1964
Eisaku Sato	Nov 1964–July 1972
Kakuei Tanaka	July 1972–Dec 1974
Takeo Miki	Dec 1974–Dec 1976
Takeo Fukuda	Dec 1976–Nov 1978
Masayoshi Ohira	Nov 1978–June 1980
Masayoshi Ito (acting)	June 1980–July 1980
Zenko Suzuki	July 1980–Nov 1980
Yashiro Nakasone	Nov 1982–Nov 1987
Noboru Takeshita	Nov 1987–June 1989
Sosuke Uno	June 1989–Aug 1989
Toshiki Kaifu	Aug 1989–Oct 1991
Kiichi Miyazawa	Oct 1991–July 1993
Morihiro Hosokawa	July 1993–Apr 1994
Tsutomo Hata	Apr 1994

LAOS

Heads of State

King
Sisavang Vong	Mar 1904–Oct 1959
Savang Vatthana	Oct 1959–Dec 1975*

President
Souphanouvong	Dec 1975–Aug 1991
Kaysone Phomvihane	Aug 1991–Nov 1992
Nouhak Phoumsavan	Feb 1993–

Heads of Government

Prime Minister
Prince Phetsarath	Sept 1945–Oct 1945
Phaya Khammao	Oct 1945–April 1946
(After April 1946 the king acted also as prime minister)	
Tiao Souvannarath	1947–Oct 1949
Boun Oum na Champassak	Oct 1949–Feb 1950
Phoui Sananikone	Feb 1950–Aug 1951
Souvanna Phouma	Aug 1951–Nov 1954
Katay Sasorith	Nov 1954–Mar 1956

---

* The monarchy was abolished on 2 Dec 1975.

Souvanna Phouma (for 2nd time)	Mar 1956–Aug 1958
Phoui Sananikone (for 2nd time)	Aug 1958–Dec 1959
Kou Abhay	Jan 1960–Jun 1960
Tiao Somsanith	Jun 1960–Aug 1960
Souvanna Phouma (for 3rd time)	Aug 1960–Dec 1960
Boun Oum	Dec 1960–June 1962
Souvanna Phouma (for 4th time)	June 1962–Dec 1975
Kaysone Phomvihane*	Dec 1975–Aug 1991
General Khamtay Siphandon**	Aug 1991–

MALAYSIA (independent as Malaya 1957; name change 1963)

Heads of State

Tunku Abdul Rahman	Aug 1957–April 1960
Sultan Hisamuddin Alam Shah	April 1960–Sept 1960
Tunku Syed Putra	Sept 1960–Sept 1965
Tunku Ismail Nasiruddin Shah	Sept 1965–Sept 1970
Sultan Abdul Halim Maudzam Shah	Sept 1970–Sept 1975
Sultan Yahya Petra	Sept 1975–Mar 1979
Sultan Ahmad Shah	Mar 1979–April 1984
Sultan Mahmud Iskander	April 1984–April 1989
Sultan Yusuff Izzuddinn	April 1989–April 1994
Tunku Jaafar Abdul Rahman	April 1994–

Heads of Government

Chief Minister

Tunku Abdul Rahman Putra	July 1955–Aug 1957

Prime Minister

Tunku Abdul Rahman Putra	Aug 1957–Feb 1959
Tun Abdul Razak bin Hussein	Feb 1959–Aug 1959
Tunku Abdul Rahman Putra (2nd time)	Aug 1959–Sept 1970
Tun Abdul Razak bin Hussein (2nd time)	Sept 1970–Jan 1976
Hussein bin Onn	Jan 1976–July 1981
Mahathir bin Mohamad	July 1981–

---

* Kaysone Phomvihane was also general secretary of the Laotian Communist Party .

** Additional powers vested in the prime minister under the country's first constitution under Communist rule.

MONGOLIA

Heads of State

Chairmen of the Presidium of the Khural (until 1990)

Gonchigiyn Bumatsende	July 1940–Sept 1953
(post vacant until July 1954)	
Zhamsarangin Sambuu	July 1954–May 1972
Sonomyn Luvsan (acting head of state)	May 1972–June 1974
Yumzhagiyn Tsedenbal	June 1974–Aug 1984
Nyamyn Jagvaral (acting head of state)	Aug 1984–Dec 1984
Zhambyn Batmunkh	Dec 1984–Mar 1990
Punsalmaagiyn Ochirbat*	Mar 1990–

Heads of Government

Prime Minister—Chairman of the Council of Ministers

Kharlogiyn Choibalsan	1939–Jan 1952
Yumzhagiyn Tsedenbal	Jan 1952–June 1974
Zhambyn Batmunkh	June 1974–Dec 1984
Dumaagiyn Sodnom	Dec 1984–Sept 1990
Dashiyn Byambasuren	Sept 1990–July 1992
Puntsagiin Jasray	July 1992–

MYANMAR (Burma until 1988)

Heads of State

President

Sao Shwe Thaik	Jan 1948–Mar 1952
Ba U (formerly U Ba Swe)	Mar 1952–Mar 1957
U Win Maung (until deposed in coup)	Mar 1957–Mar 1962
U Ne Win (formerly General Ne Win)	Mar 1962–Nov 1981
U San Yu	Nov 1981–July 1988
U Nu (briefly)	July 1988
Sein Lwin	July 1988–Aug 1988
General Saw Maung**	Aug 1988–April 1992
General Than Shwe**	April 1992–

---

* Since 3 Sept 1990 president of Mongolia.

** Chairman, State Law and Order Restoration Council—established after the military coup of 18 Sept 1988.

Heads of Government
Prime Minister

Aung San (until assassinated)	Nov 1945–July 1947
U Nu (formerly Thakin Nu)	July 1947–June 1956
U Ba Swe	June 1956–Feb 1957
U Nu (again)	Feb 1957–Oct 1958
General Ne Win (later U Ne Win)	Oct 1958–Feb 1960
U Nu (3rd time)	Feb 1960–Mar 1962
U Ne Win (2nd time)	Mar 1962–Mar 1974
U Sein Win	Mar 1974–Mar 1977
U Maung Maung Kha	Mar 1977–
General Saw Maung*	Sept 1988–April 1992
General Than Shwe*	April 1992–

NEPAL

Heads of State
King

Tribhuvana Bir Vikram Shah (briefly deposed Nov 1950–Jan 1951)	Dec 1911–Mar 1955
Mahendra Bir Vikram Shah Deva	Mar 1955–Jan 1972
Birendra Bir Vikram Shah Deva	Jan 1972–

Prime Minister

Juddha Shumshere Jung	1931–Mar 1946
Padma Shumshere Jung	Mar 1946–June 1948
Mohan Shumshere Jung	June 1948–Nov 1951
Matrika Koirala	Nov 1951–Aug 1952
King Tribhuvana	Aug 1952–Feb 1954
Matrika Koirala (2nd time)	Feb 1954–Mar 1955
King Mahendra	Mar 1955–Jan 1956
Tanka Achariya	Jan 1956–July 1957
Kunvar Singh	July 1957–Nov 1957
King Mahendra (2nd time)	Nov 1957–May 1958
Subarna Shumshere	May 1958–May 1959
Bishewar Koirala	May 1959–Dec 1960
King Mahendra (3rd time)	Dec 1960–April 1963
Tulsi Giri	April 1963–Jan 1965
Surya Thapa	Jan 1965–April 1969

---

* Chairman, State Law and Order Restoration Council—established after the military coup of 18 Sept 1988.

Kirtinidi Bista	April 1969–April 1970
King Mahendra (4th time)	April 1970–April 1971
Kirtinidi Bista (2nd time)	April 1971–July 1973
Nagendra Rijal	July 1973–Dec 1975
Tulsi Giri (2nd time)	Dec 1975–Sept 1977
Kirtinidi Bista (3rd time)	Sept 1977–May 1979
Surya Thapa (2nd time)	May 1979–July 1983
Lokendra Chand	July 1983–April 1990

(After 30 years of effective direct rule, in April 1990 a prime minister
   with political power was appointed.)

Krishna Prasad Bhattarai	April 1990–May 1991
Girija Prasad Koirala	May 1991–

NORTH KOREA (since the proclamation of the Korean People's Democratic Republic on 9 Sept 1948)

Heads of State

President*

Kim Du Bon	Sept 1948–Sept 1957
Choi Yong Kun	Sept 1957–Dec 1972
Kim Il Sung (formerly Kim Sung Ju)	Dec 1972–

Heads of Government

Prime Minister

Kim Il Sung	Sept 1948–Dec 1972
Kim Il	Dec 1972–April 1976
Pak Sung Chul	April 1976–Dec 1977
Li Jong Ok	Dec 1977–Jan 1984
Kang Song San	Jan 1984–Nov 1986
Li Gun Mo	Nov 1986–Dec 1988
Yon Hyong Muk	Dec 1988–Dec 1992
Kang Song San	Dec 1992–

---

*   Chairman of the Presidium of the Supreme People's Assembly from 1948 to 1972. The
   effective leader (and wielder of all real authority in North Korea) has been the leader of the
   Communist Party, Marshal Kim Il Sung. Kim Il Sung was chairman of the Central Committee until 1966 and has been general secretary of the Communist Party since that date.

PAKISTAN

Heads of State

Governor-General

Quaid-I-Azam Mohammed Ali Jinnah	Aug 1947–Sept 1948
Khwaja Nazimuddin	Sept 1948–Oct 1951
Ghulam Muhammed	Oct 1951–Aug 1955
Iskander Mirza	Aug 1955–Mar 1956

President

Iskander Mirza	Mar 1956–Oct 1958
Mohammed Ayub Khan	Oct 1958–Mar 1969
Agha Muhammad Yahya Khan	Mar 1969–Dec 1971
Zulfiqar Ali Bhutto	Dec 1971–Aug 1973
Fazal Elahi Chaudhri	Aug 1973–Sept 1978
Mohammed Zia ul-Haq	Sept 1978–Aug 1988
Gulam Ishaq Khan	Aug 1988–July 1993
Sardar Farooq Leghari	Nov 1993–

Heads of Government

Ali Khan Liaquat	Aug 1947–Oct 1951
Khwaja Nazimuddin	Oct 1951–April 1953
Mohammed Ali	April 1953–Aug 1955
Chaudri Mohammed Ali	Aug 1955–Sept 1956
Hussein Suhrawardy	Sept 1956–Oct 1957
Ismail Chundrigar	Oct 1957–Dec 1957
Firoz Khan Noon	Dec 1957–Oct 1958
Mohammed Ayub Khan	Oct 1958
(Post abolished later that month until Dec 1971, when briefly held by Nurul Amin. Post abolished again until Aug 1973.)	
Zulfiqar Ali Bhutto	Aug 1973–July 1977
(Post abolished again until Mar 1985)	
Mohammed Khan Junejo	Mar 1985–Nov 1988
Benazir Bhutto	Nov–Dec 1988–6 Aug 1990
Ghulam Mustafa Jatoi (interim appt.)	Aug 1990–Oct 1990
Nawar Sharif	Oct 1990–Apr 1993(dismissed)
Balakh Sher Mazari (caretaker)	April 1993–May 1993
Nawaz Sharif (reinstated, then resigned)	May 1993–July 1993
Moeen Qureshi (interim appt.)	July 1993–Oct 1993
Benazir Bhutto	Oct 1993–

PHILIPPINES

Heads of State

President

Manuel Roxas y Acuna	July 1946–April 1948
Elpidio Quirino	April 1948–Jan 1954
Ramon Magsaysay	Jan 1954–Mar 1957
Carlos Polestico Garcia	Mar 1957–Dec 1961
Diosdado Macapagal	Dec 1961–Dec 1965
Ferdinand Edralin Marcos	Dec 1965–Feb 1986
Corazon Aquino	Feb 1986–June 1992
Fidel Ramos	June 1992–

Heads of Government

Prime Minister

Ferdinand Marcos	Jan 1978–July 1981
Cesar Virata	July 1981–Feb 1986

After the February 1986 elections, parliament was abolished and a provisional government declared. A new constitution was ratified in 1987. No prime minister exists. The first vice president under Corazon Aquino was Salvador Laurel. The vice president under Ramos is Joseph Entrada.

SINGAPORE

Note: Singapore, a separate British colony after 1946, achieved full self-government in 1959. In 1963, Singapore joined the Malaysian Federation, but left in 1965, becoming an independent, sovereign republic.

Heads of State (President from August 1965)

William Goode	June 1959–Dec 1959
Yusof bin Ishak	Dec 1959–Nov 1970
Yeoh Ghim Seng	Nov 1970–Jan 1971 (acting)
Benjamin Sheares	Jan 1971–May 1981
Yeoh Ghim Seng	May 1981–Oct 1981 (acting)
C. V. Devan Nair	Oct 1981–Mar 1985
Yeoh Ghim Seng	Mar 1985–Sept 1985 (acting)
Wee Khim Wee	Sept 1985–1994
Ong Teng Cheong	1994–

Prime Minister

Lee Kuan Yew	June 1959–Nov 1990
Goh Chok Tong	Nov 1990–

SOUTH KOREA

Heads of State

President

Syngman Rhee	July 1948–April 1960
Huh Chung (acting)	April 1960–Aug 1960
Yoon Bo Sun	Aug 1960–Mar 1962
Park Chung Hee	Mar 1962–Oct 1962
Choi Kyu Hah	Oct 1979–Aug 1980
Park Choong Hoon (acting)	Aug 1980–Sept 1980
Chun Doo Hwan	Sept 1980–Feb 1988
Roh Tae-Woo	Feb 1988–Feb 1993
Kim Young-Sam	Feb 1993–

Heads of Government

Prime Minister

General Lee Bum Suk	Aug 1948–Nov 1950
John Myun Chang	Nov 1950–April 1952
Chang Taik Sang	April 1952–Oct 1952
(post vacant until April 1953)	
Paik Too Chin	April 1953–June 1954
Pyun Yung Tai	Jun 1954–Dec 1954
(post abolished until August 1960)	
Chang Myun	Aug 1960–May 1961
Chang Do Yun	May 1961–July 1961
Song Yo Chang	July 1961–June 1962
Kim Hyun Chul	June 1962–Dec 1963
Choi Too Sun	Dec 1963–May 1964
Chung Il Kwun	May 1964–Dec 1970
Paik Too Chin	Dec 1970–June 1971
Kim Chong Pil	Jun 1971–Dec 1975
Choi Kyu Hah	Dec 1975–Dec 1979
Shin Hyon Hwack	Dec 1979–May 1980
Park Choong Hoon	May 1980–Sept 1980
Nam Duck Woo	Sept 1980–Jan 1982
Yoo Chang Soon	Jan 1982–June 1982
Kim Sang Hyup	June 1982–Oct 1983
Chin Lee Chong	Oct 1983–Feb 1985
Lho Shin Yong	Feb 1985–May 1987
Kim Chung-Yul	July 1987–Feb 1988
Lee Hyun Jae	Feb 1988–Dec 1988

Kang Young Hoon	Dec 1988–Dec 1990
Ro Jai-bong	Dec 1990–May 1991
Chung Won-shik	May 1991–Oct 1992
Hyun Soong Jong	Oct 1992–Feb 1993
Hwang In Sung	Feb 1993–Dec 1993
Lee Hoi Chang	Dec 1993–

SRI LANKA (formerly Ceylon)

Heads of State

Governor-General

Sir Henry Monck-Mason Moore	Feb 1948–July 1949
Lord Soulbury	July 1949–July 1954
Sir Oliver Ernest Goonetilleke	July 1954–Mar 1962
William Gopallawa	Mar 1962–May 1972

President

William Gopallawa	May 1972–Feb 1978
Junius Richard Jayarwardene	Feb 1978–Dec 1988
Ranasinghe Premadasa	Dec 1988–May 1993
Dingiri Banda Wijetunge	May 1993

Heads of Government

Prime Minister

Donald S. Senanayake	Feb 1948–Mar 1952
Dudley S. Senanayake	Mar 1952–Oct 1953 (1st time)
Sir John L. Kotelawala	Oct 1953–April 1956
Solomon W. R. D. Bandaranaike	April 1956–Sept 1959
Wijeyananda Dahanayake	Sept 1959–Mar 1960
Dudley S. Senanayake	Mar 1960–July 1960 (2nd time)
Sirimavo Bandaranaike	July 1960–Mar 1965 (1st time)
Dudley S. Senanayake	Mar 1965–May 1970 (3rd time)
Sirimavo Bandaranaike	May 1970–July 1977 (2nd time)
Junius Richard Jayarwardene	July 1977–Feb 1978
Ranasinghe Premadasa	Feb 1978–Dec 1988
Dingiri Banda Wijetunge	Dec 1988–May 1993
Ranil Wickremasinghe	May 1993

TAIWAN

Heads of State

President

Li Zongren	Dec 1949–Mar 1950
Jiang Kaishek (Chiang Kai-shek)	Mar 1950–April 1975
Yen Jiagan (Yen Chia-kan)	April 1975–May 1978
Jiang Jinguo (Chiang Ching-kuo)	May 1978–Jan 1988
Li Denghui (Lee Teng-hui)	Jan 1988–

Heads of Government

Prime Minister

Yen Hsi-shan	Dec 1949–Mar 1950
Chen Cheng	Mar 1950–June 1954 (1st time)
Yui Hung-chun	June 1954–June 1958
Chen Cheng	June 1958–Dec 1963 (2nd time)
Yen Chia-kan (Yan Jiangan)	Dec 1963–June 1972
Chiang Ching-kuo (Jiang Jiguo)	June 1972–May 1978
Sun Yun-suan	May 1978–May 1984
Yu Kuo-hwa	May 1984–Mar 1990
Hau Pei-tsun	Mar 1990–Feb 1993
Lien Chan	Feb 1993–

THAILAND

Heads of State

King

Ananda Mahidol (Rama VIII)	Mar 1935–June 1946
Bhumibol Adulyadej (Rama IX)	June 1946–

Heads of Government

Prime Minister

Nai Thawi Bunyakat	Aug 1945–Sept 1945
Seni Pramoj	Sept 1945–Jan 1946
Kovid Aphaiwongse	Jan 1946–Mar 1946
Pridi Phanomjong	Mar 1946–Aug 1946
Dhamrong Nawasasat	Aug 1946–Dec 1947
Kovid Aphaiwongse	Dec 1947–April 1948
Pibul Songgram	April 1948–Sept 1957
Pote Sarasin	Sept 1957–Jan 1958
Thanom Khittikachorn	Jan 1958–Oct 1958

Sarit Thanarat	Oct 1958–Dec 1963
Thanom Khittikachorn	Dec 1963–Oct 1973
Sanya Dharmasaki	Oct 1973–Feb 1975
Seni Pramoj	Feb 1975–Mar 1975
Kukrit Pramoj	Mar 1975–April 1976
Seni Pramoj	April 1976–Oct 1976
Tnanin Kraivichien	Oct 1976–Oct 1977
Kriangsak Chamanand	Nov 1977–Feb 1980
Prem Tinsulanonda	Feb 1980–Aug 1988
Majben Chatichai Choonhavan	Aug 1988–Feb 1991

(In February 1991 a peaceful coup took place. A National Peacekeeping Command, headed by General Sunthorn Kompongsong, was formed, with General Suchinda Krapayoon as its most important figure. An interim prime minister, Anand Panyarachun, was appointed, who in fact continued in office until September 1992.)

Anand Panyarachun	June 1991–Sept 1992
Chuan Leekpai	Sept 1992–

TIBET

Ruler

Tenzin Gyatso (14th Dalai Lama)	Nov 1950*–Mar 1959

The 14th Dalai Lama went into exile. He was replaced (with Chinese approval) by:

Chokyi Gyaltsen (6th Panchen Lama)	Mar 1959–Sept 1966

VIETNAM

Between 1945 and 1954, the nationalist government in the north was engaged in a war with the French colonial authorities over control of the whole of Vietnam. Between 1954 and the northern victory in 1975, Vietnam was divided into the two states of South Vietnam and North Vietnam.

NORTH VIETNAM (until 1976)

Heads of State

President

Ho Chi Minh	Sept 1945–Sept 1969
Ton Duc Thang	Sept 1969–July 1976

---

* Date of enthronement. The 14th Dalai Lama was born Lhamo Tontrop in 1935.

Heads of Government

Prime Minister
(Chairman of the Council of Ministers since 1981)

Ho Chi Minh	Sept 1945–Sept 1955
Pham Van Dong	Sept 1955–1987*

Communist Party Leader

Ho Chi Minh	Sept 1945–Sept 1969
Le Duan	Sept 1969–July 1986**

SOUTH VIETNAM (until 1976)

Emperor of Vietnam†, recognized in the south until 1955
Bao Dai

President

Ngo Dinh Diem	Oct 1955–Nov 1963
Duong Van Minh	Nov 1963–Jan 1964
Nguyen Khanh	Jan 1964–Feb 1964
Duong Van Minh	Feb 1964–Aug 1964
Nguyen Khanh	Aug 1964–Sept 1964
Duong Van Minh	Sept 1964–Oct 1964
Phan Khac Suu	Oct 1964–June 1965
Nguyen Van Thieu	June 1965–April 1975
Tran Van Huong	April 1975
Duong Van Minh	April 1975
Nguyen Huu Tho‡	April 1975–July 1976

Prime Minister

Nguyen Van Xuan	May 1949–June 1949
Bao Dai	June 1949–Jan 1950
Nguyen Phan Long	Jan 1950–May 1950
Tran Van Huu	May 1950–June 1952
Nguyen Van Tam	June 1952–Dec 1953

---

*   Continued in office after unification.

**   Ho Chi Minh was chairman; Le Duan was first secretary, 1969–76, general secretary after 1976 until 1986.

†   A figurehead position, maintained by the French colonial administration.

‡   Maintained in office by the North Vietnamese until formal unification.

Buu Loc	Dec 1953–June 1954
Ngo Dinh Diem	June 1954–Nov 1963
Nguyen Ngoc Tho	Nov 1963–Feb 1964
Nguyen Khanh	Feb 1964–Oct 1964
Tran Van Huong	Oct 1964–Jan 1965
Nguyen Xuan Oanh	Jan 1965–Feb 1965
Phan Huy Quat	Feb 1965–June 1965
Nguyen Cao Ky	June 1965–Oct 1967
Nguyen Van Loc	Nov 1967–May 1968
Tran Van Huong (2nd time)	May 1968–Aug 1969
Tran Thien Khiem	Sept 1969–April 1975
Nguyen Ba Can	April 1975
Vo Van Mau	April 1975
Huynh Tan Phat*	April 1975–July 1976

VIETNAM (after unification in 1976)

Heads of State

President

Ton Duc Thang	July 1976–Mar 1980
Nguyen Huu Tho (acting)	April 1980–July 1981
Truong Chinh	July 1981–Dec 1986
Nguyen Van Linh (acting)	Dec 1986–1987
Vo Chi Cong	1987–1991
Do Muoi	Aug 1991–Sept 1992
Le Duc Anh	Sept 1992–

Heads of Government

Prime Minister

Pham Van Dong	1976–1987
Pham Hung	1987–1989
Do Muoi	1989–1991
Vo Van Kiet	1991–

Secretaries General of the Communist Party since reunification

Le Duan	Sept 1969–July 1986
Truong Chinh	July 1986–Dec 1986

---

* Maintained in office by the North Vietnamese until formal unification.

Nguyen Van Linh	Dec 1986–1990
Do Muoi	1990–

BIBLIOGRAPHICAL NOTE

Source: among the many sources available for lists of heads of state, the most invaluable are R.F. Tapsell, *Monarchs, Rulers, Dynasties and Kingdoms of the World* (Thames & Hudson, 1983); and John E. Morby, *Dynasties of the World: A Chronological and Genealogical Handbook* (Oxford UP, 1989).

CHAPTER 4

CONSTITUTIONS

AFGHANISTAN

Afghanistan began moving towards a modern political system as a monarchy in the 1960s. A constitution was promulgated in 1964 which retained the king's ultimate authority but removed the royal family from direct involvement in government.

The constitution established a bicameral parliament (the Shura). The upper chamber was the 84-member House of Elders (Meshrano Jirgah), one-third of which was appointed every five years by the king, one-third elected from constituencies every four years, and one-third elected every three years by Provincial Councils. The lower chamber was the 215-member House of the People (Wolesi Jirgah). The members were elected for four-year terms by direct universal suffrage. The cabinet, appointed by the king on the recommendation of the prime minister, was responsible to the lower house. The two houses sitting together with the chairmen of the local government Provincial Councils formed the Great Council (Loya Jirgah), which met to discuss more significant constitutional matters.

The constitution was abolished after a coup in 1978. A Communist regime was imposed following the invasion by the Soviet Union in December 1979. In April 1980 the Fundamental Principles of the Democratic Republic of Afghanistan were ratified. Ultimate state authority was vested in a Revolutionary Council and in its executive committee, the Presidium. The Revolutionary Council met twice a year, and at other times its business was conducted by the Presidium. Both bodies were presided over by a president elected from the Revolutionary Council who, as head of state, commanded the armed forces and ratified all legislation. Executive authority was vested in a Council of Ministers that was responsible to the Revolutionary Council. Though its role was not constitutionally specified, the Central Committee of the communist People's Democratic Party of Afghanistan played a significant part in setting out major policy guidelines. This constitution was succeeded by new constitutional arrangements in 1985 and 1987, and the latter was amended in 1990.

Since the fall of Najibullah, no settled constitution has yet been agreed to. In March 1993 it was agreed that President Rabbani and his archrival Gulbuddin Hekmatyar would share power. Afghan leaders also agreed to form an election commission and to hold a grand council within eight months to draft a new constitution. It was envisaged that a general election would be held in 1994.

BANGLADESH

Bangladesh was East Pakistan before it seceded to become the People's Republic of Bangladesh in December 1971. The constitution of 1972 instituted a parliamentary system, but after declaring a state of emergency in 1975 the country's founder, Sheikh Mujib ur-Rahman, abolished the parliamentary system and replaced it with a presidential system, with himself as president.

Mujib was assassinated in 1977 and replaced by General Zia ur-Rahman, who gathered power to the presidency by successive amendments to the 1972 constitution. A constitutional amendment in 1978 gave the office full executive authority as well as the role of head of state. The president was directly elected for five years by universal suffrage. This amendment retained the one-chamber legislature (Jatiya Sangsad), directly elected with legislative powers but subordinated to the authority of the president. Thirty of the chamber's 330 seats were reserved for women.

Zia was assassinated in 1981 and the military seized power in the following year. The constitution was suspended and the legislature was dissolved. A civilian president was appointed, but political authority lay with the army chief of staff and martial law administrator, General Ershad. He became president in 1983 and was confirmed in this position by a referendum in 1985.

BHUTAN

Bhutan has no formal constitution, although it operates a form of constitutional monarchy with the monarch as head of state.

A National Assembly (Tshogdu) was established in 1953 to enact legislation and to offer advice to the monarch on political and constitutional matters. The king altered the Assembly's status from that of a purely consultative to a representative body by abandoning the royal veto on its resolutions and legislation in 1968. A further amendment in 1969 made the monarch's retention of power conditional on his having the support of at least two-thirds of Assembly members. The Assembly meets twice a year, and its members are elected for three-year terms. The majority are directly elected, although seats are reserved for religious bodies, a representative of industry, and government-nominated officials.

A Royal Advisory Council (Lodoi Tsokde) was established in 1965. It is in permanent session and acts as a standing committee of the National Assembly, advising the monarch and supervising the country's administration. The Council has nine members, who serve for five years—a chairman nominated by the monarch, two monks representing the Central and District Monastic Bodies, and six popular representatives elected by the National Assembly from candidates nominated by District Development Committees.

BRUNEI

Brunei was under British "protection" from 1888 and under British administration from 1906. The framework for internal self-government was established by a written constitution in 1959. This provided for a privy council to advise the sultan, a legislative council and an executive council. The United Kingdom high commissioner retained responsibility for defense and security matters and advised the sultan on internal security.

Under the 1959 constitution the legislative council consisted of 33 members—16 elected from among district councillors by adult suffrage, six who were officials appointed by the sultan, together with a further three members appointed by him, and eight ex officio members. In 1962 both this and the executive council were temporarily replaced by an emergency council.

The constitution was amended in 1965 to allow a limited form of ministerial government. The sultan retained ultimate authority as head of state. The legislative council was made up of a speaker and 21 other members, six of whom were ex officio, five nominated, and 10 elected. The executive council became a council of ministers over which the sultan presided and which comprised the high commissioner, six ex officio members, and four assistant ministers drawn from the legislative council. One of the ex officio members of both councils is the Mentri Besar, who is responsible to the sultan for state administrative affairs.

CAMBODIA

Cambodia was part of French Indochina until becoming independent in November 1953 as a constitutional monarchy under King Norodom Sihanouk. Cambodia's constitution was promulgated in 1947. Sihanouk abdicated in 1955 in favor of his father, Norodom Suramarit, but retained direct political authority as a prince. Cambodia was effectively a one-party state.

The constitution was amended in 1960 following the death of King Suramarit. The amendment empowered the bicameral parliament to select a chief of state to exercise royal powers. Prince Sihanouk was confirmed as chief of state for an indefinite term in June 1960. Under the constitution the chief of state delegated executive powers to a Council of Ministers, under a prime minister, that was responsible to the elected National Assembly. The National Assembly was empowered to enact legislation, but the chief of state shared legislative initiative with the Council of Ministers and both houses of parliament. A National Congress, a biennial forum composed of delegates from the ruling party and other groupings, was given constitutional status in 1957.

Following a coup in March 1970, Cambodia became a republic in October. In April 1975 the Communist Khmer Rouge seized power and instituted a genocidal dictatorship. In January 1979 the regime was overthrown by Vietnamese forces. A People's Republic of Kampuchea was proclaimed on 10 January, the constitutional status of the Vietnamese-dominated state remaining fluid.

In June 1981 a new constitution was instituted. Legislative powers were vested in a 117-member National Assembly, elected by universal suffrage in 1981. In 1986 the Assembly's term was extended for a further five years. Membership was increased to 123 in 1987. A Council of State was elected by the Assembly from among its members. Executive power rested with the Council of Ministers, elected by and responsible to the National Assembly. Real political power, however, lay with the Kampuchean People's Revolutionary Party, the renamed Communist Party.

Following prolonged internal fighting, a United Nations peace plan in October 1991 proposed elections in May 1993 to a 120-member Constituent Assembly which, following agreement on a new constitution, would then become a legislative assembly. Despite threats from the Khmer Rouge, these elections were held. No party won a majority and several months of political and sometimes military conflict took place. In September 1993, Prince Sihanouk, who had occupied the titular post of president, reassumed the throne as king and appointed co-premiers in a prearranged consensus arrangement. Cambodia was again a constitutional monarchy.

CHINA, PEOPLE'S REPUBLIC OF

The People's Republic of China was proclaimed on 1 October 1949 with an Organic Law and a Common Program. A permanent constitution based on these was instituted in 1954. China was declared to be a unitary multi-national republic in which all nationalities were equal and had autonomy in national areas, which were, however, inalienably part of China. Means of production were owned collectively through the state.

Under the 1954 constitution, the head of state was the chairman of the republic. The sole legislative body, and the highest authority, was the National People's Congress. Its deputies—consisting of members of the Communist Party and eight other parties in a United Front—were elected for a five-year term by secret ballot, and met annually. The Congress, under Communist Party direction, was empowered to legislate, to amend the constitution, to elect and remove state officials, and to formulate a national plan. The Congress was convened by, and its legislation interpreted by, a permanent Standing Committee which was elected by Congress deputies and which then became the permanent legislative body. Effective power, however, lay with the Central Committee of the Communist Party. A State Council was to act as the republic's executive body, supervised by the Standing Committee of the National People's Congress.

The National People's Congress did not function during the upheaval of the Cultural Revolution of the late 1960s but was revived in 1975. A new constitution in that year reiterated the party's authority over the Congress. The 1975 constitution also replaced the single head of state with the collective Standing Committee of the Congress. In 1982 a new constitution revived the post of single head of state. Amendments to this constitution in 1988 authorized the formation of private companies and the renting of the right to use land privately.

INDIA

On independence in 1947 the Indian Independence Act retained the 1935 Government of India Act as a provisional constitution. A new constitution came into force in 1950 by which India became a federal democratic republic with a parliamentary system of government. This constitution was amended in 1951.

The head of state is the president, who is elected for a five-year term by both houses of the national parliament together with the lower houses of the state legislatures. The president's role is largely symbolic. The president appoints the prime minister, who must command a majority in the lower house of parliament, the House of the People (Lok Sabha), and with whom real authority rests.

India has a bicameral legislature—the House of the People (Lok Sabha) and the Council of States (Rajya Sabha). The lower house, the House of the People, has 525 members who are directly elected by universal adult suffrage for five years. A further 17 are elected or appointed. A temporary constitutional measure—which remains in force—provides for the reservation of 119 seats for members of the Scheduled Castes and Scheduled Tribes who have traditionally been disadvantaged in Indian society. The upper house, the Council of States, has 250 members, 12 of whom are appointed by the president, the remainder being elected by the state legislatures. They are elected for fixed terms, and a third retire every two years. The Council of States cannot be dissolved. Both houses have equal powers over legislation but only the House of the People can introduce financial bills. The Council of States' power in this area is limited to delaying financial legislation.

The states, which replaced the former provinces under the 1950 constitution, each have a legislature of one or two chambers, with the lower (or single) house sitting for five years and its members elected by direct adult suffrage. As with the central legislature, seats are specifically allocated to Scheduled Castes and Scheduled Tribes.

INDONESIA

Indonesia has had three provisional constitutions, one in 1945 and two in 1950. In 1959 the 1945 constitution was restored by presidential decree, and it was adopted permanently in 1969. By its constitution Indonesia is a republic based on the tenets of the Pancasila: belief in one god, humanity, unity, democracy and social justice. Although the constitution appears to guarantee democracy, Indonesia in practice has been an authoritarian state led by a strong president with the backing of the armed forces.

The president is the head of state, chief executive and commander of the armed forces. He is elected for a renewable five-year term by the People's Consultative Assembly and shares legislative powers with the Assembly. All ministers are responsible to the president. The People's Consultative Assembly has 1,000 members and consists of members of the House of Representatives, the Supreme Advisory Council, regional delegates, members of political organizations and other groups. The Assembly meets at least once every five years, and its main role is to set out the broad outline of state policy. The House of Representatives has 500 members, 400 of whom are directly elected and the remainder nominated by the president. It submits legislation which the president ratifies, and which he can veto. The Supreme Advisory Council assists the president and is selected by him from members of political parties and other groups.

JAPAN

The 1947 constitution, which is based on a revised version of the 1889 Meiji constitution, came into force in 1952 when Japan regained its sovereignty following a period of United States occupation. Japan is a unitary secular democracy. Under the 1947 constitution the emperor, the symbolic head of state, renounced his traditional divine status. The Japanese peerage was abolished, together with standing armed forces and the right to engage in military action. Female suffrage was instituted and safeguards for human rights guaranteed.

Executive authority rests with the prime minister and cabinet, who are responsible to a bicameral parliament, the Diet. Legislation is normally initiated by the cabinet, but it is open for Diet members to introduce bills. Most measures require the agreement of both houses, but if there is disagreement on finance bills or on the ratification of foreign treaties, the will of the lower house prevails.

Members of the lower house, the House of Representatives, are directly elected for a four-year term by the "medium constituency," which is between the local and prefectural constituencies. The members of the upper house, the House of Councillors (which replaced the former House of Peers), are elected equally by one national constituency and by prefectural constituencies. They are elected for six-year terms and half the membership is renewed every three years. There is universal adult suffrage for everyone over 20.

LAOS

Laos became part of French Indochina in 1893 and was given limited self-government in 1949. The connection with France was finally severed in 1954. The constitution promulgated in May 1947 established a constitutional monarchy. The monarch's power was exercised on his behalf by a premier and council of ministers, subject to the approval of a popularly elected National Assembly. Deputies were elected by universal popular suffrage every five years and did not represent formal political parties. The government could dissolve the National Assembly with the concurrence of the upper house—the King's Council—which also had authority to review legislation enacted by the Assembly.

In 1975 the king abdicated and Laos became a one-party communist state. The state, controlled by the Lao People's Revolutionary Party (LPRP), initially had no written constitution. The president, as head of state, had only nominal powers. Executive authority lay with the prime minister, who was concurrently secretary general of the LPRP. The legislature, the Supreme People's Council, was chaired by the president, had a majority made up of LPRP members, and had few formal legislative powers. In August 1991 a written constitution was promulgated, with proposals for a unicameral National Assembly directly elected for a five-year term and providing for an elected executive president.

MALAYSIA

The Federation of Malaya was created in 1948 within the British Empire and included all Malay territories except Singapore. The Malay rulers and the British sovereign delegated authority to a high commissioner, under whom was an Executive Council and a Legislative Council. Each state was governed by its own ruler, who acted on the high commissioner's advice. The constitution of the Federation of Malaya came into effect when Malaya became an independent monarchy in August 1957 and, with amendments, became the constitution of Malaysia in 1963. In 1965 Singapore (qv) seceded from the Federation.

The king (the Yang Di Pertuan Agong) is the head of state and acts as a constitutional monarch with few powers. He is elected to office for five years by the Conference of Rulers of the States of Malaysia by rotation from among the nine hereditary rulers. The Conference of Rulers, consisting of 13 rulers of the states and nine hereditary rulers, is consulted on state boundaries, Islamic observances and constitutional amendments.

There are two houses of parliament—the Senate (Dewan Negra) and the House of Representatives (Dewan Rakyat). All legislation must be approved by both houses. The Senate has 68 members, 42 of whom are appointed by the head of state and 26 elected by state legislatures. The members of the 176-seat House of Representatives are elected for five years by universal adult franchise. The prime minister and cabinet are appointed by the head of state from among the members of the House.

In 1993, the prime minister (Mahathir bin Mohamad) attempted to deprive the sultans (hereditary rulers) of their legal privileges and their immunity, and a constitutional battle appeared to be developing until the sultans abandoned their immunity in February 1993.

MONGOLIA

Prior to the fourth constitution of 1992, the 1960 constitution was in force. The 1960 constitution confirmed the authority of the communist Mongolian People's Revolutionary Party (MPRP), which took power in 1924. Nominally the supreme organ of government was the national legislature, the Great People's Khural, elected every four years by universal suffrage. The MPRP submitted single-candidate lists to the electorate. In fact, the Khural—the majority of whose members were MPRP members—met once a year to ratify measures submitted by the Council of Ministers. The

Council of Ministers was the highest executive body and exerted party control over government ministries, planned the economy, and controlled defense and internal security. The chair of the Council was the prime minister. The Council of Ministers was elected by the Khural. A nine-member Presidium of the Council was created in 1984 to rule in the name of the Khural when the latter was not in session. The president of the Presidium, who was the MPRP secretary, was the head of state.

A new constitution was adopted on 13 January 1992, effective from the following month. The single-chamber Mongolian Great Hural is the supreme legislative body, with 76 members elected by universal adult suffrage for a four-year term. Any presidential veto can be overruled by a two-thirds decision of the Hural.

The president is head of state and commander in chief, and must be at least 45 years old. The first direct presidential elections were held in June 1993.

MYANMAR (formerly Burma)

Myanmar (then Burma) gained its independence from Great Britain in January 1948 as a parliamentary democracy under a constitution promulgated in September 1947. Following divisions in the ruling party, the armed forces commander, General Ne Win, formed a caretaker government in 1958. In March 1962 he led an army coup and formed a government of army officers through a Revolutionary Council. Parliament was abolished and the constitution suspended.

In April 1962 a Revolutionary Council manifesto called for a one-party socialist state. The 13-man Revolutionary Council vested all executive and legislative powers in its chairman, Ne Win. As head of state, the Revolutionary Council chairman appointed the Council of Ministers. In 1964 all parties except the ruling Burma Socialist Program Party were outlawed. A civilian advisory body was formed in 1968 to formulate a new constitution, and issued its proposals for a return to civilian rule in 1969.

A new constitution was approved by referendum in December 1973 and came into force in January 1974. The constitution was intended to order the transition from military to civilian rule, with a new government structure replacing the Revolutionary Council. Executive power was vested in two bodies, the Council of State and the Council of Ministers, both of which were selected by the legislature, the People's Assembly (Pyithu Hluttaw). The Council of State had 29 members—one from each of Burma's 14 states, 14 selected from the People's Assembly, and the prime minister, who was elected by the Council of Ministers. The chairman of the Council of State took the office of president. The Council of State had broad powers, including authority to impose martial law, and assumed governing powers when the Assembly did not meet. Its members served four-year terms. The Council of Ministers was elected by the People's Assembly from a list of candidates presented by the Council of State. The People's Assembly was a one-chamber legislature that met for two sessions annually and was directly elected by universal suffrage.

Following pro-democracy demonstrations in 1988, the military formed a State Law and Order Restoration Council (SLORC) and abolished all state organs. In 1989 it enacted an Election Law, and elections for the restored People's Assembly were held in May 1990. Two months after the elections, SLORC deprived the People's Assembly of its legislative powers and announced that its members would draft a new democratic constitution. In January 1993 SLORC called a four-day national convention to lay down guidelines for a new constitution. The convention chairman, Major-General Myo Nyunt, insisted that the armed forces would continue to play a leading role in a new democratic system.

NEPAL

After a brief experiment with parliamentary democracy in 1959–60, Nepal became an absolute monarchy, with all executive, legislative and judicial powers vested in the crown and political parties forbidden. In 1961 the monarch introduced the "panchayat" system of "partyless democracy" with a four- (later three-) tiered structure from village assemblies to the national legislature. The latter comprised indirectly elected and appointed members representing the king, localities, and class and professional organizations. In 1975 the professional and class organizations were disbanded and all candidates for the legislature were selected by the government.

In 1980 the king held a national plebiscite offering a choice between the institution of multiparty government and reform of the panchayat system. The majority chose the latter. A 140-seat legislature (Rastriya Panchayat) was established, the king appointing 28 members and the remainder being elected by direct adult suffrage. Party organizations and the formation of an official opposition remained banned. The legislature was empowered to recommend the appointment of a prime minister who had the support of 60% of its members. The prime minister was responsible to the legislature rather than to the king, though the monarch had the right to dismiss him from office. Defense and royal family affairs were outside the responsibilities of the legislature and the cabinet, and the king retained the power to veto legislation. Effective power remained with the king and his immediate advisors.

In May 1990 a new constitution was promulgated, making Nepal a constitutional monarchy. The constitution guaranteed fundamental rights and movement towards a multiparty political system. It instituted a bicameral parliament with a House of Representatives to be elected by direct universal suffrage. Elections were held in May 1991.

NORTH KOREA

Following the division of Korea along the 38th parallel, the Democratic People's Republic of Korea was established in North Korea as a one-party socialist state by the constitution of 1948. The state is subordinate to the Korean Workers' Party (Communists) and carries out the political line of the party.

The 1948 constitution was replaced in 1972. The office of president as head of state was established. He is elected for renewable four-year terms by the national legislature, the Supreme People's Assembly, though in practice he is not responsible to it. The president is commander of the armed forces, chief executive of the State Administration Council (the cabinet), and has the power to issue personal edicts that have the force of law.

The members of the Supreme People's Assembly are directly elected for four-year terms by universal adult suffrage from a single slate of candidates presented by the Korean Workers' Party. The Assembly meets twice a year and is empowered to elect the president, pass legislation, amend the constitution and approve the national budget. When the Assembly is not in session a Standing Committee, elected by its deputies, functions on its behalf. A Central People's Committee, the majority of whom are party Central Political Bureau (Politburo) members and are elected for four years by the Assembly, acts as a link between the party and the state.

PAKISTAN

Pakistan became independent within the British Commonwealth in 1947. Its territory then included West and East Pakistan (now Bangladesh), which had been partitioned from British India. A constituent assembly was formed to operate as a legislature under an amended version of the 1935 (British) Government of India Act, a function it carried out until 1956. Pakistan was a federation of provinces and a parliamentary monarchy, with a governor-general representing the British crown.

The provinces were united as one unit in 1955, and in 1956 Pakistan adopted a republican constitution, with a president as head of state, with wide powers. There was provision for East and West Pakistan to have equal representation in the central parliament. In 1958 President Mohammed Ayub Khan abrogated the constitution and declared martial law.

A new constitution in 1962 introduced an executive presidency and a unicameral national assembly. There were 75 members each from East and West Pakistan, elected by limited franchise, and six women members appointed by the provincial assemblies. This constitution was overthrown and martial law imposed in 1969. In 1970 Pakistan became a federal state of four provinces, and parliamentary government was restored. The National Assembly was enlarged but the principle of parity in membership between East and West Pakistan was abandoned, seats being distributed on the basis of population. This led in December 1970 to civil war, and martial law was reimposed. East Pakistan seceded in 1971 and became Bangladesh (qv).

In 1972 Pakistan withdrew from the British Commonwealth, and in 1973 it adopted a republican federal constitution. The president became the ceremonial head of an Islamic state, while the prime minister was head of government, responsible to a bicameral parliament. The National Assembly had 200 seats, with a further 10 reserved for women. The Senate had 63 members representing the provinces, tribal areas and the capital. In 1976 six more seats were reserved for non-Muslim minorities. In 1977 martial law was reimposed, with greatly strengthened presidential powers, a situation that continued until 1985. In 1985 a new parliament was installed on the basis of the 1973 constitution. Pakistan rejoined the British Commonwealth in 1989.

PHILIPPINES

The Philippines gained its independence from the United States in 1946. It continued to be governed by the constitution of May 1935, which, with subsequent amendments, set out a centralized administration within a framework based on the American model. Executive authority was vested in a popularly elected president allowed to serve for no more than two consecutive terms. The vice-president, who had no government functions, was separately elected. The cabinet was appointed by the president. Legislative authority was vested in a bicameral Congress made up of the Senate, one-third of whose members were elected for six years every two years, and a House of Representatives elected by proportional representation every four years. The country was divided into provinces, each with an elected governor but with provincial department heads directly responsible to the central government.

In 1972 President Ferdinand Marcos placed the Philippines under martial law, abolishing the Congress, outlawing political parties and curbing personal liberties. In 1978 legislative power was nominally vested in a unicameral Interim National Assembly (Interim Batasang Pambansa) with 200 members, 146 elected by popular vote; the remainder were the president, the cabinet and government representatives. In 1981 executive power was vested in the president, with no limit on the number of six-year terms he could serve. In 1986, President Marcos was forced to flee the country following his defeat in elections. The martial law constitution remained temporarily operative, but with provisions for parliamentary government and an independent judiciary. The National Assembly became an independent policy-making body. Voting is compulsory for all citizens over 16.

SIKKIM

Sikkim became a British protectorate in the 19th century and came under the protection of India on the latter's independence in 1947. In 1950 India formally assumed responsibility for Sikkim's defense and foreign affairs with Sikkim retaining internal autonomy. Sikkim is a hereditary monarchy with executive authority vested in the Maharaja. A principal administrative officer (an Indian civil servant) presides over the Executive Council (the cabinet) and the State Council (parliament). The State Council since 1952 has been partly elected and partly appointed, and acts as an advisory body to the Maharaja. It enacts legislation with his consent but cannot discuss matters concerning the ruling family, foreign affairs or the judicial system. A People's Consultative Committee with representatives of political parties was formed in 1962.

SINGAPORE

Singapore became a separate British colony in 1946, with an executive council nominated by the governor and a partly elected legislative council. The constitution of 1955 provided for a legislative council, the majority of which was elected. Defense and external affairs remained a British responsibility. In 1963 Singapore became independent of Great Britain as part of the Federation of Malaysia (qv) but in 1965 left to become a separate, sovereign republic.

The constitution derives from four sources: the Constitution of the (Malaysian) State of Singapore, articles of the Constitution of Malaysia, the 1965 Singapore Independence Act and the Constitution (Amendment) Act. In 1965 the governor of Singapore became the president, and the State Legislature was renamed the national Parliament. By Article 52J of the Constitution (Amendment) Act, unification with any other state was prohibited.

The president is the head of state and is elected by Parliament for a four-year term. There is no limit to the number of terms the president may serve, but Parliament is empowered to remove him from office by a two-thirds vote. The position is largely formal, but the president has the power to appoint the prime minister, to refuse a dissolution of parliament and to approve legislation. A Presidential Council for Minority Rights was established in 1970 to prevent legislative discrimination against minorities. It is empowered to examine all legislation except that concerned with the budget, defense and security. Political authority is vested in the cabinet, headed by the prime minister, who is appointed by the president and is responsible to Parliament. Members of the single-chamber Parliament are popularly elected for five-year terms. It passes bills by a simple majority before submitting them to the president for approval. Voting is compulsory for all citizens and residents over 21.

SOUTH KOREA

Following the postwar division of Korea along the 38th parallel, South Korea became the Republic of Korea in 1948 under a constitution that remains in effect with amendments.

During the First Republic, from 1948–60, political power was centralized in the hands of the president, Syngman Rhee, with the elected National Assembly having little influence. Constitutional amendments allowed the president to retain authority indefinitely until he was forced to retire in 1960. During the Second Republic, more democratic rule was instituted under a new constitution in 1960. But the government was overthrown by the armed forces in 1961 and one-man rule reestablished. A further constitutional amendment in 1972 gave the president wide-ranging powers as head of state, commander of the armed forces and chief executive. Martial law was imposed and the National Assembly dissolved.

In 1980, constitutional amendments reaffirmed the power of the presidency but imposed limitations on the office. The president can assume emergency powers only with the approval of the National Assembly, and the Assembly can revoke an emergency decree. The president cannot dissolve the Assembly during its first three years, and cannot do so without consulting cabinet members and the Assembly speaker. The National Assembly, whose members are elected for a four-year term, has to approve legislation and oversee the activities of the executive.

SRI LANKA

Sri Lanka was known as Ceylon until 1972. In 1948 it became independent from Great Britain. A constitution in 1945 provided for internal autonomy, with a bicameral parliament made up of a Senate and a House of Representatives. Half the Senate members—who sat for six-year terms—were elected by the House of Representatives and half were appointed by the Governor-General (appointed by the British). The House of Representatives was elected by universal suffrage.

Following independence in 1948, Sri Lanka became a constitutional monarchy under the Ceylon Independence Act of 1947 and retained the Senate as an upper house until 1971. The prime minister was appointed by the Governor-General but was responsible to parliament. A new constitution came into effect in 1972; Sri Lanka became a republic, with a president as head of state, appointed for a four-year term by the prime minister. Executive power was vested in a council of ministers led by the prime minister. A National Assembly sitting for six years combined legislative and executive functions and was elected by all citizens over 18.

Following a period of political disorder, the constitution was amended in 1977 to create a presidential system. A new constitution was promulgated in 1978, extending the role of the president from that of head of state to exerciser of direct political authority through the prime minister. The president—who was limited to serving two six-year terms—was empowered to appoint and dismiss ministers and to dissolve parliament. Parliament became a unicameral body with the authority to enact legislation and to control public finance. Its members were to be elected for six years by proportional representation, although the president has the authority to call an election after one year.

TAIWAN

The Communist victory in the Chinese civil war in 1949 forced the Nationalists to move their capital to the island of Taiwan, where they continued to assert their legal authority as the Republic of China over the mainland as a government in exile. From 1949 to 1987 the government exercised martial law under a state of emergency.

The government structure is based on the constitution of 1946. There are five branches (Yuan) of government, controlled by the ruling party, the Kuomintang (KMT). These are the Executive, Legislative, Judicial, Examination and Control, together with a National Assembly.

The Executive is the highest administrative body and is presided over by the premier. He is appointed by the president with the approval of the Legislative Yuan. The state president is leader of the KMT and commander of the armed forces; the KMT controls the military and security forces. The vice-president of the Executive Yuan, together with the ministers, is appointed by the republic's president from candidates recommended by the Executive Yuan. The Legislative Yuan is the main lawmaking body. Its members are elected for three-year terms and it meets for eight months of the year. The function of the National Assembly is to elect the state president and vice-president and to amend the constitution. It is popularly elected and meets every six years. The Examination Yuan controls the recruitment and management of the civil service. The Control Yuan exercises an anticorruption function and oversees preparation of the national budget. It is indirectly elected by the Taiwan Provincial Assembly and smaller local bodies, together with representatives of Mongolians, Tibetans, and overseas Chinese.

The Kuomintang has a majority in all nationally elected bodies, as most seats are held by members from the mainland who hold their seats for life. The only general elections for the Legislative Yuan, the Control Yuan and the National Assembly were held in those parts of China controlled by the KMT in 1947–48. Those elected remain in office for the duration of the "state of emergency" as a symbol of the continuing claim to rule the whole of China. In 1969 the government called "partial elections" in Taiwan to replace those members who had died or left the country. This has led in successive "supplementary elections" to an increasing number of Taiwanese in "limited-term" rather than "life-term" elected office. Election laws in 1980 and 1983 added a further element of constitutionality to the electoral process.

The Taiwan Provincial Government consists of 21 commissioners appointed by the central government. A 77-seat Taiwan Popular Assembly—with a predominantly Taiwanese membership—has been popularly elected since 1959. The Assembly prepares the provincial budget and administers Taiwan within the framework of national law.

THAILAND

Thailand is nominally a constitutional monarchy with a king as head of state. Legislative power is vested in a National Assembly, comprising an elected House of Representatives and a Senate appointed by the king. The prime minister is selected by the National Assembly. However, the armed forces have dominated Thailand politically, and legislatures, parties and elections give only a nominal guide to political authority. A series of coups has been followed by the abrogation of a series of constitutions.

Elections in 1957 were followed by a coup. In 1971 martial law was imposed. Coups in 1976 and 1977 were followed in 1978 by the promulgation of a new constitution setting out an appointed Senate with 225 members and an elected 301-seat House of Representatives. This constitution was suspended following a coup in February 1991. The National Assembly was dissolved by the ruling National Peacekeeping Council (NPC). In March 1991 an interim constitution was introduced, with a military-appointed National Assembly given the role of considering legislation and drafting a new constitution within six months. A new constitution was promulgated on 9 December 1991. This involved a Legislative Assembly consisting of an elected House of Representatives and an appointed Senate. A prime minister would head the cabinet and would be appointed by the military. Following the antigovernment demonstrations of April–May 1992, the Legislative Assembly voted in May 1992 that future prime ministers would be elected by its members.

VIETNAM

In 1945, with the end of the Japanese occupation of French Indochina, the Communist Viet Minh formed a republic in northern Vietnam and introduced a constitution the following year. The French colonial power returned to southern Vietnam and recognized the north as a "free state within the Indochinese Federation." The Viet Minh, however, continued fighting for a united independent Vietnam. The country was provisionally divided by a cease-fire agreement in 1954 pending elections in 1956 that were to precede unification of the country. The elections were never held.

The northern state became the Democratic Republic of Vietnam and introduced a new constitution in 1960. This declared that the state was a socialist, democratic people's republic led by the working class. The head of state was the president, with executive powers. The National Assembly, a single-chamber legislature, was elected from a list of Communist Party candidates. A permanent Standing Committee of the Assembly had the authority to interpret the Assembly's legislation and to rule by emergency decree.

The south was organized as the Republic of Vietnam, which introduced a constitution in 1956. This provided for an elected president with executive powers and an elected National Assembly. An Assembly was elected in September 1963 and dissolved in November after a coup. Revised constitutional arrangements were followed by the election of a two-chamber Assembly in 1967, with a House of Representatives sitting for a four-year term and a Senate for six years.

After the north's victory in the war in 1975, the two states were formally united in 1976 under the northern constitution of 1960. A new constitution for the united Vietnam was introduced in 1980. This declares Vietnam a proletarian state with the Communist Party as the leading political force. A Council of State functions as a "collective presidency." Executive and administrative power is vested in a Council of Ministers. Legislative and constitutional authority is held by the National Assembly, a single chamber of 496 deputies popularly elected from a one-party list of candidates. The National Assembly is empowered to legislate, to amend the constitution and to select the members of the Council of Ministers. In practice, the Assembly's authority is limited and its role is to ratify Communist Party policy.

CHAPTER 5

INTERNATIONAL ORGANIZATIONS, TREATIES, ALLIANCES AND AGREEMENTS

INTERNATIONAL ORGANIZATIONS

ASSOCIATION OF SOUTH-EAST ASIAN NATIONS (ASEAN)

Date of formation   7 August 1967

Headquarters   Jakarta (Indonesia)

Aims
a)   To promote political, economic, social and cultural cooperation among the non-Communist states of Southeast Asia.
b)   To increase trade between ASEAN countries and with the rest of the world.

History   The foreign ministers of **Indonesia, Malaysia,** the **Philippines, Singapore** and **Thailand** met in Bangkok to discuss a regional organization, and as a result signed the Bangkok Declaration. The first summit meeting was held in 1976.

Structure

Heads of Government Meeting takes place whenever necessary.

Annual Ministerial Meeting of foreign ministers takes place in member countries on an alphabetical rotation.

Standing Committee consisting of the foreign minister of the host country and the ambassadors of the others carries on the business between meetings.

Secretariat was established in Jakarta in 1967. The post of secretary-general revolves in alphabetical order every two years; other officers remain for three years.

There are also five economic committees and three noneconomic committees.

Secretary-General
Since July 1984   Phan Wannamethee (Thailand)

Past Secretaries-General
Feb 1976–Feb 1978   Hartono Dharsono (Indonesia)
Feb–July 1978   Umarjadi Njotowijona (Indonesia)
July 1978–July 1980 Datuk Ali bin Abdullah (Malaysia)
July 1980–July 1982 Narciso Reyes (Philippines)
July 1982–July 1984 Chan Kai Yau (Singapore)

Members
Brunei (since 1984)   Philippines
Indonesia   Singapore
Malaysia   Thailand

Observers   Laos and Vietnam were granted observer status in July 1992.

COLOMBO PLAN

Date of formation   Treaty 28 November 1950; in force 1 July 1951

Headquarters   Colombo (Sri Lanka)

Aims
a)   To promote the development of member countries in Asia.
b)   To review economic and social progress and help accelerate this through cooperative effort.
c)   To encourage development aid both to and within the area.

History   The original Plan was set up by seven British Commonwealth countries and was intended to last six years. Its life was extended by five-year intervals until 1980, when it was given an indefinite span.

Although the plan endeavors to deal with development in a coordinated multilateral way, negotiations for assistance take place directly between donor and recipient countries.

Structure

Consultative Committee of ministers meets once every two years, preceded by a meeting of senior officials.

Colombo Plan Council meets three or four times a year in Colombo to review progress.

Colombo Plan Bureau is the permanent servicing, research and information-disseminating organ. Since 1973 it has been operating a drug advisory program.

Colombo Plan Staff College exists to help members with technical education.

Director   Donald R. Toussant

Members

Afghanistan	Lao People's Democratic Republic
Australia	Malaysia
Bangladesh	Maldives
Bhutan	Nepal
Burma (Myanmar)	New Zealand
Cambodia	Pakistan
Canada	Papua New Guinea
Fiji	Philippines
India	Singapore
Indonesia	Sri Lanka
Iran	Thailand
Japan	United Kingdom
Republic of Korea	United States

THE BRITISH COMMONWEALTH

Date of formation   31 December 1931 (Statute of Westminster); redefined 1949

Headquarters   London (United Kingdom)

Aims   Cooperation, consultation and mutual assistance among countries that accept the Queen "as the symbol of the free association of independent member nations and as such the Head of the Commonwealth."

History   Following resolutions at Imperial Conferences of 1926 and 1930, the Statute of Westminster affirmed that dominions are "autonomous communities within the British Empire, equal in status . . . united by a common allegiance to the Crown and freely associated as members of the British Commonwealth of Nations." This definition was modified in 1949 when member countries accepted India's intention of becoming a republic while remaining a full member of the Commonwealth. There are now 18 Queen's realms, 26 republics and six indigenous monarchies within the Commonwealth.

Structure

Commonwealth Secretariat was established in 1965 to serve all members. It has observer status at the United Nations, disseminates information, organizes meetings, coordinates activities and provides expert technical assistance.

Commonwealth Heads of Government Meetings are held biennially. Until 1946, prime ministers' meetings were attended by **Great Britain, Australia, Canada, New Zealand** and **South Africa**. In 1971 the meetings were renamed, as delegations were often led by executive presidents of newly independent countries.

Secretary-General
Since June 1990   Emeka Anyaoku (Nigeria)

Past Secretary-General
July 1965–July 1975   Arnold Smith (Canada)
Aug 1975–June 1990   Shridath Ramphal (Guyana)

THE SEVEN ASIAN MEMBERS OF THE COMMONWEALTH			
	Date of Independence	Status	Notes
Bangladesh	4 Feb 1972	R	Seceded from Pakistan as republic 16 Dec 1971; joined 18 April 1972.
Brunei	1 Jan 1984	M*	
India	15 Aug 1947	R	Republic 26 Jan 1950.
Malaysia	31 Aug 1957	M*	16 Sept 1963 as Federation of Malaysia.
Pakistan	15 Aug 1947	R	Joined 1947. Left 1972. Rejoined 1989.
Singapore	16 Sept 1963	R	Republic and independent state 9 Aug 1965.
Sri Lanka	4 Feb 1948	R	Republic 22 May 1972; formerly Ceylon.

R   Republic
M*   Country with its own monarchy

SOUTH EAST ASIA COLLECTIVE DEFENSE TREATY

On 8 September 1954 **Australia, France, Great Britain, New Zealand, Pakistan,** the **Philippines, Thailand,** and the **United States** signed a treaty in Manila that established a collective defense system and pledged the countries to form a united front against Communist domination of southeast Asia. The treaty also set up the South East Asia Treaty Organization (SEATO) with headquarters in Bangkok. A mechanism was provided under the treaty for the settlement of disputes between members, for defense against outside aggression and for cooperation in economic, social and technical fields. A Council consisting of foreign ministers met annually.

In 1973 Pakistan withdrew from SEATO, and since 1974 France has made no financial contribution, while continuing to adhere to the treaty. In 1974 changes were made to the structure to allow activity to be concentrated on Thailand and the Philippines. In 1974 the Council agreed that SEATO should be phased out, and on 30 June 1977 it was formally dissolved. The 1954 Collective Defense Treaty still remains in force, and provides for mutual support in the event of external aggression.

UNITED NATIONS

Date of formation   Charter 26 June 1945; in force 24 October 1945.

Headquarters   New York (U.S.)

Aims
a) To maintain international peace and security.
b) To cooperate in establishing political, economic and social conditions under which this task can be securely achieved.

History   A four-nation conference of foreign ministers signed an agreement in Moscow on 30 October 1943 that "a general international organization . . . for the maintenance of international peace and security" was desirable. Further discussions took place at Dumbarton Oaks (Washington, D.C.) from 21 August until 7 October 1944 among, first, the United Kingdom, the United States and the USSR and then China, the United Kingdom and the United States. These proposals were put before the United Nations Conference on International Organization held in San Francisco between 25 April and 26 June 1945, when, after amendment, the Charter was signed. It came into force on 24 October 1945 when China, France, the United Kingdom, the United States, the USSR and a majority of the other 45 signatories ratified the Charter. The first regular session was held in London from 10 January to 14 February 1946.

Structure

General Assembly consists of all members, each with five delegates but only one vote. It meets once a year starting on the third Tuesday in September. A special session can be called at the request of the Security Council by the agreement of a majority of its members or at the request of a member with the concurrence of the majority of the Security Council. The president is elected each session. Important decisions require a two-thirds majority, other decisions a simple majority of members present and voting. The Assembly has seven main committees.

Security Council is responsible for the maintenance of peace and security and can call on the armed forces of member states to help achieve that purpose. It consists of 15 members, each with one representative and one vote. China, France, the United Kingdom, the United States and Russia are permanent members. Others are elected by a two-thirds majority in the General Assembly. They serve for two years and are not immediately eligible for reelection. The Council functions continuously and its president serves for one month in alphabetical rotation. Procedural questions must be agreed on by at least nine of its members. On other matters the nine concurring votes must include the five permanent members.

Economic and Social Council is responsible for economic, social, cultural, educational, health and related matters. There are 15 specialized intergovernmental agencies, and consultation takes place with numerous international nongovernmental agencies and national organizations. It consists of 54 members elected by a two-thirds majority of the General Assembly. Eighteen are elected each year for a three-year period and can be reelected immediately. It holds two sessions a year. Its president is elected for one year and may be reelected. Decisions are made by a majority vote of those present and voting. The Council has numerous commissions and standing committees.

Trusteeship Council is responsible for the interests of territories that are not yet fully self-governing. There were formerly 11 of these trust territories. The members of the Council are the permanent members of the Security Council; they meet in regular session once a year, and votes are by a majority of members present and voting.

International Court of Justice consists of 15 independent judges, each of a different nationality, elected by the Security Council and the General Assembly sitting independently. They meet at The Hague, Netherlands, in permanent session and serve for nine-year terms, after which they may be reelected. The president and vice-president are elected by the Court for three-year terms. Decisions are made by a majority of judges present, and a quorum of nine is sufficient to constitute the Court. All members of the UN are parties to the Statute of the Court. Judgments are final and without appeal.

Secretariat in New York is administered by the Secretary-General, who is appointed by the General Assembly for a five-year term that may be renewed.

Membership

The following are the Asian members of the United Nations (with date of joining in parenthesis).

Afghanistan	(1946)
Bangladesh	(1974)
Bhutan	(1971)
Brunei	(1984)
Cambodia	(1955)
China	(1945)
India	(1945)
Indonesia	(1950)
Japan	(1956)
Laos	(1955)
Malaysia	(1957)
Mongolia	(1961)
Myanmar (Burma)	(1948)
Nepal	(1955)
North Korea	(1991)
Pakistan	(1947)
Philippines	(1945)
Singapore	(1965)
South Korea	(1991)
Sri Lanka	(1955)
Thailand	(1946)
Vietnam	(1977)

MAJOR TREATIES AND AGREEMENTS

Note

This section is arranged alphabetically by country. It does not attempt to include the multitude of cultural, educational or commercial treaties, which would occupy a large volume. It is confined to major diplomatic and military agreements of political significance.

AFGHANISTAN

4 Jan 1950	Treaty of peace and friendship with **India**
18 Dec 1955	Ten-year extension to 1931 treaty of neutrality and nonaggression with **Soviet Union** (extended further on 6 Aug 1965 and 10 Dec 1975)
27 Aug 1960	Treaty of friendship and nonaggression with **China**
24 Nov 1963	Boundary treaty with **China**
5 Dec 1978	Treaty of friendship, cooperation and good-neighborliness with **Soviet Union**
4 April 1980	Agreement with **Soviet Union** formalizing presence of Soviet troops in Afghanistan
25 June 1981	Treaty of friendship with **Czechoslovakia**
23 May 1982	Treaty of friendship with **East Germany**
14 May 1988	Geneva accord with **Pakistan** guaranteed by **United States** and **Soviet Union**, for noninterference in each other's affairs

CAMBODIA (KAMPUCHEA)

23 Dec 1950	Agreement with **France, Laos, Vietnam** and **United States** for mutual defense assistance in Indochina
21 July 1954	Geneva Agreements on **Indochina**
27 Nov 1960	Treaty of friendship and cooperation with **Czechoslovakia**
19 Dec 1960	Treaty of friendship and cooperation with **China**
23 July 1962	Declaration on the neutrality of **Laos** at Geneva
28 May 1978	Treaty of friendship and cooperation with **Romania**
18 Feb 1979	Treaty of peace, friendship and cooperation with **Vietnam**
7 July 1982	Agreement with **Vietnam** defining territorial waters
20 July 1983	Border treaty with **Vietnam**
23 Oct 1991	Peace agreement (signed in Paris) ending 13-year civil war. UN is mandated to supervise the peace and prepare for elections in 1993
Mar 1994	Cambodia and the **Vatican** agree to establish diplomatic relations.

CHINA

23 May 1951	Agreement with **Tibet** regarding that country's autonomy
21 July 1954	Geneva declaration on **Indochina**
25 Dec 1955	Treaty of friendship with **East Germany**

27 Aug 1957	Treaty of friendship with **Czechoslovakia**
6 May 1959	Treaty of friendship with **Hungary**
28 Jan 1960	Treaty of friendship and nonaggression with **Burma**
21 Mar 1960	Border agreement with **Nepal**
28 April 1960	Treaty of peace and friendship with **Nepal**
31 May 1960	Treaty of friendship and mutual economic aid with **Mongolia**
27 Aug 1960	Treaty of friendship and nonaggression with **Afghanistan**
13 Sept 1960	Treaty of friendship with **Guinea**
1 Oct 1960	Border agreement with **Burma**
19 Dec 1960	Treaty of friendship and nonaggression with **Cambodia**
1 April 1961	Treaty of friendship with **Indonesia**
11 July 1961	Treaty of friendship, cooperation and mutual assistance with **North Korea**
18 Aug 1961	Treaty of friendship with **Ghana**
5 Oct 1961	Border agreement with **Nepal**
23 July 1962	Declaration on neutrality of **Laos** at Geneva
26 Dec 1962	Border agreement with **Mongolia**
2 Mar 1963	Border agreement with **Pakistan**
24 Nov 1963	Border agreement with **Afghanistan**
9 June 1964	Treaty of friendship with **Yemen Republic**
2 Oct 1964	Treaty of friendship with **Congo**
3 Nov 1964	Treaty of friendship with **Mali**
20 Feb 1965	Treaty of friendship with **Tanzania**
26 Mar 1965	Border agreement with **Pakistan**
7 July 1965	Treaty of friendship and good-neighborly relations with **North Vietnam**
8 Aug 1969	Agreement with **Soviet Union** on the navigation of the Amur and Ussuri rivers
15 Nov 1969	Agreement with **Tanzania** and **Zambia** to build the Tan-Zam railway
20 April 1976	Military aid protocol with **Egypt**
12 Aug 1978	Treaty of peace and friendship with **Japan**
17 Sept 1980	Treaty for the normalization of relations with **United States**
19 Dec 1984	Agreement with **Great Britain** on the future of Hong Kong
7 April 1985	Military cooperation agreement with **Italy**
13 April 1987	Agreement with **Portugal** on the return of Macao in 1999
July 1990	**Saudi Arabia** recognizes China
Aug 1990	Diplomatic relations with **Indonesia** reestablished
Oct 1990	Diplomatic relations with **Singapore** established
April 1991	Official end of "state of war" between China and **Taiwan**

10 Nov 1991	Diplomatic relations with **Vietnam** reestablished
24 Aug 1992	Diplomatic relations established with **South Korea**
7 Sept 1993	Border peace deal with **India** signed, reducing troop numbers along border and establishing a cease-fire line

INDIA

8 Aug 1949	Treaty of peace and friendship with **Bhutan**
4 Jan 1950	Treaty of peace and friendship with **Afghanistan**
31 July 1950	Treaty of peace and friendship with **Nepal**
5 Dec 1950	Treaty with **Sikkim** for continuation of its status as an autonomous protectorate of India
11 July 1952	Treaty of peace and friendship with **Philippines**
29 April 1954	Nonaggression treaty with **China**
28 Feb 1956	Five-year agreement with **Indonesia** on mutual aid between air forces
3 Dec 1958	Naval cooperation agreement with **Indonesia**
3 June 1960	Agreement with **Indonesia** for military cooperation and mutual assistance in developing armies
19 Sept 1960	Indus Waters Treaty with **Pakistan**
23 July 1962	Declaration on the neutrality of **Laos** at Geneva
27 Nov 1962	Agreement for supply of arms by **Great Britain**, only for defense against Chinese aggression
13 Jan 1965	Military assistance agreement with **United States**
10 Jan 1966	Declaration of conference with **Pakistan** on the restoration of "normal and peaceful relations"
19 Mar 1967	Border agreement with **Burma**
9 Aug 1971	Twenty-year treaty of peace, friendship and cooperation with **Soviet Union**
19 Mar 1972	Twenty-five year defense agreement with **Bangladesh**
3 July 1972	Peace treaty with **Pakistan**
11 Dec 1972	Agreement with **Pakistan** defining "line of control" in Kashmir
28 Aug 1973	Agreement with **Pakistan** on repatriation of prisoners of war
24 Sept 1974	Agreement with **Portugal** over Goa and other former Portuguese Indian territories
29 July 1987	Accord with **Sri Lanka** on future of its Tamil population
28 Jan 1993	Weapons and debt agreement with **Russia**
7 Sept 1993	Border peace deal with **China** signed, reducing troop numbers and establishing a cease-fire line
22 Nov 1993	Diplomatic relations with **South Africa** reestablished

INDONESIA

15 Aug 1950	Agreement with **United States** for military assistance
17 April 1959	Treaty of friendship with **Malaya**
1 April 1961	Treaty of friendship with **China**
16 Aug 1962	Agreement with the **Netherlands** on western New Guinea
5 Aug 1963	Manila Declaration concerning formation of confederation with **Malaya** and **Philippines**
8 Aug 1967	Association of South-East Asian Nations
17 Mar 1970	Treaty of friendship with **Malaysia**
18 Aug 1970	Exchange of notes with **United States** on furnishing combat equipment to Indonesia
15 Feb 1972	Agreement with **Philippines** on military cooperation
4 April 1972	Agreement with **Singapore** on status and supervision of Straits of Malacca
6 April 1972	Agreement with **Malaysia** on closer antiguerrilla cooperation in border areas (agreement revised 3 Dec 1984)
11 Mar 1975	Border cooperation and control agreements with **Philippines**
25 Feb 1982	Maritime treaty with **Malaysia**
Aug 1990	Diplomatic relations with **China** reestablished

JAPAN

8 Sept 1951	Peace treaty with the Allied powers
8 Mar 1954	Mutual defense assistance agreement with **United States**
20 Jan 1958	Reparations agreement with **Indonesia**
13 May 1959	Reparations agreement with **South Vietnam**
13 Aug 1959	Agreement to repatriate North Koreans
19 Jan 1960	Treaty of mutual cooperation and security with **United States**
9 Dec 1960	Treaty of friendship, commerce and navigation with **Philippines**
22 June 1965	Treaty on basic relations with **South Korea**
16 June 1966	Membership of Asian and Pacific Council
5 April 1968	Agreement with **United States** for the return to Japan of Bonin and Volcano islands, together with Rosario, Parece and Marcus islands
17 June 1971	Agreement with **United States** for transfer of sovereignty over Ryukyu Islands
16 June 1976	Treaty of friendship and cooperation with **Australia**

10 Aug 1977	Agreement to promote political, economic and cultural cooperation with **Malaysia**
12 Aug 1978	Treaty of peace and friendship with **China**
10 May 1979	Revised treaty of friendship, commerce and navigation with **Philippines**
26 Dec 1984	Agreement with **United States** on a joint military operational plan
24 Sept 1990	Agreement with **South Korea** settling differences arising from World War II
6 Nov 1992	Normalization of economic ties with **Vietnam**

LAOS

23 Dec 1950	Mutual defense assistance agreement with **United States, France, Cambodia** and **Vietnam**
31 Dec 1951	Agreement with **United States** on economic and military aid
21 July 1954	Geneva Agreements on **Indochina**
23 July 1962	Declaration on the neutrality of **Laos** at Geneva
21 Feb 1973	Peace treaty with the Pathet Lao insurgents
18 July 1977	Twenty-five year treaty of friendship with **Vietnam**
4 Oct 1979	Treaty of friendship and cooperation with **Bulgaria**
8 Dec 1979	Treaty of friendship and cooperation with **Mongolia**
17 Feb 1980	Treaty of friendship and cooperation with **Czechoslovakia**
22 Sept 1982	Twenty-five year treaty of friendship and cooperation with **East Germany**

MALAYSIA

12 Oct 1957	Treaty of defense and mutual assistance with **Great Britain**
17 April 1959	Treaty of friendship with **Indonesia**
31 July 1961	Association of Southeast Asian States formed with **Thailand** and **Philippines** (dissolved 29 Aug 1967)
5 Aug 1963	Manila Declaration concerning formation of confederation with **Indonesia** and **Philippines**
1 June 1966	Agreement with **Indonesia** ending "confrontation"
16 June 1966	Member of Asian and Pacific Council
8 Aug 1967	Member of Association of South-East Asian Nations (further treaty on 24 Feb 1976)

11 Nov 1969	Agreement with **Thailand** to establish a joint command to combat insurgents on their border
7 Mar 1970	Agreement with **Thailand** for military cooperation against insurgents operating on their border
17 Mar 1970	Treaty of friendship with **Indonesia**
9 Jan 1971	Agreement with **Great Britain, Australia, New Zealand** and **Singapore** on five-power arrangements for defense of Malaysia and Singapore
6 April 1972	Agreement with **Indonesia** on closer antiguerrilla cooperation
4 Mar 1977	Agreement with **Thailand** for combined operations against Communist guerrillas
10 Aug 1977	Agreement with **Japan** to promote political, economic and cultural cooperation
25 Feb 1982	Maritime treaty with **Indonesia**
June 1983	Agreement with **Thailand** on combined operations against guerrillas
3 Dec 1984	Revised security accord with **Indonesia**

NORTH KOREA

27 July 1953	Armistice with **South Korean** and UN forces
6 July 1961	Treaty of friendship, cooperation and mutual assistance with **Soviet Union**
11 July 1961	Treaty of friendship, cooperation and mutual assistance with **China**
9 Nov 1979	Twenty-year treaty of friendship and cooperation with **Guinea-Bissau**
12 Oct 1980	Twenty-year treaty of friendship and cooperation with **Guinea**
12 Oct 1980	Ten-year treaty of friendship and cooperation with **Zimbabwe**
19 Oct 1981	Treaty of friendship and cooperation with **Angola**
1984	Treaty of peace and friendship with **East Germany**
1984	Treaty of peace and friendship with **Bulgaria**
11 Oct 1984	Treaty of friendship and cooperation with **South Yemen**
24 Oct 1984	Agreement with **Nigeria** on establishment of joint defense programs
12 Dec 1991	Terms of draft nonaggression pact with **South Korea** agreed on
1 Jan 1992	Pact with **South Korea** banning nuclear weapons from Korean peninsula

| 1992 | Diplomatic relations with **Philippines** established |
| Feb 1994 | Agreement with **Iran** to intensify military and nuclear co-operation |

PAKISTAN

30 Aug 1950	Treaty of friendship with **Syria**
25 June 1952	Treaty of peace and friendship with **Burma**
2 April 1954	Treaty of friendly cooperation with **Turkey**
8 Sept 1954	South-East Asia Collective Defense Treaty
23 Sept 1955	Membership of the Baghdad Pact
8 July 1957	Treaty of friendship with **Spain**
28 Aug 1958	Treaty of friendship with **Thailand**
5 Mar 1959	Treaty of defense and cooperation with **United States**
19 Sept 1960	Indus Waters Treaty with **India**
2 Mar 1963	Border treaty with **China**
21 July 1964	Agreement on regional cooperation for development with **Iran** and **Turkey**
26 Mar 1965	Border treaty with **China**
10 Jan 1966	Declaration of conference with **India** on restoration of "normal and peaceful relations"
3 July 1972	Peace treaty with **India**
11 Dec 1972	Agreement with **India** defining the "line of control" in Kashmir
28 Aug 1973	Agreement with **India** on repatriation of prisoners of war
14 May 1988	Geneva accord with **Afghanistan**, guaranteed by **United States** and **Soviet Union**, for noninterference in each other's affairs

PHILIPPINES

14 Mar 1947	Agreement with **United States** concerning military bases
30 Aug 1951	Mutual defense treaty with **United States**
11 July 1952	Treaty of peace and amity with **India**
26 June 1953	Military assistance agreement with **United States**
8 Sept 1954	South-East Asia Collective Defense Treaty
27 April 1955	Military assistance agreement with **United States**
15 May 1958	Agreement with **United States** for establishment of a Mutual Defense Board
9 Dec 1960	Treaty of friendship, trade and navigation with **Japan**
31 July 1961	Association of Southeast Asian States formed with **Malaya** and **Thailand** (dissolved 29 Aug 1967)

5 Aug 1963	Manila Declaration concerning formation of confederation with **Malaya** and **Indonesia**
16 June 1966	Member of Asian and Pacific Council
8 Aug 1967	Member of Association of South-East Asian Nations
15 Feb 1972	Agreement on military cooperation with **Indonesia**
11 Mar 1975	Border cooperation and control agreements with **Indonesia**
6 Jan 1979	Agreement with **United States** for continued use of bases
10 May 1979	Revised treaty of friendship, trade and navigation with **Japan**
27 Aug 1991	Agreement on future of U.S. bases; Senate in Philippines refuses to ratify (Sept) but compromise formula agreed (2 Oct)
1992	Diplomatic relations with **North Korea** established

SOUTH KOREA

26 Jan 1950	Mutual defense assistance agreement with **United States**
27 July 1953	Armistice with **North Korea**
1 Oct 1953	Mutual defense treaty with **United States**
22 June 1965	Treaty on basic relations with **Japan**
16 June 1966	Member of Asian and Pacific Council
2 July 1981	Military and economic cooperation agreements with **Singapore**
12 Dec 1991	Terms of draft nonaggression pact with **North Korea** agreed on
1 Jan 1992	Pact with **North Korea** banning nuclear weapons from Korean peninsula
24 Aug 1992	Diplomatic relations with **China** reestablished
22 Nov 1992	Diplomatic relations with **Vietnam** reestablished

THAILAND

1 Jan 1946	Peace treaty with **Britain** and **India**
17 Oct 1950	Military assistance agreement with **United States**
8 Sept 1954	South-East Asia Collective Defense Treaty
31 July 1961	Formation with **Malaya** and **Philippines** of Association of Southeast Asian States (dissolved 29 Aug 1967)
6 Mar 1962	Declaration with **United States** on support against aggression
23 July 1962	Declaration on neutrality of **Laos** at Geneva
16 June 1966	Member of Asian and Pacific Council

8 Aug 1967	Member of Association of South-East Asian Nations
7 Mar 1970	Agreement with **Malaysia** for combined operations against insurgents on their border
4 Mar 1977	Agreement with **Malaysia** for joint operations against insurgents
June 1983	Agreement with **Malaysia** for joint operations against guerrillas
1991	Diplomatic relations established with **North Korea**

VIETNAM

23 Dec 1950	Agreement for mutual defense assistance in Indochina with **France, Cambodia, Laos** and **United States**
21 July 1954	Geneva Agreements on Indochina
13 May 1959	World War II reparations agreement between **Japan** and **South Vietnam**
30 Nov 1961	Treaty of amity with **United States** (South Vietnam)
23 July 1962	Declaration on the neutrality of **Laos** at Geneva
7 July 1965	Treaty of friendship and good-neighborly relations with **China** (North Vietnam)
16 June 1966	South Vietnam joins Asian and Pacific Council
27 Jan 1973	Agreement to end the war and restore peace in Vietnam between **United States, North Vietnam, South Vietnam** and South Vietnam Provisional Revolutionary Government
18 July 1977	Twenty-five-year treaty of friendship with **Laos**
4 Dec 1977	Treaty of friendship and cooperation with **East Germany**
3 Nov 1978	Twenty-five-year treaty of friendship and cooperation with **Soviet Union**
18 Feb 1979	Treaty of peace, friendship and cooperation with **Kampuchea**
3 Dec 1979	Twenty-five-year treaty of friendship and cooperation with **Mongolia**
7 July 1982	Agreement with **Kampuchea** defining territorial waters
20 July 1983	Border treaty with **Kampuchea**
21 Oct 1991	Agreement with **Great Britain** on repatriation of "boat people" from Hong Kong
10 Nov 1991	Diplomatic relations with **China** resumed in general "peace accord"
6 Nov 1992	Normalization of economic ties with **Japan**, ending 14-year Japanese embargo

14 Dec 1992   Easing of 17-year American embargo on economic ties with the **United States**

22 Dec 1992   Establishment of diplomatic relations with **South Korea**

ASIA AND THE GREAT POWERS

UNITED STATES

14 Mar 1947   Agreement with **Philippines** concerning US military bases

3 Sept 1947   Agreement with **China** relating to the presence of US armed forces

26 Jan 1950   Mutual defense assistance agreement with **South Korea**

15 Aug 1950   Agreement with **Indonesia** for military assistance

30 Aug 1951   Security treaty for mutual defense with **Philippines**

8 Sept 1951   Security treaty with **Japan**

5 July 1953   Agreement on military assistance with **Philippines**

27 July 1953   Korean War armistice

1 Oct 1953   Mutual defense treaty with **South Korea**

8 Mar 1954   Mutual defense assistance agreement with **Japan**

19 May 1954   Mutual defense assistance agreement with **Pakistan**

21 July 1954   Geneva agreements on **Indochina**

8 Sept 1954   South-East Asia Collective Defense Treaty

2 Dec 1954   Mutual defense treaty with **Taiwan** (Nationalist China)

27 April 1955   Military assistance agreement with **Philippines**

15 May 1958   Agreement with **Philippines** for the establishment of a mutual defense board

5 Mar 1959   Agreement for cooperation with **Pakistan**

19 Jan 1960   Treaty of mutual cooperation and security with **Japan**

23 July 1962   Geneva declaration on the neutrality of **Laos**

13 Jan 1965   Military assistance agreement with **India**

30 Dec 1966   Agreement with **Great Britain** on American use of certain Indian Ocean islands for defense purposes

1 April 1967   Agreement with **Great Britain** on the joint use of the British Indian Ocean Territory for defense purposes

5 April 1968   Agreement with **Japan** for return of Bonin and Volcano islands, and Rosario, Parece and Marcus islands

19 Aug 1970   Exchange of notes with **Indonesia** on furnishing of combat equipment

17 June 1971   Agreement with **Japan** on transfer of sovereignty over the Ryukyu Islands

27 Jan 1973   Agreement to end the war in Vietnam with **North** and

South Vietnam and the **South Vietnamese Provisional Revolutionary Government**

25 Feb 1976   Exchange of notes with **Great Britain** on a US naval support facility on Diego Garcia

6 Jan 1979   Agreement with **Philippines** on use of bases

17 Sept 1980   Agreement for normalization of relations with **China**

1 June 1983   Agreement with **Philippines** for continued use of bases

26 Dec 1984   Agreement with **Japan** on joint military operational plan

27 Aug 1991   Agreement with Philippines over future of U.S. bases

14 Dec 1992   Agreement to ease 17-year-old embargo on economic ties with Vietnam

UNITED KINGDOM

28 Aug 1947   Defense agreement with **Burma** (abrogated by Burma on 3 Jan 1953)

9 Nov 1947   Agreement with **Nepal** on employment of Gurkha troops in the British army

11 Nov 1947   Defense agreement with **Ceylon**

30 Oct 1950   Treaty of peace and friendship with **Nepal**

1 Jan 1953   Agreement with **Maldive Islands** by which Great Britain retained the right to establish and maintain defense facilities

21 July 1954   Geneva declarations on Indochina

8 Sept 1954   South-East Asia Collective Defense Treaty

3 Jan 1957   Agreement with **Maldive Islands** on reestablishment of wartime airfield on Gan

14 Feb 1960   Agreement with **Maldive Islands** granting Great Britain use of Gan airfield for 30 years retroactive to December 1956 (reconfirmed under independence agreement of 26 July 1965)

23 July 1962   Declaration on neutrality of **Laos** at Geneva

27 Nov 1962   Agreement with **India** for supply of arms to be used against China only

1 April 1967   Agreement with **United States** on joint use of British Indian Ocean Territory for defense purposes

15 Dec 1970   Agreement with **United States** to start work in 1971 on a naval communications station on the Indian Ocean island of Diego Garcia

9 Jan 1971   Agreement with **Australia, New Zealand, Malaysia** and **Singapore** on five-power arrangements for defense of Malaysia and Singapore

23 Nov 1971	Defense agreement with **Brunei**
5 Feb 1974	Agreement with **United States** to expand military facilities at Indian Ocean base of Diego Garcia
25 Feb 1976	Exchange of notes with **United States** on an American naval support facility on Diego Garcia
7 Jan 1979	Independence agreement with **Brunei**
19 Dec 1984	Agreement with **China** on the future of Hong Kong
21 Oct 1991	Agreement with **Vietnam** for forcible repatriation from Hong Kong of Vietnamese "boat people" (qv)

UNION OF SOVIET SOCIALIST REPUBLICS (until 1991)

27 Feb 1946	Treaty of friendship and mutual assistance with **Mongolia**
14 Feb 1950	Treaty of friendship, alliance and mutual assistance with **China**
21 July 1954	Geneva Declaration on Indochina
12 Oct 1954	Agreement on political cooperation with **China**
18 Dec 1955	Ten-year extension of 1931 treaty of neutrality and nonaggression with **Afghanistan** (further extensions 6 Aug 1965 and 10 Dec 1975)
6 July 1961	Treaty of friendship, cooperation and mutual assistance with **North Korea**
23 July 1962	Declaration on the neutrality of **Laos** at Geneva
15 Jan 1966	Treaty of friendship, cooperation and mutual assistance with **Mongolia**
8 Aug 1969	Agreement with **China** on the navigation of the Amur and Ussuri rivers
20 Oct 1976	Agreement with **Mongolia** for closer cooperation
3 Nov 1978	Twenty-five-year treaty of friendship and cooperation with **Vietnam**
5 Dec 1978	Treaty of friendship, good-neighborliness and cooperation with **Afghanistan**

CHAPTER 6

WARFARE, COUPS AND CONFLICT

WARS SINCE 1945

China: Civil War, 1945–49

Combatants Communists versus Kuomintang

Key dates Civil war between the national military government of Jiang Kaishek and his Kuomintang and Communist forces led by Mao Zedong resumed after the defeat of Japan in August 1945. Through the mediation of U.S. Army General George C. Marshall, a truce was arranged on January 14, 1946. It broke down, and American supplies to the Nationalists were halted on July 29, 1946. A Nationalist offensive in Shensi took the Communist capital, Yenan, on March 19, 1947, but it was retaken in April 1948. Beijing fell to the Communist advance on January 22, 1949, Nanjing on April 22, and Shanghai on May 27. Mao Zedong proclaimed the People's Republic of China on October 1, 1949. The Nationalists withdrew to Taiwan on December 7, 1949.

Casualties No statistics available.

Indonesia: War of Independence, 1945–49

Combatants Indonesian People's Army versus Dutch, British and (British colonial) Indian armed forces.

Key dates The independence of the Republic of Indonesia (formerly the Netherlands East Indies) was proclaimed by the nationalist leaders Sukarno and Hatta on August 17, 1945. British, British Indian, and Dutch troops began to arrive on September 29, 1945. British troops captured the rebel capital of Surabaya on November 29, 1945. The Dutch recognized the Indonesian Republic (comprising Java, Sumatra and Madura) on November 13, 1946. The withdrawal of British troops was completed on November 30, 1946. A nationalist uprising on West Java on May 4, 1947 led to Dutch military action on Java on July 20, 1947. A truce arranged under UN auspices on January 17, 1948 broke down, and the Dutch occupied the rebel capital, Jogjakarta, on December 19, 1948. International opposition and guerrilla warfare led to the Dutch decision to withdraw and recognize the independence of Indonesia on December 27, 1949.

Casualties Indonesians: 80,000 killed and wounded; Dutch: 25,000 killed and wounded; British and Indian: 556 killed and 1,393 wounded.

Philippines: Hukbalahap Insurgency, 1946–54

Combatants Philippine armed forces versus Hukbalahap (Huk) insurgents.

Key dates When the Philippines became independent on July 4, 1946, the wartime Communist Anti-Japanese People's Liberation Army, or Hukbalahaps (Huks), waged a guerrilla campaign against the government of the republic. By 1950 the Hukbalahaps, with an army of 15,000 men and support of the peasantry, had established control over central Luzon. However, with American backing, a new defense secretary, Ramon Magsaysay, revitalized the Philippine armed forces. Counterinsurgency operations, together with a program of land reform and the resettlement of dissidents, ensured that by 1954 the revolt had petered out. The Hukbalahap leader, Luis Taruc, surrendered on May 17, 1954.

Casualties No statistics available.

Vietnam: First Indochina War, 1946–54

Combatants French armed forces versus Viet Minh insurgents.

Key dates Following the surrender of Japan, Ho Chi Minh proclaimed the Democratic Republic of Vietnam at Hanoi on September 2, 1945. French and British forces regained control in Saigon, and after negotiations French troops entered Hanoi on March 16, 1946. After French naval forces shelled the Vietnamese quarter of Haiphong on November 23, 1946, an abortive Viet Minh uprising took place in Hanoi on December 19, 1946. Guerrilla warfare grew into full-scale conflict between the French and the Viet Minh forces under General Giap. On November 20, 1953 the French established a forward base at Dien Bien Phu to lure the Viet Minh into a set-piece battle, but the garrison of 15,000 men was overwhelmed on May 7, 1954. An agreement for a cease-fire, the temporary division of the country, and nationwide elections to determine the future government of a reunited country in 1956, was signed at the Geneva Conference on July 27, 1954.

Casualties   No statistics available.

India: Kashmir Conflict with Pakistan, 1947–49

Combatants   Kashmiri and Indian armed forces versus Muslim insurgents and Pakistani armed forces.

Key dates   A rebellion by the Muslim majority in Kashmir led the Hindu maharajah to accede to the Indian Union, and Indian troops were flown into Kashmir on October 27, 1947. Pakistan sent aid to the Muslim Azad ("free") Kashmir irregulars, and Pakistani army units crossed into Kashmir in March 1948. An undeclared state of war between India and Pakistan continued until UN mediation brought about a cease-fire on January 1, 1949. India formally annexed Kashmir on January 26, 1957.

Casualties   No statistics available.

Malaya: Communist Insurgency, 1948–60

Combatants   British Commonwealth armed forces versus "Malayan Races Liberation Army."

Key dates   The Federation of Malaya was proclaimed on February 1, 1948. Communist guerrilla activity began, and a state of emergency was declared on June 16, 1948. In April 1950 General Sir Harold Briggs was appointed to coordinate antiguerrilla operations. He inaugurated the Briggs Plan for settling Chinese squatters in new villages to cut them off from the insurgents. General Sir Gerald Templer became high commissioner and director of military operations on January 15, 1952, and a new offensive was launched on February 7, 1952. British authorities announced that the Communist Party's high command in Malaya had withdrawn to Sumatra on February 8, 1954. The emergency was officially ended on July 31, 1960.

Casualties   Commonwealth: 2,384 killed and 2,400 wounded; Communist forces: 6,705 killed, 1,286 wounded and 2,696 captured; civilian casualties numbered 4,668.

Myanmar (Burma): Civil War, 1948–55

Combatants   Burmese armed forces versus Communists, ethnic minorities, People's Volunteer Organization, Mujahids and Chinese Kuomintang refugees.

Key dates   In the year after gaining independence on January 4, 1948, the Burmese government faced armed opposition from a wide range of dissident groups: the Communists, themselves divided into the White Flag Stalinists and the Red Flag Trotskyites; a private army of wartime "old comrades" known as the People's Volunteer Organization, who made common cause with army mutineers; ethnic minorities seeking autonomy, such as the Mons and Karens; and bands of Muslim fighters called Mujahids, in the north of Arakan. By March 12, 1949, when Mandalay fell to the Karen National Defense Organization and the Communists, most of Burma was in rebel hands. But the rebels were disunited, and Mandalay was retaken by government forces on April 24, 1949. The rebel capital, Toungoo, was captured on March 19, 1950. The government held the initiative and was able to deal with a new threat posed by Chinese Kuomintang refugees in the eastern Shan states. An offensive in November 1954 broke the Mujahid campaign, and Operation "Final Victory" was launched against the Karens on January 21, 1955. Outbreaks of fighting have occurred since 1955, but never on the scale of the early years of independence.

Casualties   No statistics available.

Chinese Offshore Islands: Bombardment by People's Republic of China, 1950–62

Combatants   Nationalist Chinese (with United States' support) versus Communist Chinese.

Key dates   When the defeated Chinese Nationalist forces took refuge on Taiwan on December 7, 1949, they also retained strong garrisons on Quemoy, Matsu and the Tachen Islands, only a few miles from the mainland. Communist artillery carried out heavy bombardments of Quemoy. On February 6, 1955 the U.S. Seventh Fleet began the evacuation of 25,000 troops and 17,000 civilians from the Tachen Islands in the face of mounting Communist threats. Heavy shelling of Quemoy resumed on August 23, 1958, but threats of invasion were countered by an American military buildup. Sporadic shelling continued until 1962.

Casualties   No statistics available.

Indonesia: Civil War, 1950–62

Combatants   Indonesian armed forces versus Darul Islam, South Moluccan guerrillas, and dissident Indonesian military officers.

Key dates   In 1950, prolonged guerrilla campaigns were begun by a fanatical Muslim sect, Darul Islam, and by the South Moluccans, who proclaimed their independence on April 26, 1950. In 1957, objections to Javanese domination of Indonesian affairs and suspicion of President Sukarno's left-wing policies led the military commanders in Borneo, Sumatra and Celebes to repudiate the authority of the government. A Revolutionary Government of the Indonesian Republic was proclaimed on February 15, 1958. The authorities took military action against the right-wing rebels, capturing their headquarters at Bukittingi on May 5, 1958, and their capital, Menado, on June 26, 1958. The rebel movement finally collapsed when an amnesty was offered on July 31, 1961, and the civilian leaders surrendered. Opposition from Darul Islam was also suppressed by 1962.

Casualties   No statistics available

Korea: Korean War, 1950–53

Combatants   North Korean and Chinese armed forces versus South Korean armed forces and UN command, comprising combat troops primarily from the United States, with contingents from Australia, Belgium, Britain, Canada, Colombia, Ethiopia, France, Greece, Luxembourg, Netherlands, New Zealand, Philippines and Thailand, and medical units from India, Italy, Norway and Sweden.

Key dates   North Korean troops invaded the south on June 25, 1950. The United Nations decided to intervene following an emergency session of the Security Council, which was being boycotted by the Soviet Union. The first U.S. troops landed at Pusan airport on July 1, 1950. U.S. Army General Douglas MacArthur, the UN commander, mounted an amphibious landing at Inchon on September 15, 1950, and recaptured Seoul on September 26. The advance of the UN forces into North Korea on October 1, 1950 led to the entry of China into the war on November 25, 1950. Seoul fell to the Chinese on January 4, 1951, but was retaken by UN forces on March 14, 1951. General MacArthur was relieved of his command on April 11, 1951 after expressing his desire to expand the war into China. Truce talks began on July 10, 1951, and an armistice was finally signed at Panmunjon on July 27, 1953.

Casualties   South Korea: 47,000 dead, 183,000 wounded and 70,000 missing or taken prisoner; United States: 33,699 dead, 103,284 wounded in action and 13,000 missing or taken prisoner (of whom 5,000 returned); other members of UN command: 3,194 dead, 11,297 wounded; North Korea: 520,000 dead or wounded.

Tibet: Chinese Annexation, 1950–59

Combatants   Tibetan nationalists versus Chinese armed forces.

Key dates   The Chinese invaded across the eastern frontier of Tibet on October 7, 1950. An agreement was signed on May 23, 1951 giving China control of Tibet's affairs, and Chinese troops entered Lhasa in September

1951. The Dalai Lama remained as a figurehead ruler, but there was widespread guerrilla activity against the Chinese occupation. The last serious resistance came on March 10, 1959, when an uprising took place in Lhasa. It was suppressed by Chinese tanks, and on March 30 the Dalai Lama fled to asylum in India.

Casualties   No statistics available.

Laos: Civil War, 1959–75

Combatants   Civil war among royalist-neutralists, rightists and the Communist Pathet Lao (with involvement by the United States, Thailand, and North and South Vietnam).

Key dates   The arrest of Prince Souphanouvong and other leaders of the Communist Pathet Lao on July 28, 1959 marked the end of attempts at coalition government and the beginning of a three-way conflict among neutralists under Premier Prince Souvanna Phouma, rightists under General Phoumi Nosavan, and the Pathet Lao. International efforts to find a settlement led to a cease-fire on May 3, 1961 and recognition of the neutrality of Laos at a conference in Geneva on July 23, 1962. But fighting resumed in Laos, with growing involvement by North Vietnam, Thailand and the United States. The South Vietnamese army attacked Laos on February 8, 1971 in an attempt to disrupt the Ho Chi Minh trail. A new cease-fire agreement was reached on February 21, 1973, and a coalition government formed in 1974. But Communist victories in Vietnam and Cambodia in April 1975 opened the door to a takeover by the Pathet Lao in Laos. The Pathet Lao declared Vientiane liberated on August 23, 1975, and Laos was proclaimed the Lao People's Democratic Republic on December 2, 1975, with Prince Souphanouvong as president.

Casualties   No statistics available.

Vietnam: Second Indochina War (Vietnam War), 1959–75

Combatants   South Vietnamese armed forces (supported by the United States, with detachments from South Korea, Australia, New Zealand, Thailand and Philippines) versus Viet Cong guerrillas and North Vietnamese armed forces.

Key dates   Following the interim division of Vietnam at the Geneva Conference in 1954, Ngo Dinh Diem became prime minister, then president of South Vietnam and secured American support for a permanent South Vietnamese state, contrary to the Geneva accords. His government became increasingly authoritarian and repressive, and unrest grew widespread. The Communists in South Vietnam built up a guerrilla force (the

Viet Cong) and launched their first attack on the South Vietnamese armed forces on July 8, 1959 near Bien Hoa, killing two American advisers. A state of emergency was proclaimed in the south on October 19, 1961. After alleged attacks on the U.S. Navy ships *Maddox* and *Turner Joy*, Congress passed the Gulf of Tonkin resolution on August 7, 1964, giving President Lyndon B. Johnson wide military powers in South Vietnam. The sustained bombing of North Vietnam by US aircraft (Operation Rolling Thunder) began on February 7, 1965. The first American combat troops landed at Da Nang on March 8, 1965 and engaged the Viet Cong on June 15. On January 30, 1968 Communist forces launched their Tet offensive with heavy attacks on Saigon, Hué and 30 provincial capitals. On March 31, 1968 President Johnson announced the end of the bombing of the north, and on May 13, 1968 peace discussions began in Paris. On January 25, 1969 these discussions were transformed into a formal conference. American and South Vietnamese troops invaded Cambodia in 1970, and the South Vietnamese made an incursion into Laos in 1971. A new Communist offensive in the south began on March 30, 1972, and this led to a resumption of American bombing of the north on April 6. The last American ground combat units were withdrawn on August 11, 1972. American bombing was halted on January 15, 1973, and a peace agreement was signed in Paris on January 27. In 1975 a North Vietnamese offensive, which had begun on January 6, overran the south, and Saigon was occupied on April 30.

Casualties   (1964–73) United States: 47,239 killed in action, 10,446 non-combat deaths, 152,303 wounded and 695 missing; South Vietnamese armed forces: 183,528 dead and 500,000 wounded; South Korea: 4,407 dead; Australia: 492 dead; New Zealand: 35 dead; Thailand: 351 dead; North Vietnamese armed forces and Viet Cong: 950,000 dead. Civilian casualties were very high in both north and south, but reliable statistics are unavailable.

Brunei: Pro-Indonesian Revolt, 1962

Combatants   Brunei armed forces (with British support) versus Brunei People's Party rebels.

Key dates   On 8 December 1962, A. M. Azahari, leader of the Brunei People's Party, staged a revolt in opposition to Brunei's proposed entry into the Federation of Malaysia. British and Gurkha troops were flown in from Singapore, and the rebellion was suppressed by 17 December 1962.

Casualties   No statistics available.

India: Himalayan Conflict with China, 1962

Combatants   Indian armed forces versus Chinese armed forces.

Key dates   After a series of incidents in disputed border areas, Chinese forces attacked on October 20, 1962 and drove Indian forces back on the northeast frontier and in the Ladakh region. India declared a state of emergency on October 26, 1962, and launched an unsuccessful counteroffensive on November 14, 1962. On November 21, the Chinese announced that they would cease fire all along the border and withdraw 12½ miles behind the line of actual control that existed on November 7, 1959.

Casualties   Indian losses: 1,383 killed, 1,696 missing and 3,968 captured; no Chinese casualty statistics available.

Indonesia: Conflict over Irian Jaya, 1962–continuing

Combatants   Dutch armed forces versus Indonesian armed forces; Indonesian armed forces versus Free Papua Movement guerrillas.

Key dates   Following a clash between Indonesian and Dutch naval forces on January 15, 1962, President Sukarno ordered military mobilization and sent armed units into West New Guinea. In a settlement negotiated through the United Nations, the Dutch agreed on August 15, 1962 to hand over Western New Guinea, which was incorporated into Indonesia as Irian Barat on 1 May 1963. The Free Papua Movement, opposed to Indonesian control and desiring unification with Papua New Guinea, undertook small-scale guerrilla operations. Fighting in 1984 led to the movement of over 11,000 refugees to Papua New Guinea.

Casualties   No statistics available.

Malaysia: Confrontation with Indonesia, 1963–66

Combatants   Malaysian Federation (with British Commonwealth support) versus Indonesian armed forces.

Key dates   When the Federation of Malaysia was established on 16 September 1963, President Sukarno of Indonesia announced a policy of "confrontation" on the grounds that it was "neocolonialist." A campaign of propaganda, sabotage and guerrilla raids from Indonesia into Sarawak and Sabah followed. After Sukarno had handed over power to General Suharto on 12 March 1966, "confrontation" came to an end, with a peace agreement signed in Bangkok on 1 June 1966.

Casualties   Commonwealth forces: 114 killed and 181 wounded; Indonesia: 590 killed, 222 wounded and 771 captured.

India: Conflict with Pakistan, 1965

Combatants   Indian armed forces versus Pakistani armed forces and Muslim irregulars.

Key dates   Border clashes took place in the Rann of Kutch in April 1965, but a cease-fire agreement came into effect on 1 July. More serious fighting in Kashmir and the Punjab began on 5 August 1965, when Muslim irregulars invaded eastern Kashmir. The Indian army contained these incursions, but on 1 September 1965 Pakistani regular forces crossed the frontier. India launched a three-pronged attack towards Lahore on 6 September. As a military stalemate developed, the UN Security Council called for a cease-fire, which came into effect on 23 September 1965.

Casualties   Indian losses: 2,212 killed, 7,636 wounded and 1,500 missing; no Pakistani casualty statistics available.

Indonesia: Attempted Communist Coup, Followed by Campaign of Repression, 1965–66

Combatants   Indonesian army forces versus PKI (Communist Party of Indonesia) with support from rebel military commanders.

Key dates   An attempted coup by the PKI was launched on 1 October 1965 with the killing of six army generals. Details remain very obscure. The coup was quickly crushed in Jakarta, but in parts of Java insurgents took control; they briefly seized the city of Jogjakarta in central Java. Fighting was subsequently reported in north Sumatra, Celebes and Kalimantan (Borneo). Violence continued into 1966 in central Java, especially around Jogjakarta, Surakarta and Semarang, where the army attempted to impose order by executing thousands of people alleged to be Communists. After this the army and its supporters attacked virtually the entire population of Java and Bali in a bloody, indiscriminate massacre.

Casualties   An estimated 500,000–750,000 dead.

Philippines: Communist and Muslim Insurgencies, 1968–continuing

Combatants   Philippine armed forces versus New People's Army and Bangsa Moro Army (Army of the Moro Nation).

Key dates   The Hukbalahap (Huk) insurgency had faded by the mid–1950s, but in December 1968 a congress of reestablishment was held on Luzon, which reconstituted the Communist Party. Its New People's Army (NPA) began a guerrilla campaign. The government also faced armed opposition from Muslim separatists of the Moro National Liberation Front

(MNLF) on Mindanao. President Ferdinand Marcos declared martial law on 23 September 1972. A cease-fire with the MNLF was announced on 22 December 1976 after talks held in Libya, but fighting continued. President Corazon Aquino signed a 60-day truce with the NPA on 27 November 1986, but fighting resumed when it expired in 1987.

Casualties   No statistics available.

China: Border Conflict with Soviet Union, 1969

Combatants   Chinese armed forces versus Soviet armed forces.

Key dates   Long-standing Sino–Soviet border disputes erupted into serious fighting on Damansky Island in the Ussuri River on 2 March 1969. Each side blamed the other for the clash, in which 31 Soviet frontier guards were killed. The fighting spread further west to the border between Sinkiang and Kazakhstan. On 11 September 1969 Soviet Prime Minister Alexei Kosygin, who was returning from the funeral of Ho Chi Minh in Hanoi, stopped briefly at Beijing Airport for a meeting with Zhou Enlai. Talks were arranged, and tension on the border subsided.

Casualties   No statistics available.

Cambodia (Kampuchea): Civil War 1970–75

Combatants   Cambodian, South Vietnamese and U.S. armed forces versus Khmer Rouge, North Vietnamese and Viet Cong.

Key dates   On 18 March 1970, Lieutenant General Lon Nol ousted the head of state, Prince Norodom Sihanouk, who was out of the country. Sihanouk allied himself with his former enemies, the Maoist Khmer Rouge, to form the National United Front of Cambodia. Lon Nol appealed for aid on 14 April 1970, and on 29 April, U.S. and South Vietnamese troops mounted an incursion into Cambodia to attack North Vietnamese, Viet Cong and Khmer Rouge forces. The last U.S. troops withdrew on 29 June 1970. The Communists took control of the countryside and in 1975 cut supply routes to the capital, Phnom Penh. Lon Nol left the country on 1 April 1975 and the Khmer Rouge occupied Phnom Penh on 17 April.

Casualties   No statistics available. Estimates of 500,000 to two million deaths in the Khmer Rouge's effort to consolidate their rule between 1975 and 1979.

Bangladesh: War of Independence, 1971

Combatants   Pakistani armed forces and *razakar* irregulars versus Mukti Bahini and Indian armed forces.

Key dates   Elections in December 1970 resulted in a landslide victory in

East Pakistan for the Awami League. On 26 March 1971, Sheikh Mujib ur-Rahman, the head of the League, proclaimed East Pakistan an independent republic under the name of Bangladesh. He was arrested, and West Pakistani troops and locally raised irregulars—*razakars*—put down large-scale resistance by 10 May 1971. Awami League fighters—the Mukti Bahini—began a guerrilla campaign, and clashes grew between India and Pakistan as millions of refugees fled into India. President Yahya Khan declared a state of emergency in Pakistan on 23 November 1971. On 3 December 1971 the Pakistani air force launched surprise attacks on Indian airfields. On 4 December some 160,000 Indian troops invaded East Pakistan. Pakistani forces in East Pakistan surrendered on 16 December 1971, and a general cease-fire came into effect the following day.

Casualties   India: 3,037 killed, 7,300 wounded and 1,561 captured and missing; Pakistan: 7,982 killed, 9,547 wounded and 85,000 captured and missing, including 15,000 wounded. No figures are available for Bangladeshi casualties.

Sri Lanka: JVP Revolt, 1971

Combatants   Sri Lankan security forces versus Janata Vimukti Peramuna (People's Liberation Front).

Key dates   A state of emergency was declared in Sri Lanka on 16 March 1971 following the disclosure of a plot to overthrow the government by the ultra-left JVP. An abortive uprising began on 5 April 1971, but by May some 4,000 rebels were in custody and resistance had ceased.

Casualties   1,200 killed, including 60 members of the security forces.

East Timor: Civil War and Indonesian Annexation, 1975–continuing

Combatants   Timor Democratic Union (UDT) versus Revolutionary Front for the Independence of Timor (FRETILIN), with intervention by Indonesian armed forces.

Key dates   In June 1975 Portugal announced its intention of holding independence elections in its colony of East Timor. On 11 August 1975 the moderate UDT, which favored continuing links with Portugal, attempted to stage a coup, but by 20 August, civil war had broken out with the Communist group FRETILIN. As increasing numbers of refugees fled into Indonesian West Timor, Indonesian troops invaded East Timor on 7 December 1975 to forestall a FRETILIN victory. By 28 December the Indonesians were in control, and East Timor was officially integrated into Indonesia on 17 July 1976. This annexation is not recognized by the international community and anti-Indonesian guerrilla activity has continued. The guerrilla leader, Xanana Gusmao, was captured in 1993. The Indonesian massacre of 1991 at the Santa Cruz cemetery provoked an international outcry.

Casualties No statistics available. Estimates of over 100,000 deaths to date in the continuing Indonesian effort to maintain control.

Sri Lanka: Communal Strife, 1977–continuing

Combatants Sri Lankan armed forces and Indian Peacekeeping Force (IPKF) versus Tamil separatists and JVP (see p. 128).

Key dates Tension between the Tamil minority and the Sinhalese majority in Sri Lanka led to rioting in the northern town of Jaffna, beginning on 14 August 1977, in which 125 people died. The situation grew more serious in the 1980s. Acts of terrorism by the Tamil Liberation Tigers provoked violence by the army against the Tamil community. A state of emergency was declared on 4 June 1981. Sri Lanka signed an accord with India on 29 July 1987, regarding a Tamil homeland, and an IPKF was established in Sri Lanka. Hostilities took place between the IPKF and Tamil separatists. The JVP objected to the Indian presence, and began a guerrilla campaign against the government. India withdrew its last troops on 24 March 1990. Civil strife continued into the 1990s.

Casualties No statistics available.

Cambodia, Vietnamese Invasion and Civil War, 1978–continuing

Combatants Vietnamese armed forces and Kampuchean troops of the Heng Samrin government versus the Khmer Rouge, Khmer People's National Liberation Front, and guerrillas loyal to Prince Sihanouk.

Key dates After a series of clashes on the border, Vietnamese forces and Kampuchean rebels launched an invasion of Kampuchea on 25 December 1978. The capital, Phnom Penh, was occupied on 7 January 1979, and a People's Republic of Kampuchea, with Heng Samrin as president, was proclaimed. Guerrilla operations against the Vietnamese occupying forces were carried out by three groups: the Khmer Rouge; guerrillas loyal to the former head of state, Prince Sihanouk; and the non-Communist Khmer People's National Liberation Front. The three groups formed a unified military command on 14 March 1989, with Prince Sihanouk as head but the Khmer Rouge as the dominant partner. Vietnam completed the withdrawal of its forces from Kampuchea on 26 September 1989. Civil war continued, with the Khmer Rouge making significant advances. A new cease-fire agreement was signed on 27 August 1991 and a United Nations Transitional Authority established. Elections were successfully held in 1993, but there has been continuing fighting between government troops and Khmer Rouge guerrillas. In March 1994, government troops captured the headquarters of Pol Pot at Pailin in western Cambodia.

Casualties   No statistics available.

Afghanistan: Soviet Occupation and Civil War 1979–continuing

Combatants   Soviet and Afghan government forces versus Mujaheddin guerrillas.

Key dates   The instability of the Soviet-backed regime, and growing resistance to its reforms, led to a full-scale Soviet invasion of Afghanistan on 27 December 1979. A new government was installed under Babrak Karmal, but a very considerable Soviet military presence had to be maintained in the country to combat the Mujaheddin guerrillas. Following Babrak Karmal's resignation on 4 May 1986, his successor, Major General Najibullah, announced a six-month cease-fire on 15 January 1987, but this was rejected by the mujaheddin. Withdrawal of Soviet forces from Afghanistan began on 15 May 1988, and was completed on 15 February 1989. Divisions within the Mujaheddin and an effective performance by the Afghan army meant that President Najibullah remained in power, and the civil war continued.

Renewed fighting raged in early 1993. Fighting had claimed 3,000 lives by February in a struggle between the government of President Burhanuddin Rabbani and the Hezb-i-Islami of Gulbuddin Hekmatyar, and the pro-Iranian, mainly Shi'ite, Islamic Unity Party (Hezb-i-Wahdat). Intermittent fighting continued into 1994 between Rabbani's forces and those of General Abdul Rashid Dostam.

Casualties   Official casualty figures for the Soviet armed forces were 15,000 killed and 37,000 wounded. In fighting in 1993 alone, an estimated 20,000 were killed.

Vietnam, Chinese Invasion, 1979

Combatants   Vietnamese armed forces versus Chinese armed forces.

Key dates   Chinese forces launched an invasion of Vietnam on 17 February 1979 in retaliation for Vietnam's intervention in Cambodia (see p. 103). Following the fall of the provincial capital, Lang Son, on 3 March 1979, the Chinese government announced that it had accomplished its aims, and the withdrawal of its forces was completed by 16 March 1979.

Casualties   No statistics available.

MAJOR TERRORIST ACTIVITY IN ASIA SINCE 1970

1971	21 August	Philippines: Ten are killed and 74 are wounded by terrorist grenades at a preelection rally of opposition Liberal Party in Manila.
1974	30 August	Japan: Bomb explosion in front of the Mitsubishi Heavy Industries building in Tokyo kills eight.
1975	4 August	Malaysia: Five Japanese Red Army guerrillas attack the American and Swedish embassies in Kuala Lumpur. The terrorists and four hostages are flown to Libya.
1975	2 December	Indonesia: South Moluccan terrorists demanding independence from Indonesia for their homeland seize a train near Beilin in the Netherlands, killing two people and holding 50 hostages. The six terrorists surrender on 14 December.
1975	4 December	Indonesia: South Moluccans seize the Indonesian consulate in Amsterdam. One hostage killed, but terrorists surrender on 19 December.
1977	23 May	Indonesia: South Moluccans seize a train at Assen and a school at Bovinsmilde in the Netherlands. The siege at the school ends on 27 May. Two hostages and six terrorists are killed in an army attempt to rescue train hostages on 11 June.
1977	28 September	Air piracy: A Japan Air Lines DC-8 en route from Paris to Tokyo is hijacked by five Japanese Red Army terrorists off Bombay and forced to land at Dacca in Bangladesh. The aircraft is eventually flown to Algiers, after stops at Kuwait and Damascus. The passengers are then set free in return for the release of six prisoners in Japan and a ransom of $6 million.
1978	13 March	Indonesia: South Moluccans seize a government building in Assen, killing one man and taking 71 hostages. Marines storm the building on 14 March and capture the terrorists; five hostages are wounded.
1978	6 August	Pakistan: Gunmen attack the PLO office in Islamabad, killing three PLO members and a police guard.

1979	14 February	Afghanistan: Adolph Dubs, U.S. ambassador, is kidnapped by Muslim extremists and dies together with the four kidnappers when Afghan police storm the room in the Kabul Hotel where he is being held.
1981	2 March	Air piracy: A Pakistan International Airlines Boeing 720 on a domestic flight from Karachi to Peshawar is hijacked by three Al-Zulfikar terrorists and forced to land at Kabul in Afghanistan. A Pakistani diplomat, Tariq Rahim, is shot dead. The aircraft is flown to Damascus, where the hostages are set free on 14 March in return for the release of 55 prisoners in Pakistan.
1981	28 March	Air piracy: A domestic Indonesian flight is hijacked by five armed men and forced to fly to Bangkok, Thailand. On 30 March the aircraft is stormed by Indonesian and Thai commandos, who kill four of the hijackers and release the hostages.
1983	9 October	Burma: A bomb explosion in Rangoon kills 21 people, including four South Korean ministers on an official visit.
1984	2 August	India: A bomb explosion at Madras Airport kills 29 people.
1985	24 July	Burma: Some 70 people are killed when a mine explodes under a passenger train traveling from Rangoon to Mandalay.
1986	31 May	Sri Lanka: At the end of a month of violence, a bomb planted by Tamil extremists on a Colombo-bound train kills eight.
1986	14 September	South Korea: A bomb blast at Seoul's Kimpo Airport kills five and wounds 26.
1987	17 April	Sri Lanka: Tamil separatists ambush three buses and two trucks near Trincomalee, killing 120.
	21 April	Sri Lanka: A bomb explosion in Colombo kills over 100.
	6 July	India: Sikh militants kill 40 Hindu bus passengers in the Punjab. A further 32 are killed in the neighboring state of Haryana on 7 July.
	14 July	Pakistan: Two bomb explosions in Karachi, blamed on Afghan agents, kill 70.
	18 August	Sri Lanka: Grenade attack in the parliament fails to assassinate the president, but kills one member of parliament and injures 15.

	28 October	Philippines: Three U.S. servicemen killed by Communists near Clark Field Air Base.
	9 November	Sri Lanka: Tamil separatist bombing in Colombo kills 32, injures over 100.
	29 November	Korea: A bomb on a Korean plane kills all 116 passengers.
1988	1 May	Sri Lanka: More than 26 bus passengers killed by a land mine.
	17 August	Pakistan: President Zia killed by a bomb placed on his aircraft, together with more than 30 passengers, including the U.S. ambassador, Arnold L. Raphel.
1989	13 April	Sri Lanka: Forty-five killed in Tamil bombing in Trimcomalee.
1990	3 April	India: Bomb planted by Sikh separatists kills 32 and injures 50 in Punjab.
1991	March	Sri Lanka: Ranjan Wijeratne, deputy minister of defense, killed by a car bomb.
	21 May	India: Leader of the Congress (I) Party, Rajiv Gandhi, is assassinated near Madras in a bomb attack during an election rally.
	15 June	India: Sikh terrorists in Punjab kill 74 in attack on two passenger trains.
1992	December	Philippines: Muslim separatists in Zamboanga del Sur province massacre 40 villagers.
1993	12 March	India: Bombs in Bombay kill 225 and injure 1100.

COUPS AND REVOLUTIONARY CHANGES OF GOVERNMENT IN ASIA SINCE 1949

21 September 1949	China (Communist revolution)
20 October 1958	Thailand
28 October 1958	Burma
9 August 1959	Laos
16 May 1961	South Korea
3 July 1961	South Korea
2 March 1962	Burma
1 November 1963	South Vietnam
30 January 1964	South Vietnam
20 December 1964	South Vietnam
27 January 1965	South Vietnam
22 January 1967	Indonesia
18 March 1970	Cambodia
17 November 1971	Thailand

16 December 1971	East Pakistan (Bangladesh)
20 December 1971	West Pakistan
22 September 1972	Philippines
17 October 1972	South Korea
17 July 1973	Afghanistan
17 April 1975	Cambodia
30 April 1975	South Vietnam
30 April 1975	Laos
15 August 1975	Bangladesh
3 November 1975	Bangladesh
7 November 1975	Bangladesh
5 July 1976	Pakistan
10 October 1976	Thailand
27 April 1978	Afghanistan
16 September 1979	Afghanistan
27 December 1979	Afghanistan
24 March 1982	Bangladesh
25 February 1986	Philippines
17 September 1988	Burma
8 August 1990	Pakistan
4 December 1990	Bangladesh
23 February 1991	Thailand

Source: Patrick Brogan, *World Conflicts*

MAJOR ASSASSINATIONS IN ASIA SINCE 1945

1947	19 July	Aung San, Burmese leader, and seven associates.
1948	30 January	Mahatma Gandhi.
1949	29 April	Widow of President Quezon of the Philippines, her daughter, son-in-law, and 10 others.
1951	31 July	General Charles-Marie Chanson and Thai Lap Thanh, governor of South Vietnam.
	6 October	Sir Henry Gurney, British high commissioner in Malaya.
	16 October	Liaquat Ali Khan, prime minister of Pakistan.
1959	25 September	Solomon West Ridgway Diaz Bandaranaike, prime minister of Ceylon.
1960	12 October	Asanuma Inejiro, chairman, Japanese Socialist Party.

1963	1 April	Quinim Pholsen, foreign minister of Laos.
	2 November	Ngo Dinh Diem, president of South Vietnam, and his brother Ngo Dinh Nhu.
1965	1 October	General Achmad Yani, Indonesian chief of staff, and five other generals.
	22 November	Dipa Nusantara Aidit, Indonesian Communist party leader.
1974	15 August	Attempted assassination of President Park Chung Hee of South Korea; his wife killed.
1975	15 August	Sheikh Mujib ur-Rahman, president of Bangladesh.
	7 November	General Khalid Musharaf, Bangladesh head of government.
1978	27 April	Mohammed Daoud, president of Afghanistan.
1979	14 February	Adolph Dubs, U.S. ambassador to Afghanistan.
	4 April	Zulfikar Ali Bhutto, former president of Pakistan, executed after 1977 coup.
	8 October	Nur Mohammed Taraki, president of Afghanistan.
	26 October	General Park Chung Hee, president of South Korea.
	27 December	Hafizullah Amin, president of Afghanistan.
1981	30 May	Zia Rahman, president of Bangladesh.
1983	21 August	Benigno Aquino, Philippine senator and opposition leader.
	9 October	Four South Korean government ministers killed by a bomb in Rangoon, Burma.
1984	5 June	Sant Bhindranwale, Sikh terrorist leader, killed by Indian army.
	20 August	Sant Harchand Singh Longowal, moderate Sikh leader.
	31 October	Indira Gandhi, prime minister of India.
	27 November	Percy Norris, British deputy high commissioner in India.
1986	11 August	Indian General Arun Vaidya.
1987	2 August	Jaime Ferrer, minister of local government, Philippines.
	18 August	Attempted assassination of Junius Jayewardene, president of Sri Lanka.
1988	5 August	Allama Arif al-Hussaini, Pakistani Shi'ite leader.
	17 August	Mohammed Zia ul-Haq, president of Pakistan, U.S. ambassador Arnold Raphel and others in a plane crash, possibly sabotage.
1989	13 July	Appapillai Amirthalingam, leader of the Tamil United Liberation Front, Sri Lanka.

	13 November	Rohana Wijeweera, Sinhalese terrorist leader, killed by security forces.
1991	21 May	Rajiv Gandhi, former Indian prime minister.
1993	1 May	Sri Lankan president, Ranasinghe Premadasa.

UNITED NATIONS PEACEKEEPING OPERATIONS IN ASIA SINCE 1949

UNMOGIP: United Nations Military Observer Group for India and Pakistan, 1949–Continuing

Established to supervise the cease-fire of January 1949 between India and Pakistan in Kashmir.

Participants: Australia, Belgium, Canada, Chile, Denmark, Ecuador, Finland, Italy, Mexico, New Zealand, Norway, Sweden, United States, Uruguay.

UNCI: United Nations Commission for Indonesia, 1949–51.

Established in January 1949 to supervise the truce between the Republic of Indonesia and the Netherlands. The UN mission was disbanded after the transfer of full sovereignty to Indonesia.

Participants: Australia, Belgium, China, France, Great Britain, United States.

UNTEA–UNSF: United Nations Temporary Executive Authority—United Nations Security Force, West Irian, 1962–63.

Established in September 1962 to administer West New Guinea (West Irian) until Indonesia took over full sovereignty from the Netherlands in May 1963.

Participants: Canada, Pakistan, United States (observers provided before the arrival of UNTEA–UNSF by Brazil, India, Ireland, Nigeria, Sri Lanka and Sweden).

UNIPOM: United Nations India–Pakistan Observation Mission, 1965–66.

Established in September 1965 to supervise the cease-fire between India and Pakistan. Disbanded on completion of its mission in March 1966.

Participants: Australia, Belgium, Brazil, Burma, Canada, Chile, Den-

	Geneva Protocol on Poison Gas and Bacteriological Warfare	Antarctic Treaty	Partial Nuclear Test-Ban Treaty	Outer Space Treaty	Nuclear Nonproliferation Treaty	Sea Bed Treaty	Biological Warfare Convention	Environmental Modification Convention	"Inhumane Weapons" Convention
Afghanistan	1986		1964	1988	1970	1971	1975	1985	
Bangladesh	1989		1985	1986	1979		1985	1979	
Bhutan	1979		1978		1985		1978		
Brunei Darus-Salam					1985				
Burma (Myanmar)			1963	1970					
Cambodia (Kampuchea)	1983								
China	1929	1983		1983			1984		1982
India	1930	1983	1963	1982		1973	1974	1978	1984
Indonesia	1971		1964	(1967)	1979		(1972)		
Japan	1970	1960	1964	1967	1976	1971	1982	1982	1982
Laos	1989		1965	1972	1970	1971	1973	1978	1983
Malaysia	1970		1964	(1967)	1970	1972	(1972)		
Mongolia	1968		1963	1967	1969	1971	1972	1978	1982
Nepal	1969		1964	1967	1970 SA	1971	(1972)		
North Korea	1988	1987	1988	1968	1985		1987	1984	
Pakistan	1960		1965	(1967)			1974	1986	1985
Philippines	1973		1968	1976	1972 SA		1973		
Singapore			1968		1976 SA	1976	1975		
South Korea	1988	1986	1964	1967	1975	1987	1987	1986	
Sri Lanka	1954		1964	1986	1979 SA		1986	1978	
Taiwan			1964	1970	1970	1972	1973		
Thailand	1931		1963	1968	1972 SA		1975	1980	
Vietnam	1980		1964	1980	1982	1980	1980		

DEFENSE EXPENDITURE IN ASIA

Country	U.S. Dollars (millions) (1985 Exchange Rates) 1990	U.S. Dollars per capita (1985 Exchange Rates) 1990	Percentage of GDP/GNP 1990	Numbers in Armed Forces (thousands) 1985	Numbers in Armed Forces (thousands) 1991	Reservists (thousands) 1991	Paramilitary (thousands) 1991
Afghanistan	n/a	n/a	n/a	47.0	45.0	n/a	97.0
Bangladesh	251	2	1.5	91.3	107.0	n/a	55.0
Brunei	n/a	n/a	n/a	4.1	4.2	0.9	2.7
Cambodia	n/a	n/a	n/a	35.0	111.8	n/a	50.0
China	10,617	9	3.1	3,900.0	3,030.0	1,200.0	12,000.0
India	8,506	10	3.2	1,260.0	1,265.0	655.0	1,280.5
Indonesia	1,776	10	1.4	278.1	283.0	400.0	480.0
Japan	16,059	130	1.0	243.0	246.0	48.4	n/a
Laos	138	35	3.6	53.7	55.1	n/a	n/a
Malaysia	1,557	89	3.7	110.0	127.5	44.3	22.7
Mongolia	262	120	10.9	33.0	15.5	200.0	10.0
Myanmar (Burma)	335	8	4.9	186.0	286.0	n/a	85.3
Nepal	37	2	1.3	25.0	35.0	n/a	28.0
North Korea	5,434	235	25.2	838.0	1,132.0	540.0	200.0
Pakistan	2,803	25	7.2	482.8	580.0	513.0	270.0
Philippines	878	14	2.2	114.8	106.5	131.0	90.0
Singapore	1,313	485	4.9	55.0	55.5	292.0	111.6
South Korea	6,637	150	4.4	598.0	633.0	4,500.0	3.5
Sri Lanka	361	21	5.5	21.6	105.9	12.0	57.2
Taiwan	5,304	254	5.4	444.0	360.0	1,657.5	25.0
Thailand	1601	28	2.6	235.3	283.0	500.0	139.5
Vietnam	2,311	34	16.0	1,027.0	1,041.0	1,000.0	2,600.0

mark, Ethiopia, Finland, Ireland, Italy, Nepal, Netherlands, New Zealand, Nigeria, Norway, Sri Lanka, Sweden, Uruguay, Venezuela.

UNTAC: United Nations Transitional Authority in Cambodia, 1992–September 1993

Established following the signing of the Cambodia peace settlement of 23 October 1991, the force became operational on 15 March 1992. It supervised the elections of May 1993.

Participants: Infantry battalions from Bangladesh, Bulgaria, France, Ghana, India, Indonesia, Malaysia, Netherlands, Pakistan, Tunisia and Uruguay. Military observers from Algeria, Argentina, Austria, Bangladesh, Belgium, Bulgaria, Cameroon, China, France, Ghana, India, Indonesia, Ireland, Malaysia, New Zealand, Pakistan, Poland, Russia, Senegal, Tunisia, United Kingdom and United States.

CHAPTER 7

POLITICAL PARTIES

AFGHANISTAN

Prior to the fall of the Communist government of Najibullah in 1992, the dominant party was the People's Democratic Party of Afghanistan (PDPA). Formed in 1905, it had two main factions after a 1967 split: the Parcham faction, which sought to work within a parliamentary system, and the Khalq faction, which advocated more direct class struggle. The Khalq faction mounted a successful coup in 1978 and began widespread agrarian reform, provoking mounting opposition, which the PDPA met with repression. The Soviet Union invaded Afghanistan in 1979 to support PDPA rule. In 1981 the PDPA formed a National Fatherland Front in an attempt to build wider political support. The PDPA was renamed the Homeland Party (Hezb-i-Watan) in June 1990. At the fall of Najibullah in 1992, the main Mujaheddin groups (with their leaders) were:

Hezb-i-Islami: Led by Gulbuddin Hekmatyar, a radical Islamic fundamentalist. Believed to be one of the best-armed and best-organized groups.

Jamiat-i-Islami: Led by Burhanuddin Rabbani, a moderate. Controls much of northern Afghanistan. Has produced some of the most effective rebel commanders.

Ittehad-e-Islami: Led by Abdul Rasul Sayyaf. Closely aligned to the militant Muslim Brotherhood and heavily financed by Saudi Arabia's radical Islamic groups.

Hezb-i-Islami: Breakaway faction of Hekmatyar's group led by Younus Khalis, a Muslim fundamentalist cleric.

Harakat-e-Inquilab-e-Islami: Led by Muhammad Nabi Muhammadi, a moderate Sunni Muslim cleric.

National Islamic Front of Afghanistan: Led by Syed Ahmed Gailani, a spiritual leader of Afghanistan's mystic Sufi Islamic sect.

Afghan National Liberation Front: Led by Sibghatullah Mojadidi, former professor of Islamic philosophy.

Hezb-i-Wahadat: Coalition of eight, mostly Shi'a, guerrilla groups headquartered in Iran.

Harakat-e-Islami and *Shura-ye-Itefaq-i-Islami:* Two smaller Shi'a-dominated groups based in Pakistan.

BANGLADESH

Awami League (AL)   Formed in East Pakistan in 1949, the League led the movement for independence. It was the ruling party in independent Bangladesh from 1971 until 1975, when it was banned. On its revival in 1978 the League advocated a return to parliamentary democracy and moderate socialism.

Bangladesh National Party (BNP)   Founded in 1978 by the merger of factions from the National Democratic Party, the National Awami Party, the United People's Party, the Muslim League, and Hindu caste groupings. It advocates rapid economic development, expansion of health services and population planning, nationalism, and presidential government.

National Party   Formed in 1985 by the People's Party with former members of the BNP and the Awami League. The party has abandoned an earlier platform of Islamization, and its policies are now broadly similar to those of the BNP, with a program for the privatization of state property.

National Socialist Party (NSP)   A pro-Chinese Marxist party formed in 1972 by dissidents from the Awami League who favored more rapid moves toward socialization of the economy.

Muslim League   Grew out of factions of the Pakistan Muslim League, which ruled East Pakistan from 1947–54. Outlawed when Bangladesh achieved independence for supporting Pakistan but revived in 1977. The League advocates moderate Islamization of the state. A section left in 1978 to join the BNP.

Islamic Democratic League (IDL)   The IDL opposes westernization and secularization and calls for the formation of an Islamic state. Formed by groupings of Islamic fundamentalists, it was outlawed on independence for allegedly cooperating with Pakistan. The ILP was revived in 1977.

BHUTAN

Political parties are banned, and candidates stand for election as individuals.

Bhutan Congress Party   A predominantly Nepalese party in exile in India that advocates political democracy and closer relations with India but has little influence.

Bhutan People's Party   Founded in 1990, the party advocates a constitutional monarchy, freedom of the press, other basic freedoms, equal rights for all ethnic groups, and the release of all political prisoners.

The United Liberation People's Front was also founded in 1990.

BRUNEI

Brunei People's Party   A left-wing nationalist party that won all the seats on a new legislative council in 1962. The party was banned following its involvement in an Indonesian-supported rebellion that was put down with British assistance.

People's Independence Party   Formed in 1966 advocating independence and constitutional government. The party was outlawed.

People's United Party   Founded in 1968 by the government to support the ruling sultanate.

Brunei National Democratic Party (BNDP)   A party formed in exile in Singapore in 1985 but with apparent Brunei government acquiescence.

CAMBODIA

People's Socialist Community   Formed in 1955 by Prince Norodom Sihanouk as a party of national unity and socialist democracy.

People's Group   A small communist party supported largely by Cambodia's Vietnamese population.

Kampuchean People's Revolutionary Party (KPRP)   Formed in 1979 by former Khmer Viet Minh and former Khmer Rouge exiles under Vietnamese auspices. The party aimed at developing industry and restoring agriculture to achieve self-sufficiency in food. Divided into two main factions. It was the main force in the Kampuchean United Front for National Construction and Defense, which nominated all candidates for election.

The post-1979 KPRK government faced armed opposition from three main groups: the Khmer People's National Liberation Front (KPNLF), an anticommunist republican group appealing to the prerevolutionary elite; the Cambodian National Liberation Movement, a peasant-backed group associated with Prince Sihanouk; and the Khmer Rouge, remnants of the Pol Pot regime.

The two strongest parties to emerge from the 1993 elections were the incumbent Cambodian People's Party and the royalist Funcinpec (the United National Front for an Independent, Neutral, Peaceful and Cooperative Cambodia) (led by Prince Norodom Ranariddh).

CHINA

Chinese Communist Party (CCP)   Formed in 1921 as a workers' party in urban areas on the Leninist model. Allied with the Kuomintang until 1927, when CCP members were massacred. Transformed by Mao Zedong into a revolutionary peasant army that became the ruling party following victory in the civil war in 1949. Torn by constant conflicts between radicals and pragmatists, the latter having control since the late 1970s following Mao's death.

There are also eight small parties that are of minor political significance: Revolutionary Committee of the Kuomintang (founded in 1948); China Democratic League (1944); China Democratic National Construction Association (1945); China Association for Promoting Democracy (1945); Chinese Peasants' and Workers' Democratic Party (1947); China Zhi Gong Dang (1947); Jin San Society (1946); Taiwan Democratic Self-Government League (1947).

HONG KONG

A British colony that will be returned to China in 1997, it has a consultative Legislative Council. None of its members was elected until 1985. Political parties were late to develop in Hong Kong, although two associations, the Reform Club and the Civic Association, fielded candidates after 1985.

INDIA

Indian National Congress   Founded in 1885, the party led the movement for Indian independence. It governed India from 1947 until 1977. Although internally divided, it stood for democratic and secular government, with left-of-center domestic policies and nonalignment internationally. Congress divided in 1978, a section of the party going into government coalition with the Janata party.

Indian National Congress (I)   Formed in 1978 from the Indian National Congress by supporters of Indira Gandhi, Congress (I) advocated industrialization, land reform, a moderately socialist planned economy, secularism and a neutralist foreign policy. But under Mrs. Gandhi and her successor, Rajiv Gandhi, there were increasing moves toward a more market-oriented economy and an expansion of the private sector.

Swatantra (Freedom) Party   Formed in 1959, Swatantra supports economic development through the private sector.

Praja Socialist Party   A democratic socialist party formed in 1952 by the merger of the Socialist Party and the left wing of the Indian National Congress. The party joined with the Samyuka Socialist Party from 1965–66.

Samyuka Socialist Party   Formed in 1964 on a platform of democratic socialism and the encouragement of foreign investment in the Indian economy.

Communist Party of India (CPI)   Founded in 1920. Advocated secularism, industrialization, land reform including the nationalization of larger-scale agriculture and collectivization. The party split in 1964, a pro-China section (the CPM) leaving a more moderate pro-Soviet group that supported the Indian National Congress. The schism weakened the CPI.

Communist Party of India (Marxist) (CPM)   A pro-Chinese breakaway from the CPI in 1964. CPM supporters demanded militant opposition to the Congress government and peasant- rather than worker-based organization. The CPM's anti-Congress position attracted significant support. In 1977 the party was loosely allied with the governing Janata coalition. Although its foreign policy position remained anti-Western, the CPM was increasingly critical of China in the 1980s.

Communist Party of India (Marxist-Leninist)   A pro-Chinese party formed in 1969 by Naxalites in West Bengal who supported a peasant revolt against the pro-Soviet Communist-dominated state government. The party is divided between factions supporting armed revolution and those favoring electoral politics.

Indian People's Party (BJP)   Founded in 1980 as a successor to the Jan Sangh (People's) Party, via the Janata Party. A militant Hindu nationalist party that has moved gradually to a moderate socialist economic policy. The BJP believes that India should have nuclear weapons and finds its main support among middle-class Hindus. Increased its support significantly through participation in anti-Congress (I) National Front in the 1989 general elections.

Jan Sangh (People's) Party Formed in 1950 as the party of Hindu cultural nationalism, strongest in the Hindi-speaking areas of north-central India. Jan Sangh became one of the founding groups within the conservative Janata Party, formed in 1977, but its followers left in 1980 to form the BJP.

People's Party (Janata Dal) Formed in 1988 by the merger of a number of other parties on a platform of eradication of poverty and a nonaligned foreign policy. The party led an anti-Congress (I) National Front that won the 1989 general elections.

Akali Dal A Sikh party in Punjab that seeks greater autonomy for the Sikh community, part of which advocates an independent state of Khalistan.

Bharatiya Janata Party Founded in 1977 by the four largest opposition parties—the India National Congress (Organization), which broke away from the National Congress in 1964; the Bharatiya Lok Dal; the Bharatiya Jan Sangh, or Indian People's Union; and the Socialist Party—it merged with the Congress for Democracy. Internal divisions subsequently arose. In 1980 the Janata Party and its allies gained 33 out of 542 seats in Parliament to Congress (I)'s 375, but lost support in 1984.

INDONESIA

Indonesian Nationalist Party (PNI) Formed in 1927 as a secular nationalist party. After independence became a radical populist party supported by the majority of the bureaucracy. Its strength waned after the removal of Sukarno.

People's Party A socialist party banned in 1965 but rehabilitated in 1967.

There have also been a variety of smaller parties, including the Muslim Scholars' Party (NU), a conservative Islamic party formed in 1952; the United Islamic Party of Indonesia (PSII); the Indonesian Islamic Party (formed in 1967); the Protestant Party; and the Catholic Party.

After 1973 only three parties were allowed by law:

Golkar Formed in 1964 by army officers to combat radical nationalism and communism. Became the state party in 1969, the vehicle of President Suharto's New Order. A pro-Western anticommunist grouping that has a majority in parliament and that provides all cabinet ministers, it is the political wing of the bureaucracy.

Development Unity Party (PPP) Formed in 1973 by a government-enforced merger of four main Islamic factions. The PPP's major policy interests are in religion, and it forms the main opposition to the government.

Indonesian Democracy Party (PDI)　A minor party created by enforced government merger in 1973 of the Indonesian Nationalist Party, the Protestant and Catholic parties, and two smaller nationalist organizations. Internally divided.

JAPAN

Liberal Democratic Party (LDP)　Formed in 1955 by the merger of the conservative Liberal and Democratic parties, the LDP and its predecessors governed Japan for all but a year from 1947 to 1993. The LDP, which is dominated by competing faction leaders, stands for private enterprise, alliance with the U.S., and the expansion of Japanese interests in Asia. Recently it has been weakened by a series of corruption scandals and defections and in the 1993 elections it was removed from office.

Japan Socialist Party (JSP)　First organized in 1925, the present party was reformed in 1955 by the amalgamation of several postwar socialist parties, one of which briefly headed a coalition government in 1947–48. The JSP advocated a rapid but peaceful transition to socialism, with the nationalization of banking and industry, and opposed the security treaty with the United States in favor of a neutralist foreign policy. In 1991 the party changed its name to the Social Democratic Party of Japan as a preliminary to an apparent shift to the center.

Social Democratic Party of Japan (SDPJ)　The successor in 1991 to the Japan Socialist Party (see above).

Democratic Socialist Party (DSP)　Formed in 1961 by defectors from the right wing of the JSP who advocated a mixed economy, economic and security ties with the United States, and an easing of relations with China and the USSR.

Komeito ("Clean Government") Party　The political arm of the Nicheren Buddhist sect, formed in 1964. Komeito called for greater morality in political life, national self-sufficiency in food, social reform in the

---

Note: On 22 August 1991, General Dharsono announced the formation of a "Forum for the Purification of the People's Sovereignty," bringing together various strands of the opposition. In 1993 the daughter of Sukarno, Megawati Sukarnoputri Kiemas, was elected chairman of the Party of Democracy.

interests of the poor, and nonaggression pacts with China and the Soviet Union. The party's identification with a particular religious stance has limited its potential for wider support.

Japan Communist Party (JCP)   Formed in 1922, declared illegal in the late 1920s, the JCP revived in 1945. Divided over the Sino–Soviet dispute in the 1960s, the leadership attempted to take a neutral position in the 1970s. More recently the JCP has abandoned advocacy of violent revolution, concentrating on environmental issues and social reform.

Prior to the 1993 elections, a number of LDP breakaway parties were formed. These included the Japan Renewal Party (Shinseito) led by Tsutomu Hata, the Sakigake (Pioneer Party) and the Japan New Party, a non-LDP center-right party.

LAOS

Neutralist Party   Formed in 1961 by Souvanna Phouma.

Lao Patriotic Front (NLHS)   The political arm of the communist movement, formed in 1956.

Patriotic Neutralists   A left-wing breakaway faction from the Neutralist Party that linked itself with the NLHS.

Lao People's Revolutionary Party (LPRP)   Established in 1972 from the Pathet Lao Liberation Movement. The LPRP has ruled Laos as the sole legal political party since the Communist victory in Vietnam in 1976. It seeks to build a communist state through nationalization of all major industries and agricultural collectivization.

MALAYSIA

United Malays National Organization (UMNO)   Founded in 1946 to promote Malay unity. The largest national party, with a dominant role in the National Front ruling coalition of 11 parties, each of which retains a separate identity. Anticommunist domestically and internationally, UMNO adopted a New Economic Policy in the 1980s to promote economic development.

Malayan Chinese Association (MCA)   Formed in 1949 to represent the interests of the Chinese population. Cooperated with UMNO in an Alliance Party from 1952. Increasingly divided internally between older moderates and younger radicals.

Alliance Party   Electoral alliance formed in 1952 by the United Malays National Organization (UMNO) and the conservative Malayan Chinese Association (MCA). The Alliance was joined in 1955 by the Malayan Indian Congress.

Democratic Action Party   A predominantly Chinese party founded in 1966 when Singapore left the Malaysian Federation as an offshoot of the People's Action Party of Singapore. Supported by the urban Chinese working class, the Democratic Action Party advocates democratic socialism.

Malaysian People's Movement   A democratic socialist party formed in 1968, supported mainly by intellectuals. The Movement has some Malay members but is generally viewed as a Chinese party.

Malayan Indian Congress (MIC)   Formed in 1946 to represent the interests of the Indian community. Cooperated with UMNO and the MCA in the Alliance Party from 1955. The MIC appears internally divided.

Sabah People's Union   Founded in 1975, its initial popularity waned as Christians saw it becoming increasingly a Muslim party.

United People Party (PPBB)   Formed in Sarawak in 1973 to represent the Malay population.

Sarawak National Party (SNAP)   Founded in 1961 and supported by Sarawak's indigenous population.

Sarawak Dayak Party (PBDS)   PBDS broke away from SNAP in 1983 and represents the interests of the Dayak population of Sarawak.

Pan-Malaysian Islamic Party (PAS)   A Malay nationalist party combining Islamic traditions with advocacy of moderate socialism and modernization, founded in 1955. A member of the ruling National Front coalition from 1973–77, PAS has developed an increasingly stronger Islamic fundamentalist faction.

Among other parties are the People's Progressive Party of Malaysia (PPP); the Sarawak United People's Party (SUPP), a predominantly Chinese party formed in 1959; and the Malaysian Islamic People's Front, a breakaway from PAS in 1977.

MONGOLIAN PEOPLE'S REPUBLIC

Until the advent of political pluralism after 1990, there was only one party in the Mongolian People's Republic—the Mongolian People's Revolutionary Party (MPRP), founded in 1920 as a pro-Soviet communist party. Over a dozen parties now exist, including the Mongolian Democratic Party (founded 1990), the Greens, the Capitalists, the People's Party and a Farmer's Party.

MYANMAR (BURMA)

Anti-Fascist People's Freedom League (AFPFL)   A coalition of nationalist groups that ruled Burma under U Nu from independence in 1948 until the AFPFL split off in 1958. After a period of military rule, the AFPFL then became the opposition party following elections in 1960.

Union Party   The ruling party under U Nu that won the 1960 elections following a period of military rule.

National Unity Party   A procommunist party affiliated with the Burmese Workers' Party.

Military rule was imposed in 1962, and all parties except the ruling Burmese Socialist Program Party were banned in 1964.

Burmese Socialist Program Party (BSPP)   Formed by the Revolutionary Council and remaining under predominantly military leadership. Based on a mixture of Marxism, Buddhism and "humanism," the BSPP advocates a centrally controlled socialist economy in a single-party system. It is neutralist in foreign policy.

NEPAL

Political parties were banned by royal decree in December 1960, but since 1979 they have been active, and tolerated in practice.

Congress Party   Formed in the late 1940s, the party won an absolute majority in the first general elections, held in 1959. Parliament was dissolved in 1960 and the party went underground, its leadership going into exile in India. However, it took part in the 1985 local elections and succeeded in electing one of its activists as mayor of Katmandu.

Communist Party   Originally pro-Soviet, the party went underground and came under the dominance of Maoist factions. It remained influential among students. It now participates, at least unofficially, in both local and national elections.

NORTH KOREA

Korean Workers' Party (KWP)   The governing party in a one-party state. The KWP was formed in 1949 by a merger of the New National Party with Communists active in internal resistance and others previously based in China and the Soviet Union. It modeled itself on the Soviet Communist Party, under the increasingly personal domination of Kim Il Sung. Its policy of "self-reliance" is an adaptation of Marxism to Korean conditions, and it has become increasingly nationalist.

PAKISTAN

Political parties were banned in 1958 and allowed to resume activity in 1962. A military government took power in 1977, once again outlawing political activity. The right to form parties was restored in 1986.

Pakistan Muslim League   The successor party to the pre-independence All-India Muslim League, revived in 1962 to form the main political support for Ayub Khan.

Pakistan People's Party (PPP)   Formed in 1967 as a socialist party by Zulfikar Ali Bhutto. The PPP was divided between grass-roots left-wing activists and wealthy landowning supporters. After returning to power in 1988 under the leadership of Bhutto's daughter Benazir Bhutto, the PPP was defeated in the 1990 elections. After the 1993 elections it led a coalition government.

National Awami Party   A peasant-and-workers' party that found the bulk of its support in East Pakistan before Bangladesh became independent.

Six-Point Awami League   A predominantly middle-class party advocating universal suffrage and East Pakistan autonomy before Bangladesh achieved independence.

Islamic Party   A party with largely lower-middle-class support that advocates the supremacy of Islamic principles.

Pakistan Democratic Party   A right-wing Islamic party formed in 1969 by the merger of four parties.

Islamic Democratic Alliance   A coalition of nine right-wing Islamic parties united by their opposition to the PPP, this party won power in the 1990 elections. It was ousted in 1993.

Among other parties are the Awami National Party, a socialist party formed by the merger of several parties in 1986; and the Muhajir Qaumi Mahaz, a party of Muslim immigrants to Pakistan, formed in 1986.

PHILIPPINES

Except for the period of Japanese occupation from 1942 to 1945, the Philippines was a multiparty semi-autonomous colony, then an independent state (after 1946) until 1972, when parties were outlawed. They were legalized once more in 1978.

Nacionalista Party   Founded in 1907, divided in 1946 when a left-center faction split away. The Nacionalista Party was dominated by sugar interests and advocated strict control over foreign investment. The party was revived in 1988 by the Aquino government's right-wing opponents and absorbed UNIDO.

Liberal Party   Formed in 1946 by the left-center breakaway section of the Nacionalista Party, whose ideological position it shared, though the Liberal Party was more favorably disposed toward foreign investment.

New Society Movement (KBL)   Formed by President Marcos in 1978 as a political organization to lessen his dependence on military support, the KBL stood for capitalist economic development and for strong ties with the United States.

Social Democratic Party   Formed in 1981, the SDP favored a mixed economy, with the nationalization of key industries, a presidential system modeled on that of the United States, and a pro-Western foreign policy.

United Democratic Organization (UNIDO)   A coalition of five anti-Marcos groupings formed in 1981, including remnants of both the Nacionalista and Liberal parties. UNIDO advocated a return to democracy, economic development, and a nonaligned foreign policy. Absorbed into the revived Nacionalista Party in 1988.

Filipino Democratic Party   A pro-Aquino party formed in 1988 by the merger of People's Struggle (formed in 1987) and the People's Power movement.

Philippine Communist Party (PKP)   Founded in 1930 as a pro-Soviet party, advocates agrarian reform and the nationalization of banking and mining.

Communist Party of the Philippines (CCP)   A pro-Chinese party founded in 1968 that was conducted rural guerrilla warfare since 1970.

Among other parties is the Moro National Liberation Front, a Muslim separatist party in the southern Philippines founded in 1970; and the Mindanao Alliance, a regional party founded in 1978.

SIKKIM

Sikkim National Party   A conservative party financed by Sikkim's monarch, the maharajah, and supported mainly by Bhutia and Lepcha segments of the population.

Sikkim National Congress   A party that supports political reform and the creation of a constitutional monarchy.

Sikkim State Congress   A predominantly Nepalese party that advocates constitutional reform, abolition of the landlord system and closer relations with India.

SINGAPORE

People's Action Party (PAP)   Formed in 1954, the ruling party since 1963. A procommunist faction left in 1961, leaving a moderate state-socialist party that sought economic development, social welfare policies and the creation of a sense of national identity. Strongly anticommunist and antiunion, the PAP has repressed all dissent.

Socialist Front   Formed in 1961 by breakaway PAP activists who created a pro-Chinese and pro-Indonesian party with a revolutionary program. In 1966 its members resigned from parliament and the Front mounted a terrorist campaign that lost it support.

Workers' Party   Founded in 1955 as a moderate socialist party advocating freedom of the press, free trade unions, and the protection of civil liberties from government infringement.

Singapore Malays National Organization (SMNO)   An associate party of the United Malays National Organization in Malaysia, the SMNO supports reunification of Singapore with Malaysia.

United People's Front   Opposition group formed in late 1974 from seven former opposition parties, including the United National Front (formed 1970), the Singapore Justice Party and the Singapore Chinese Party.

Among other parties are the Singapore People's Alliance (SPA), a small right-wing party formed in 1958; and the Singapore Democratic party, founded in 1981.

SOUTH KOREA

South Korea began to develop a multiparty system in 1961. All currently active political parties, however, date only from 1980, when a ban on political activity was lifted.

Democratic Republican Party (DRP)   Formed in 1963 as a platform on which the military rulers of South Korea could stand for election.

Korean National Party (KNP)   Formed in 1981 by former DRP supporters who demanded a popularly elected presidency. It was weakened by defections to the NKDP in 1985. It then merged with the New Korea Democratic Party.

New Korea Democratic Party (NKDP)   Formed by dissident opposition groupings, including defectors from the Korean National Party, in 1985 during a period of political liberalization. The NKDP sought an end to military rule and the establishment of democracy under a directly elected president.

New Democratic Party   Formed in the 1960s by a fusion of moderate opposition groupings.

Democratic Justice Party (DJP)   Founded in 1980 on a platform of clean government and the elimination of corruption, it advocated economic growth, expansion of social and health services and mild political liberalization.

Democratic Liberal Party   Formed in 1990 through the merger of the Democratic Justice Party, the New Democratic Republican Party, and the Reunification Democratic Party (active since 1981).

Among other parties are the Peace and Democracy Party; the Civil Rights Party (CRP); the Democratic Korea Party; and the Socialist Democratic Party, which was reorganized in 1982.

SRI LANKA

United National Party (UNP)   Formed in 1946, originally as a conservative party, the UNP adopted a democratic socialist program in 1958, although it remained in favor of private enterprise and foreign investment and opposed the nationalization of foreign-owned estates. The UNP supports a nonaligned foreign policy and an accommodation with the minority Tamil population.

Sri Lanka Freedom Party (SLFP)   Founded in 1951 as a democratic socialist alternative to the UNP. It advocates the nationalization of some industries, state intervention in the economy, redistribution of wealth, a neutralist foreign policy, and the preservation of Sinhala as the official language but with safeguards for minority population interests.

People's United Front (MEP)   A strongly Sinhalese and Buddhist left-wing party that supports the nationalization of foreign-owned estates. United with the JVP until 1966.

Tamil Congress   A Tamil party, strongest in north and east Sri Lanka, that advocated a policy of cooperation with the Sinhalese majority population.

Tamil United Liberation Front (TULF)   Formed in 1972 by the alliance of a number of Tamil groupings, including the Tamil United Front, the National Liberation Front, the Muslim United Front, and the Tamil Congress. The TULF seeks the creation of an autonomous Tamil region to be known as Eelam, though an extreme wing favors outright independence.

Federal Party   The main Tamil party, advocating a federal constitution and noncooperation with the Sinhalese community.

Ceylon Equal Society Party (Lanka Sama Samaja Party—LSSP)
Founded in 1935, the LSSP had become a Trotskyist party by the late 1930s, advocating nationalization of foreign-owned estates and companies. The high point of its support was in the 1940s. The LSSP formed a coalition government with the SLFP in 1964.

Ceylon Communist Party   Supports the withdrawal of Sri Lanka from the British Commonwealth and the nationalization of banks, factories and estates.

People's Liberation Front (JVP)   A breakaway grouping from the MEP in 1966, the JVP was a Marxist youth organization that led an armed insurrection in 1971 and was banned in 1983.

Among smaller parties are the Ceylon Workers' Congress, the party of Indian Tamils; and the Communist Party of Sri Lanka, formed in 1943 as a pro-Soviet breakaway from the LSSP. In 1964 the CPSL divided into pro-Soviet and pro-Chinese factions.

TAIWAN (REPUBLIC OF CHINA)

National People's Party—Kuomintang (KMT)　　The dominant governing party. Formed in 1910, initially as a party advocating democratic and socialist reform, sympathetic to the Soviet Union in the early 1920s. Transformed by Jiang Kaishek into an authoritarian anticommunist party. Since defeat in the civil war in 1949, the KMT has been the party of industrial development and capitalism in Taiwan. There are divisions between military "hard-liners" and pragmatic "technocrats."

With the lifting of martial law in July 1987, ending a 38-year period when no new political parties had officially been allowed to form, a welter of political parties began to emerge. The Democratic Progressive Party had in fact been founded in September 1986 without government interference. It was followed by such parties as the Chinese Freedom Party (founded July 1987), the Democratic Liberal Party (September 1987) and the Labor Party (also founded in 1987 by a breakaway from the DPP).

THAILAND

Political parties were banned following the 1957 coup but were allowed to revive in 1968. The 1974 constitution authorized the existence of noncommunist parties only.

United Thai People's Party (UTPP)　　Formed in 1968 as the official governing party, standing for national unity, anticommunism, and capitalist economic development.

Democratic Party　　The oldest political party in Thailand, founded in 1946. Its moderate socialist program advocates a liberal constitution, devolution of power to local government, legalization of trade unions and aid to farmers. A right-wing faction was expelled in 1974, but the party remains divided.

Democratic Front　　Formed in 1968 as a socialist party supporting a neutralist foreign policy.

Economist United Front　　A coalition of a number of preexisting parties. Moderately socialist with a neutralist foreign policy.

National Democracy Party (NDP)   Formed in 1981, the NDP's ideological position remains ill-defined because of the number of competing factions contained within it.

Social Democratic Force   A predominantly intellectual party, formed in 1974 as New Force, that called for the withdrawal of United States troops, land reform, the nationalization of major industries and friendlier relations with China and Vietnam.

VIETNAM

From 1945 until 1976 Vietnam was divided between the north and the south. The South Vietnamese government fell in 1975, and the next year Vietnam was unified into the Socialist Republic of Vietnam, a one-party state.

Pre-1976 North Vietnam

Worker's Party   Formed in 1951 as the successor party to the Indochinese Communist Party, which had been founded in 1930 and dissolved in 1945. Its aim was the reunification of Vietnam under Communist control.

The Worker's Party was the dominant member of a National Fatherland Front umbrella organization that included two minor parties: the Socialist Party, a small party of intellectuals formed in 1951; and the Democratic Party, a party of businessmen and intellectuals formed in 1944.

Pre-1976 South Vietnam

National Social Democratic Front (NSDF)   An anticommunist conservative coalition of six parties formed in 1969. The main components of the NSDF were the People's Alliance for Social Revolution (founded in 1969); the Liberal and Democratic Front; the Workers' and Peasants' Party; and the National Salvation Front.

Greater Solidarity Force   A conservative Roman Catholic party led by refugees from North Vietnam.

Humanist Socialist Party   A conservative party.

Social Democratic Party.   A party of the Hoa Hao sect in the Mekong delta.

Vietnamese Nationalist Party   Formed in the 1920s as an anti-French party modeled on the Chinese Kuomintang. The party later reemerged as the Greater Vietnam Revolutionary Party, with its supporters concentrated in central and northern South Vietnam.

The government in the south faced a number of opponents:

People's Revolutionary Party (PRP)   Formed in 1962 as the southern branch of North Vietnam's ruling Worker's Party. The PRP controlled the insurgent National Front for the Liberation of South Vietnam (NLF), a coalition of 20 groups aiming at the reunification of Vietnam, and in 1969 identified itself as a Provisional Revolutionary Government.

Alliance of Nationalist, Democratic and Peace Forces
Formed in 1968 by neutralists and pacifists, advocating an independent South Vietnam under coalition government.

Post-1976 Vietnam

Vietnam Communist Party   The successor party in 1976 to the North Vietnamese ruling Worker's Party. Its aim was agricultural collectivization and the transformation of Vietnam into an industrialized society on the Soviet and East European model. Under the pressure of events in the Soviet bloc there were increasing divisions between hard-liners and pragmatists.

CHAPTER 8

ELECTIONS

BANGLADESH

Since independence in December 1971, five elections have been held in Bangladesh (up to and including the general election of 27 February 1991). With 120 million people, Bangladesh is in theory the world's third largest democracy (after India and the United States). However, the 1991 elections were the only genuinely free contest. The elections of 1973 were dominated by the Awami League, the 1979 contests by the BNP. In 1986 and 1988, the Jatiyo Dal swept the board.

1973

Awami League	292
JSD	1
Others	7
	300

1979

BNP	207
Awami League	42
JSD	9
Muslim League	20
Others	22
	300

1986

Jatiyo Dal	153
Awami League	76
JSD	7
Muslim League	4
Jamaat-i-Islami	10
Others	50
	300

1988

Jatiyo Dal	251
JSD	2
COG	18
Others	29
	300

The elections of 27 February 1991 saw the Bangladesh National Party (BNP) of Begum Khaleda Zia emerge as the strongest political force, but without an overall majority in the 300-seat parliament.

Party	Seats Won	Led By
BNP	138	Begum Khaleda Zia
Awami League	88	Sheikh Hasina
Jatiya	35	Hussain Muhammed Ershad
Jamaat-i-Islami	18	
Independents and others	18	
Seats repolling	38	
	300	

CAMBODIA (KAMPUCHEA)

Cambodia has no tradition of democratic elections. Prior to January 1979, when the People's Republic of Kampuchea (PRK) was proclaimed following the military invasion by Vietnam, no free elections had taken place. After 1979, a one-party state was in existence. Thus, the elections of May 1981 to the National Assembly were contested only by 148 candidates nominated and approved by the Kampuchean United Front for National Construction and Defense (KUFNCD). It was claimed that over 99% of the 3,417,000 electorate voted. In 1986 the National Assembly voted to extend its first term for another five years (until 1991).

Under the UN peacekeeping operation, free elections took place in May 1993. Of the 4.2 million electorate, there was a 90% turnout. FUNCINPEC attracted 45.3%, the CPP 38.6%.

CHINA

China has no tradition of democratic elections, either before the Communist takeover in 1949 or since. Under the Communists, elections have been held in the following years:

1954
1959
1965
(Elections scheduled for 1971 were postponed because of the internal crisis in China)
1975
1978
1983
1988

In 1993, over 800 million voters in China were eligible to vote for local and national offices.

INDIA

India is the world's most populous democracy. Although frequently marred by violence, independent India has a strong tradition of multiparty elections. The first general election after independence took place in 1952. Up to 1992, 10 general elections have taken place. The results are summarized below.

1952

Congress Party	362
Socialist Party	12
KMPP	9
Jan Sangh	3
CPI and allies	27
Others	39
Independents	37
	489

1957

Congress Party	369
PSP	21
CPI	27
Jan Sangh	4
Independents and others	73
	494

1962

Congress Party	361
Swatantra	18
Jan Sangh	14
DMK	7
Samyuka Socialists	6
Communists	29
Praja Socialists	12
Others	47
	494

1967

Congress Party	282
Communists	42
Swatantra	44
Jan Sangh	35
Praja Socialists	13
DMK	25
Samyuka Socialists	23
Others	54
	518

1971

Congress Party	366
Communists	48
Swatantra	8
Jan Sangh	22
Telengana Praia Samiti	10
DMK	23
Samyuka Socialists	3
Others	38
	518

1977

Janata Party	271
Congress Party	153
Congress for Democracy	28
Communists (Marxist)	22
DMK	19
Akali Dal	8
Communist Party of India	7
Others	32
	540

1980

Congress Party (I) (and allies)	374
Lok Dal	41
Janata (and allies)	34
Congress	13
Left Front (inc. Communists)	54
Others	9
Vacant	19
	544

1984

Congress Party (I)	413
Communists	22
Telugu Desam	30
Janata	13
Others	64
	542

1989		1991	
Congress Party	192	Congress Party (I)	227
Janata Dal	141	Bharatiya Janata Party	119
Bharatiya Janata Party	88	Janata Dal	55
Communists (and allies)	51	Communists (Marxist)	35
Sikh Nationalists	9	Communists (CPI)	13
Others	44	Telugu Desam	13
		Others	51
		Vacant	32
	525 *		545

* Excluding vacant seats

INDONESIA

Since independence, Indonesia has had no tradition of truly free elections. Golkar has been the dominant force in the political life of the country for over two decades. The following table summarizes results since 1977.

2 May 1977	Golkar	232
	Indonesian Democracy Party	29
	United Development Party	99
	Total (of elective seats)	360
4 May 1982	Golkar	246
	Indonesian Democracy Party	24
	United Development Party	94
	Total (of elective seats)	364
23 April 1987	Golkar	299
	Indonesian Democracy Party	40
	United Development Party	61
	Total (of elective seats)	400
9 June 1992	Golkar*	282
	United Development Party	62
	Indonesian Democracy Party	56

* Golkar won all 27 provinces.

JAPAN

Since the first general election in postwar Japan (on 10 April 1946), the country has had a continuous period of competitive multiparty elections, albeit dominated by the ruling Liberal Democratic Party since its formation in 1955. Up to the end of 1993, 19 general elections had been held. Table I summarizes the results from 1946 to 1979. Table II gives more detailed results for the period since 1980.

Table I: Election Summary 1946–1979

10 April 1946   Liberals, 140; Progressives, 94; Socialists, 92; Communists, 5; Others, 133 (total, 464)

25 April 1947   Socialists, 143; Liberals, 131; Progressives, 121; Communists, 4; Others, 67 (total, 466)

23 Jan 1949   Liberals, 264; Progressives, 69; Socialists, 48; Communists, 35; Others, 50 (total, 466)

1 Oct 1952   Liberals, 240; Progressives, 85; Right-wing Socialists, 57; Left-wing Socialists, 54; Others, 30 (total, 466)

9 April 1953   Liberals (Yoshida faction), 199; Liberals (Hatoyama faction), 35; Progressives, 76; Right-wing Socialists, 66; Left-wing Socialists, 72; Communists, 1; Others, 17 (total, 466)

27 Feb 1955   Democratic Party, 185; Liberals (Yoshida faction), 112; Left-wing Socialists, 89; Right-wing Socialists, 67; Communists, 2; Others, 12 (total, 467)

22 May 1958   Liberal Democratic Party (LDP), 287; Socialists, 166; Communists, 1; Others, 13 (total, 467)

20 Nov 1960   LDP, 296; Socialists, 145; Democratic Socialists, 17; Communists, 3; Others, 6 (total, 467)

21 Nov 1963   LDP, 283; Socialists, 144; Democratic Socialists, 23; Communists, 5; Others, 12 (total, 467)

29 Jan 1967   LDP, 277; Socialists, 140; Democratic Socialists, 30; Komeito, 25; Communists, 5; Others, 9 (total, 486)

27 Dec 1969   LDP, 288; Socialists, 90; Komeito, 47; Democratic Socialists, 31; Communists, 14; Others, 16 (total, 486)

10 Dec 1972   LDP, 271; Socialists, 118; Communists, 38; Komeito, 29; Democratic Socialists, 19; Others, 16 (total, 491)

5 Dec 1976   LDP, 249; Socialists, 123; Komeito, 55; Democratic Socialists, 29; Communists, 17; Others, 38 (total, 511)

7 Oct 1979   LDP, 248; Socialists, 107; Komeito, 57; Communists, 39; Democratic Socialists, 35; Others, 25 (total, 511)

Table II: Elections in Japan: June 1980–July 1993

22 June 1980 (turnout 74.6%)

Party	Seats Won	% of Vote
Liberal Democratic Party	284	47.9
Japan Socialist Party	107	19.3
Clean Government Party (Komeito)	33	9.0
Democratic Socialist Party	32	6.6
Japan Communist Party	29	9.0

	12	3.0
New Liberal Club	12	3.0
Others	14	5.2
	511	100.0

18 December 1983 (turnout 67.0%)

Party	Seats Won	% of Vote
Liberal Democratic Party	251	45.8
Japan Socialist Party	110	19.5
Clean Government Party (Komeito)	59	10.1
Democratic Socialist Party	39	7.3
Japan Communist Party	25	9.3
New Liberal Club	8	2.4
Others	19	5.6
	511	100.0

6 July 1986 (turnout 71.4%)

Party	Seats Won	% of Vote
Liberal Democratic Party	304	48.7
Japan Socialist Party	86	18.7
Clean Government Party	57	9.6
Japan Communist Party	27	9.7
Democratic Socialist Party	26	6.2
New Liberal Club	6	1.5
Others	6	5.6
	512	100.0

18 February 1990 (turnout 73.3%)

Party	Seats Won	% of Vote
Liberal Democratic Party	275	46.1
Japan Socialist Party	136	24.4
Clean Government Party	45	8.0
Japan Communist Party	16	8.0
Democratic Socialist Party	14	4.8
Minor parties	5	1.4
Independents	21	7.3
	512	100.0

18 July 1993

Party	Seats Won	% of Vote
Liberal Democratic Party	223	36.6
Japan Socialist Party	70	15.4
Clean Government Party	51	8.1
Japan Communist Party	15	7.7
Democratic Socialist Party	15	3.5
Renewal Party*	55	10.1
Japan New Party*	35	8.1
Harbinger Party*	13	2.6

*All basically "new" conservatives formed by LDP rebels.

LAOS

As in neighboring Cambodia, Laos has no tradition of democratic elections. Indeed, prior to the elections that began on 26 June 1988 for district-level People's Councils, no nationwide elections had ever been held.

MALAYSIA

Prior to the formation of Malaysia, the only general election held in the independent Malayan Federation took place in August 1959. The multiracial Alliance Party, led by Tunku Abdul Rahman, won a landslide victory (it had earlier come to power in the pre-independence elections in 1955). The results were:

Party	Seats Won
Alliance	73
Islamic Party of Malaya	13
Other parties	14
Vacant seats	1

Following the creation of Malaysia, seven general elections have been held (through the elections of 20–21 October 1990). The results have been:

	1964	1969	1974	1978	1982	1986	1990
Alliance/National Front	89	76	135	131	132	148	127
Democratic Action Party	–	13	9	16	9	24	20
Islamic Party of Malaysia	9	12	—[2]	5	5	1	7
Other parties	6	12	10	1	–	–	22[3]
Independents	–	–	–	1	8	4	4
Vacant	–	31[1]	–	–	–	–	–
	104	144	154	154	154	177	180[4]

1   Polling took place in only 113 seats. Elections in Sarawak and Sabah were abandoned.

2   Fought as part of the National Front.

3   Includes 14 from the Parti Bersatu Sabah and 8 from Semangat '46.

4   An amendment to the constitution increased the number of seats to 180 in 1990 (132 from peninsular Malaysia, 27 from Sarawak and 21 from Sabah).

MONGOLIA

The first general election under the country's fourth constitution (see p. 64) took place in June 1992, when 76 members were elected from 26 constituencies. The outcome was:

Party	Seats Won
Mongolian Peoples Revolutionary Party (MPRP)	70
Mongolian Democratic Party (MDP)	1
Mongolian National Progress Party (MNPP)	1
Mongolian Social Democratic Party	1
United Party	1
Independents	2*

* One supporting the MPRP, one supporting the MDP.

The first direct presidential elections were held on June 6 1993 when Pulsalmaagiyn was reelected with 60% of the vote.

MYANMAR (BURMA)

Democracy in Myanmar has had only a brief and troubled history. On independence, universal adult suffrage was adopted, the voting age was 18, and candidates for the People's Assembly had to be 28 or over. Three elections took place between independence and 1962, after which only the Burma Socialist Program Party (BSPP) was allowed to organize political activities. The results were:

June 1951

	Seats Won
Anti-Fascist People's Freedom League (AFPFL)	180
Burma Workers and Peasants Party (BWPP)	6
People's Peace Front/People's Democratic Front (PPF/PDF)	14
Others and independents	33
	233

April 1956

Anti-Fascist People's Freedom League	145
National United Front	47
Others and independents (including allies of the AFPFL and NUF)	48
	240

February 1960

AFPFL ("Clean" faction, led by U Nu)	163
AFPFL ("Stable" faction, led by U Ba Swe)	24
National United Front	7
Others and independents	17
	211

Following the September 1988 coup (and the abolition of the People's Assembly), Myanmar appeared to enjoy a democratic resurgence with the general election of 27 May 1990. The military, however, ignored the result. Parties winning four or more seats were:

	% of Vote	Seats Won
National League for Democracy	59.9	392
Shan Nationalities League for Democracy	1.7	23
Arakan League for Democracy	1.2	11
National Unity Party	21.2	10
Mon National Democratic Front	1.0	5
National Democratic Party for Human Rights	0.9	4
Others (including independents)	14.1	40
	100.0	485

NEPAL

Nepal has very little tradition of democratic elections. However, the elections of February 1959 were contested by political parties and resulted in a sweeping victory (at least in terms of seats) for the Nepali Congress. The Congress, with 37% of the vote, won 74 of the 109 seats. The election of May 1986 was effectively a non-party contest. The result of the election of 12 May 1991 produced another sweeping victory for the Nepali Congress Party, but with a very strong showing by the Communist Party of Nepal. The results were as follows:

Party	Seats Won
Nepali Congress Party	110
Communist Party of Nepal (Unified Marxist-Leninist—UML)	69
United People's Front	9
Nepali Sadbhavana Party	6
National Democratic Party (Chand)	3
Nepal Workers' and Peasants Party	2
Communist Party of Nepal (CPN) (Democratic-Manandhar)	2
National Democratic Party (Thapa)	1
Independents	3
	205

NORTH KOREA

North Korea has been a Communist dictatorship since its establishment in 1948. Under the constitution, the people (in theory) exercise power through the Supreme People's Assembly. With 655 members, this assembly is directly elected every four years from a single list of candidates, all of whom are selected by the Korean Workers' Party (KWP) and its affiliates. All are unopposed. Voting is compulsory, and in all recent elections the government claims that every single person turned out to vote.

PAKISTAN

Democracy in Pakistan has a checkered history. Few elections have been free in the Western sense, and the results have always been much disputed. From independence until the creation of Bangladesh in December 1971, three elections were held—on 21 June 1955 to the Constituent Assembly, on 21 March 1965, and on 7 December 1970 (to the National Assembly). The elections of December 1970 were the first to be held on a real one-man-one-vote basis. The results of all three elections are as follows:

21 June 1955	Seats Won
Awami League	13
Pakistan Muslim League	25
United Front	16*
Others	14
Independents	4
	72

* The alliance of the Awami League and the Krishak Sramik Party in East Pakistan.

21 March 1965	Seats Won
Convention Muslim League	126
Combined Opposition Parties	13
Others	10
Independents	6
	155

7 December 1970	Seats Won
Awami League	151
Pakistan People's Party	81
Qayyum Muslim League	9
Council Muslim League	7
Ahle Sunnat	7
Others	36
	291

Since 1972, multiparty elections have been held on three occasions. The first election (in 1977), after the breakaway of East Pakistan, resulted in the ruling Pakistan People's Party winning 155 seats, the Pakistan National Alliance 36, the Qayyum Muslim League 1, and Independents 8. The results were much disputed. No further multiparty elections took place until 16

November 1988. The outcome then was a major victory for the Pakistan People's Party led by Benazir Bhutto:

Party	Seats Won
Pakistan People's Party	93
Islami Jamhoori Ittehad	54*
Muhajir Qaumi Mahaz	13
Minor parties	18
Independents	27
	205

* Incorporating the Muslim League, the National People's Party and a variety of religious groups.

The elections on 24 October 1990 produced the following outcome:

Party	Seats Won
Islamic Democratic Alliance	106
People's Democratic Alliance	45*
Muhajir Qaumi Movement	15
Jamiat-e-Ulema-e-Islam	6
Awami National Party	6
Other parties	8
Independents	21
	207

* Comprising the Pakistan People's Party, Pakistan Muslim League, etc.

The third elections in five years were held in October 1993. The Pakistan People's Party of Benazir Bhutto won 86 seats in the 217-seat assembly, the Pakistan Muslim League 72, while minor parties and independents took 49. Turnout was only 40%. On 19 October, Benazir Bhutto was elected prime minister by 121 votes to 72.

PHILIPPINES

Prior to September 1972, when martial law was imposed by President Ferdinand Marcos, presidential elections had been held as follows (with the winning party indicated):

1946 Liberal Party
1949 Liberal Party
1953 Nationalist Party
1957 Nationalist Party

1961   Liberal Party
1965   Nationalist Party
1969   Nationalist Party

During the Marcos regime, various plebiscites were held in the 1970s to approve of the exercise of martial law by Marcos and to endorse his continuation in office.

In 1978, elections to the Interim National Assembly resulted in Marcos's New Society Movement winning 152 of the 166 seats.

After the lifting of martial law, presidential elections were held in June 1981, but were boycotted by the major opposition grouping (UNIDO). It was claimed that Marcos received 88.8% of the votes cast. In elections to the National Assembly in May 1984 it was claimed that the government won 110 of the 183 elective seats. The 1986 elections were held amid opposition charges of blatant fraud, and heralded the fall of Marcos. Subsequent elections to the legislature in May 1987 gave 180 seats to the pro-Aquino parties (Lakas ng Bayan) and 20 to the opposition.

The outcome of the elections of 11 May 1992 was as follows:

Presidential Election

Candidate	Vote	% of Vote
Gen. Fidel Ramos (Lakas-NUCD)	5,340,839	23.6
Miriam Defensor Santiago (PRP)	4,466,184	19.7
Eduardo Cojuangco (Nationalist People's Coalition)	4,114,980	18.2
Ramon Mitra (LDP)	3,316,255	14.6
Imelda Marcos (KBL)	2,337,417	10.3
Jovito Salonga (Liberal Party)	2,301,141	10.2
Salvador Laurel (Nacionalista Party)	769,935	3.4
	22,646,751	100.0

General Election

Party	Seats Won
Laban ng Demokratikong Philipino (LDP)	89
Lakas ng EDSA–National Union of Christian Democrats	33
Nationalist People's Coalition	42
Liberal Party/PDP–Laban	15
Nacionalista Party	7
Kilusan Bagong Lipunan (KBL)	3
Others	11
	200

SINGAPORE

Apart from the victory of the left-wing Labor Front under David Marshall in the April 1955 elections, the People's Action Party (PAP) under Lee Kwan Yew has exercised a virtual stranglehold over elections in Singapore. In the election of 1968 (the first since Singapore became an independent republic after its withdrawal from the Federation of Malaysia) the PAP won all 58 seats. The PAP won all the seats in 1972, 1976 and 1980. In 1984, PAP's share of the vote fell to 63% and two opposition MPs were returned (one each from the Workers' Party and the Singapore Democratic Party). The most recent elections (on 31 August 1991) saw four opposition MPs returned (three Singapore Democratic Party, one Workers' Party). Elections since 1955 are summarized below.

Date	Number of Seats[1]	Number of Parties Contesting	Winning Party	Number of Seats Won	Percentage of Vote Won
		Legislative Assembly			
1955 April 2	25[2]	5 and 11 independents	Labor Front	10	26.74
1959 May 30	51	10 and 39 independents	PAP	43	53.40
1963 Sept 21	51	8 and 16 independents	PAP	37	46.46
		Parliament			
1968 April 13	7 (51)	2 and 5 independents	PAP	58	84.43
1972 Sept 2	57 (8)	6 and 2 independents	PAP	65	69.02
1976 Dec 23	53 (16)	7 and 2 independents	PAP	69	72.40
1980 Dec 23	38 (37)	8	PAP	75	72.55
1984 Dec 22	49 (30)	9 and 3 independents	PAP	77	62.94
1988 Sept 3	70 (11)	8 and 4 independents	PAP	80	61.76
1991 Aug 31	40 (41)	7 and 7 independents	PAP	77	59.31

1   Uncontested seats shown in parentheses.
2   Elected members. There were also three ex-officio and four appointed members, and the Speaker.

Source: *Singapore Yearbook, 1992*

Note: In the first direct presidential elections held in August 1993, the government candidate, Ong Teng Cheong, secured 58.7% of the votes cast.

SOUTH KOREA

Conditions for elections in South Korea have varied enormously under the differing constitutions. The table below summarizes results for three eras: 1950 until the proclamation of the Third Republic; the elections of the Third and Fourth Republic, 1963–79; and a more detailed analysis of the results of the 1980s.

1950–63	May 1950	May 1954	May 1958	July 1960 (House)
Agrarian Party	11	–	–	–
Democratic Nationalist Party	23	15	–	–
Democratic Party	–	–	79	175
Korean Nationalist Party	22	–	–	–
Korean Youth League	10	–	–	–
Liberal Party	–	109(+27)	125	2
National Union Party	10	–	–	–
Other parties	13	5	1	7
Independents	130	74	28	49
	219	203	233	233

1963–78	Nov 1963	June 1967	May 1971	Feb 1973	Dec 1978
Civil Rule Party	41	–	–	–	–
Democratic Republican Party	110	130	113	146	145
New Democratic Party	–	44	89	52	61
Other parties	24	1	2	2	3
Independents	–	–	–	19	22
	175	175	204	219	231

The results of the last four National Assembly elections have been:

25 March 1981

Democratic Justice Party	151
Democratic Korea Party	81
Korean Nationalist Party	25
Others	8
Independents	11
	276

12 February 1985

Democratic Justice Party	148
New Korea Democratic Party	67
Democratic Korea Party	35
Korea National Party	20
Independents and others	6
	276

26 April 1988

Democratic Justice Party	125
New Democratic Republican Party	35
Party for Peace and Democracy	70
Reunification Democratic Party	59
Other parties	1
Independents	9
	299

24 Martch 1992

Democratic Liberal Party	149
Democratic Party	97
Unification National Party	31
Party for New Political Reform	1
Independents	21
	299

In presidential elections, the results since 1987 (the first direct presidential election since 1971) have been:

16 December 1987

Candidate	Vote	% of Vote
Roh Tae-Woo	8,282,738	35.9
Kim Young-Sam	6,337,581	27.5
Kim Dae-Jung	6,113,375	26.5
Others	2,337,054	10.1
	23,070,748	100.0

18 December 1992 (the first all-civilian elections for over 30 years)

Candidate	% of Vote	Party
Kim Young-Sam	42	Democratic Liberal Party
Kim Dae-Jung	34	Democratic Party
Chun Ju Yung	16	United Peoples Party
Others	6	

Of the electorate of 29,422,658 some 81.9% voted.

SRI LANKA

1956 (April)	Seats Won	% of Vote
Mahajana Eksath Peramuna	51	40.0
United National Party	8	27.4
Lanka Sama Samaja Party	14	10.5
Federal Party (FP)	10	5.4
Communists (CP)	3	3.0
Tamil Congress (TC)	1	0.3
Independents and others	8	11.7
	95	

1960 (March)	Seats Won	% of Vote
United National Party	50	29.6
Sri Lanka Freedom Party	46	21.1
Lanka Sama Samaja Party	10	10.5

Mahajana Eksath Peramuna	10	10.6
Communist Party	3	4.6
Federal Party	15	5.8
Tamil Congress	1	1.3
Independents and others	16	16.5
	151	

1960 (July)	Seats Won	% of Vote
United National Party	30	37.6
Sri Lanka Freedom Party	75	33.6
Lanka Sama Samaja Party	12	7.4
Mahajana Eksath Peramuna	3	3.6
Communist Party	4	4.0
Federal Party	16	7.2
Tamil Congress	1	1.5
Independents and others	10	6.4
	151	

1965 (March)	Seats Won	% of Vote
United National Party	65	38.9
Sri Lanka Freedom Party	41	30.2
Lanka Sama Samaja Party	10	7.5
Mahajana Eksath Peramuna	1	2.7
Communist Party	4	4.0
Federal Party	14	5.4
Tamil Congress	3	2.4
Independents and others	12	10.2
	150	

1970 (27 May)	Seats Won	% of Vote
United National Party	17	37.9
Sri Lanka Freedom Party	91	36.7
Lanka Sama Samaja Party	19	8.8
Communist Party	6	6.0
Federal Party	13	5.0
Tamil Congress	3	2.3
Independents and others	2	6.0
	151	

1977	Seats Won	% of Vote
United National Party	140	50.1
Sri Lanka Freedom Party	8	29.7
Federal Party/Tamil United Liberation Front	18	6.8
CWC	1	1.0
Others	1	12.4
	168	

A new constitution was adopted in 1978 and elections were not held. The most recent contests are summarized below:

Presidential Election: 19 December 1988

Candidate	Vote	% of Vote	Party
Ranasinghe Premadasa	2,569,199	50.4	UNP
Sirimavo Bandaranaike	2,289,860	44.9	SLFP
Ossie Abeygoonasekera	235,719	4.6	SLMP[1]

1   Sri Lanka Mahajana Party

General Election: 15 February 1989	Seats Won
United National Party	125
Sri Lanka Freedom Party	67
Eelam Revolutionary Organization of Students	13
Tamil United Liberation Front Alliance	10
Sri Lankan Muslim Congress	4
United Socialist Alliance	3
Mahajana Eksath Peramuna	3
	225

TAIWAN

Prior to the elections of 18 December 1992, no free or fully representative elections had ever taken place in Taiwan. The island remained in the stranglehold of those elected in 1947–48 to represent constituencies on the mainland (see below). Since 1972, elections have been held to fill seats in both the Yuan and the National Assembly for Taiwan. Only in 1988 was a plan begun to phase out mainland representation and give a corresponding increase to members in areas actually ruled by Taiwan.

Election Summary

1947–48	Two thousand candidates contest elections in KMT-controlled areas (1,750 KMT candidates, others from Young China Party or the China Democratic Socialist Party).
1972	Partial elections to seats representing Taiwan. KMT won 38 of 53 seats in the National Assembly and 59 of 73 seats in the Yuan.
1980	Elections postponed from 1978. KMT won 58 of 70 seats in the Yuan, 65 of 76 in the National Assembly.
1983	KMT win 62 of 71 seats in the Yuan.
1986	The first elections to be contested by an organized opposition (the Democratic Progressive Party). The outcome:

	Yuan	National Assembly
KMT	59	68
DPP	12	11
Others	2	5
	73	84

1991/92   KMT support fell to 71% in the National Assembly elections
                 (21 December 1991). In the Yuan election of December 1992
                 the outcome was:

Party	Seats Won	% of Vote
KMT	96	53
Democratic Progressive Party	50	31
Others	15	16
	161	100

THAILAND

Frequent military coups, accompanied by changes to the constitution, have
ensured that Thailand's electoral history has been a checkered one. The
following summary up to 1986 gives the year of the election and seats won.
More detailed figures are given for 1988 onwards.

1948   Democratic Party, 54; other parties, 46 (including the Peo-
              ple's Party and the Justice Sovereignty Party)

1957 (1 st)   Government Party, 83; Democratic Party, 28; others (includ-
              ing the Economist Party), 8; Independents, 41

1957 (2nd)   Unionist Party, 45; Democrat Party, 39; others, 7; inde-
              pendents, 73

1969   United Thai People's Party/Thai United Party, 75; Demo-
              crat Party, 57; others (including Democratic Front Party
              and the Economist United Front), 14; independents, 73

1975   Democrat Party, 72; Social Justice Party, 45; Thai Nation
              (Chart Thai), 28; Social Agrarian Party, 19; Social Ac-
              tion Force, 18; New Force Party, 12; others, 75

1976   Democrat Party, 114; Social Action Force, 45; Thai Nation,
              56; Social Justice Party, 28; others, 36

1979   Social Action Force, 82; Thai Nation, 38; Democrat Party,
              32; Thai Citizens Party, 32; Free Justice Party, 23; other
              parties, 31; independents, 63

1983   Social Action Force, 92; Thai Nation, 73; Democrat Party,
              56; Thai Citizens Party, 36; Free Justice Party/National
              Democracy Party, 15; other parties, 28; independents, 24

1986   Thai Nation, 63; Social Action Force, 51; United Democrat
              Party, 38; Thai Citizens Party, 24; United Thai People's Party,
              19; Citizens Party, 18; Community Action Party, 15; others, 19

The results of elections since 1988 have been:

1988	**Seats Won**
Thai Nation Party	87
Social Action Force	54
Democrat Party	48
Thai Citizens Party	31
United Thai People's Party	35
Citizens Party	21
People Party	19
Thai People's Party	17
Righteous Force	14
Other parties	31
	357

September 1992	**Seats Won**
Democrat Party	79
Chart Thai	77
Chart Pattana	60
New Aspiration Party	51
Palang Dharma	47
Social Action Party	22
Others	24
	360

CHAPTER 9

POPULATION AND URBANIZATION

POPULATION OF INDIVIDUAL COUNTRIES

AFGHANISTAN		

	Population Total Population	Percentage of Population Urban
1950	8,420,000	5.8
1955	9,125,000	
1960	10,016,000	8.0
1965	11,115,000	
1970	12,457,000	11.0
1975	14,038,000	13.1
1979	15,551,358	
1988	10 to 12 million	20.0
1991 (est)	16,450,000	21.7

Cities					
	1948	1964	1973	1979	1982
Kabul	154,000	400,000	318,000	913,164	1,127,417
Kandahar		119,000	140,000	178,409	191,345
Herat			108,000	140,323	150,497
Mazar-i-Sharif		40,000		103,372	110,367
Jalalabad		44,000		53,915	57,824
Kunduz				53,251	
Baghlan			105,944*	39,228	41,240
Maimana				38,251	
Pul-i-Khumri				31,101	
Ghazni				30,425	31,985

* 1971 figure

Population Density (Per Square Kilometer)	
1975	1985
30	30

AFGHANISTAN (Continued)

Ethnic Composition

1963

Pathans/Pashtuns	8,800,000
Tadzhiks	4,300,000
Uzbeks	800,000
Nomads	650,000
Hazarahs	440,000

BANGLADESH

	Population	
	Total Population	**Percentage of Population Urban**
1961	50,854,000*	
1965	62,500,000*	5.6
1970	72,000,000*	7.6
1974	71,479,000	
1981	89,912,000	
1988	106,600,000	13.0
1991 (est)	116,601,000	13.6

* East Pakistan.

	Cities			
	1961	**1972**	**1981**	**1987**
Dhaka	556,712	1,500,000	3,430,312	4,770,000
Chittagong	364,205	680,000	1,391,877	1,840,000
Khulna	127,970	500,000	646,359	860,000
Rajshahi			253,740	430,000

Population Density (Per Square Kilometer)

1975	**1988**
533	740

BHUTAN

	Population	
	Total Population	**Percentage of Population Urban**
1961	700,000	
1988	1,400,000	5.0

Cities

	1987
Thimphu	15,000

BRUNEI

Population
Total Population

1972	141,500
1981	192,832
1988	241,400
1991 (est)	397,000

Cities

	1971	1981
Bandar Seri Begawan	72,481	49,902
Seria		23,415
Kuala Belait		19,335

Ethnic Composition

	1972	1988
Malays	65%	105,700
Chinese	23%	43,400
Indigenous	7%	
Others	5%	

CAMBODIA

Population

Total Population		Percentage of Population Urban
1962	5,728,771	
1981	5,756,141	
1985	6,232,000	11.0
1991 (est)	7,146,000	

Cities

	1962	1983	1986
Phnom Penh	393,995	500,000	700,000

Population Density (Per Square Kilometer)

1975	1988
45	37

Ethnic Composition

	1962	1981
Khmer	5,334,000	93%
Vietnamese	218,000	4%
Chinese	163,000	3%
Others	14,000	

CHINA

	Population Total Population*	Percentage of Population Urban
1953	590,195,000	
1965	700,000,000	
1975	933,000,000	20.2
1982	1,008,175,288	
1990	1,110,000,000	21.4
1993	1,180,000,000	

Cities

	1953	1958	1970	1987
Shanghai		6,900,000*	10,820,000	7,100,000
Beijing		4,010,000*	7,570,000	5,970,000
Tianjin			4,280,000	5,460,000
Shenyang		2,420,000		4,290,000
Wuhan		2,230,000		3,490,000
Guangzhou	180,000			3,360,000
Chongqing		2,160,000		2,830,000
Harbin		1,590,000		2,670,000
Chengdu	1,107,000	1,130,000		2,640,000
Xian				2,390,000

* 1957 figure

Population Density (Per Square Kilometer)

1975	1987
86	113

Ethnic Composition

	1953	1982
Han Chinese	547,280,000	936,700,000
Zhuang	6,610,000	1.3%
Hui	3,560,000	0.7%
Uighur	3,640,000	0.6%
Yi	3,250,000	0.54%
Miao	2,510,000	0.5%
Manchu	2,420,000	0.43%
Tibetan	2,770,000	0.39%
Mongolian	1,460,000	0.34%
Puyi	1,250,000	
Korean	1,120,000	
Other	6,720,000	

* Includes Tibet

TIBET (FORMALLY, AN AUTONOMOUS REGION OF THE PEOPLE'S REPUBLIC OF CHINA)

	Population Total Population	Percentage of Population Urban
1988 (est)	2,080,000	Unk.

	Cities 1982	1987
Lhasa	343,200	130,000

Population Density (Per Square Kilometer)
1987

2

Ethnic Composition 1988	
Tibetan	2,000,000
Han	73,000

HONG KONG

	Population Total Population	Percentage of Population Urban
1961	3,226,400	
1971	3,950,000	
1987	5,613,000	
1989	5,761,400	93.0

Population Density (Per Square Kilometer)	
1975	1985
4,179	5,337

Ethnic Composition 1989	
Vietnamese	56,810

Note: This is the only numerically significant minority group in Hong Kong.

INDIA

	Population Total Population	Percentage of Population Urban
1951	361,088,090	17.3
1961	439,234,771	18.0
1971	548,159,052	19.9
1981	685,184,692	23.3
1984	748,000,000	
1988	789,120,000	27.5
1991 (est)	866,000,000	28.0

INDIA *(Continued)*

Cities

	1951	1961	1971	1981
Calcutta	4,578,000	4,405,000	7,005,362	9,194,018
Bombay	2,839,000	4,152,000	5,968,546	8,243,405
Delhi	1,384,000	2,359,000	3,629,842	4,884,234
Madras	1,416,000	1,729,000	2,470,288	3,276,622
Bangalore	779,000	1,207,000	1,648,232	2,914,000
Ahmedabad	794,000	1,206,000	1,746,111	2,059,725
Hyderabad		1,252,337*	1,798,910	2,187,262
Kanpur	705,000	971,000	1,273,016	1,481,789
Nagpur	449,000	690,000	930,000	1,219,461
Pune	345,000	737,000	1,123,399	1,203,351

* Provisional figure

Population Density (Per Square Kilometer)

1951	1961	1971	1981
117	142	177	216

Ethnic Composition

Religion	1951	1961	1971	1981
Hindu	303,200,000	366,418,701	453,436,630	549,724,717
Muslim	35,400,000	46,939,592	61,418,269	75,571,514
Christian	8,200,000	10,725,273	14,225,045	16,174,498
Sikh	6,200,000	7,845,843	10,378,891	13,078,146
Jain	1,600,000	2,027,262	2,604,837	3,192,572
Buddhist	200,000	3,206,142	3,874,942	4,719,900
Zoroastrian	100,000			
Other religions (tribal)	1,700,000			
Other religions (nontribal)	100,000			
Others		1,498,895	2,184,955	2,766,285

Mother Tongue	1951	1961
Hindu		133,433,207
Urdu	149,944,311	23,323,399
Hindustani		
Punjabi		10,950,660
Telugu	32,999,916	37,668,106
Marathi	27,049,522	33,286,710
Tamil	26,546,764	30,562,671
Bengali	25,121,674	33,888,279
Gujurati	16,310,771	20,304,461
Kannada	14,471,764	17,415,826
Malayalam	13,380,109	17,015,674

Source: India Reference Annuals 1953, 1962, 1971–72, 1988–89, Ministry of Information and Broadcasting, Government of India.

INDONESIA

	Population Total Population	Percentage of Population Urban
1950	79,538,000	12.4
1955	86,552,000	
1961	97,387,000	
1965	107,041,000	
1971	118,460,000	17.1
1975	135,666,000	19.4
1980	147,490,298	
1988	175,600,000	28.5
1991 (est)	193,000,000	28.8

Cities	1955	1961	1971	1980	1983
Jakarta	1,865,000	3,694,000	5,849,000	6,503,449	7,636,000
Surabaya	929,000	1,008,000	1,269,000	2,027,913	2,289,000
Medan	308,000	479,000	620,000	1,378,955	1,966,000
Bandung	833,000	973,000	1,152,000	1,462,637	1,602,000
Semarang	371,000	503,000	633,000	1,026,671	1,269,000
Palembang	285,000	475,000	614,000	787,187	
Ujung Padang				709,038	888,000
Padang		144,000	187,000	480,922	726,000
Malang	280,000	341,000	429,000	511,780	560,000
Surakarta				469,888	

Population Density (Per Square Kilometer)	
1975	1985
69	90

JAPAN

	Population Total Population	Percentage of Population Urban
1950	83,200,000	37.5
1960	93,419,000	
1970	103,720,000	72.1
1980	117,060,000	76.2
1985	121,047,196	77.0
1988	122,783,000	
1991 (est)	124,017,000	77.5

	Cities				
	1955	**1966**	**1970**	**1975**	**1988**
Tokyo	7,867,000	11,005,000	8,841,000	11,663,000	8,156,000
Yokohama	1,144,000	1,860,000	2,238,000	2,620,000	3,122,000
Osaka	2,547,000	3,133,000	2,980,000	2,780,000	2,544,000
Nagoya	1,337,000	1,954,000	2,036,000	2,080,000	2,100,000
Sapporo	427,000	815,000	1,010,000	1,240,000	1,582,000
Kobe	979,000	1,228,000	1,289,000	1,360,000	1,427,000
Kyoto	1,204,000	1,379,000	1,419,000	1,460,000	1,419,000
Fukuoka	544,000	778,000	853,000	1,000,000	1,157,000
Kawasaki	445,000	856,000	973,000	1,020,000	1,114,000
Hiroshima			542,000		1,043,000

Population Density (Per Square Kilometer)

1975	1985
297	324

LAOS

Population

	Total Population	**Percentage of Population Urban**
1972	3,106,000	9.6
1986	3,722,000	
1987	3,830,000	18.5
1991	4,113,000	18.6

Cities

	1970	**1973**	**1985**
Vientiane	150,000		377,409
Savannakhet		50,690	
Pakse		44,860	
Luang Prabang		44,244	

Population Density (Per Square Kilometer)

1975	1985
14	16

MACAO

Population

	Total Population	**Percentage of Population Urban**
1970	248,636	
1981	261,680	
1987	434,300	

MALAYSIA

Population

	Total Population	Percentage of Population Urban
1960	10,992,000	
1970	10,440,770*	27.0
1980	13,745,241	
1989	17,363,000	42.3
1991 (est)	17,981,000	

* Excludes Singapore, which became a separate state in 1965.

Cities

	1971	1980	1986
Kuala Lampur	452,000	937,875	1,000,000
Ipoh		300,727	
Penang		250,578	
Johor Baharu		249,880	
Petaling Jaya		207,805	
Kelang		192,080	
Kuala Terengganu		186,608	
Kota Baharu		170,559	
Taiping		146,002	
Kuantan		136,625	

Population Density (Per Square Kilometer)

1975	1985
36	50

Ethnic Composition

	1970	1980
Malay	4,888,000	47%
Chinese	3,555,000	32%
Indian	933,000	8%
Others		13%

MONGOLIA

Population

	Total Population	Percentage of Population Urban
1972	1,301,600	45
1989	2,001,000	52
1991 (est)	2,247,000	51.2

Cities

	1985	1988
Ulan Bator		500,000
Darkhan		80,000
Erdenet	42,900	

Population Density (Per Square Kilometer)
1987

1.28

MYANMAR (BURMA)

Population

	Total Population	Percentage of Population Urban
1970	27,584,000	22.8
1983	35,313,905	
1988	39,840,000	24.6
1991 (est)	42,112,000	

Cities

	1970	1983
Rangoon (Yangon)		2,458,712
Mandalay	401,633	532,985
Henzada	84,898	283,658
Moulmein	172,569	219,991
Pegu	124,643	150,447
Bassein	136,429	144,092
Sittwe (Akyab)	82,313	107,907
Taunggye		107,607
Monywa		106,873
Prome	148,000*	

* 1973 figure

Population Density (Per Square Kilometer)

1975	1985
45	57

NEPAL

Population

	Total Population	Percentage of Population Urban
1971	11,289,968	3.9
1981	15,022,839	
1985	16,625,439	8.0
1990 (est)	19,611,000	9.6

Cities

	1971	1981
Katmandu	353,756	235,160
Morang (Biratnagar)		93,544
Patan (Lalitpur)		79,875
Bhadgaon (Bhaktapur)		48,472

Population Density (Per Square Kilometer)

1975	1985
89	122

Ethnic Composition

	1981
Nepali-speaking	52.4%
Bihari-speaking	18.5%

NORTH KOREA

	Population Total Population	Percentage of Population Urban
1960	10,789,000	
1965	11,100,000	
1970	13,892,000	50.1
1975	16,000,000	
1985	21,185,000	
1989	22,420,000	67.4

		Cities		
	1960	**1966**	**1981**	**1984**
Pyongyang	635,100	1,364,000	1,280,000	2,639,448
Hamhung		420,000*	775,000	
Chongjin	184,300			754,128
Nampo		•		691,284
Sinuiju			305,000	500,000
Wonsan			398,000	350,000
Kaesong	139,900			345,642
Kimchaek				281,000
Haeju				131,000
Sariwon				130,000

* 1972 figure

Population Density (Per Square Kilometer)

1975	1989
132	186

PAKISTAN

	Population Total Population	Percentage of Population Urban
1951	75,842,000*	10.4
1961	93,832,000	13.1
1972	64,980,000	25.5
1981	84,250,000	
1984	93,290,000	29.1
1989	105,400,000	32.0
1991 (est)	117,490,000	

* 1951 and 1961 figures include the population of East Pakistan, which became Bangladesh in 1971.

PAKISTAN *(Continued)*

Cities

	1951	1961	1972	1981
Karachi	1,126,000	1,912,598	3,499,000	5,103,000
Lahore	849,000	1,296,477	2,165,000	2,922,000
Faisalabad	179,000		823,000	1,092,000
Rawalpindi	237,000	340,175	615,000	928,000
Hyderabad	242,000	434,537	628,000	795,000
Multan	190,000	358,201	542,000	730,000
Gujranwala	121,000	196,154	360,000	597,000
Peshawar	152,000	218,691	268,000	555,000
Sialkot		164,346		296,000
Dargodha				294,000

Population Density (Per Square Kilometer)

1975	1981
87	105.8

PHILIPPINES

Population

	Total Population	Percentage of Population Urban
1948	19,234,182	26.6
1955	23,858,000	
1960	27,087,685	30.2
1965	32,941,000	
1970	36,684,486	31.8
1975	42,070,660	31.6
1980	48,098,460	37.3
1990	60,684,887	42.4
1991 (est)	65,758,000	

Cities

	1948	1960	1970	1980	1990
Quezon City	108,000	398,000	754,452	1,165,865	1,666,766
Manila	983,906	1,138,611	1,330,788	1,630,485	1,598,918
Davao City	111,000	226,000	323,020	610,375	849,947
Kalookan City		146,000	326,000*	467,816	761,011
Cebu City	168,000	251,000	347,116	490,281	610,417
Makati				372,631	452,734
Zamboanga City				343,722	442,345
Pasig				268,570	397,309
Pasay City				287,770	366,623
Bacolod City				262,415	364,180

* 1973 Figure

Population Density (Per Square Kilometer)

1948	1960	1970	1980	1990
64.1	90.3	122.3	160.3	202.3

PHILIPPINES *(Continued)*

Ethnic Composition

Mother Tongue (Other Than English)	1948	1960	1970	1975	1980*
Tagalog	3,730,028	5,694,072	8,979,719	10,019,214	2,552,561
Cebuano	4,759,772	6,529,882	8,844,996	10,262,735	2,083,335
Ilokano	2,340,221	3,158,560	4,150,596	4,685,896	886,319
Hiligaynon/Ilongo	2,373,566	2,817,314	3,745,333	4,204,825	788,479
Bicol	1,467,874	2,108,837	2,507,156	2,928,245	479,472
Lineyte/Samarron (Waray)	1,203,963	1,488,668	1,767,829	1,945,005	342,987
Pampango	641,795	875,531	1,212,024	1,442,607	238,715
Pangasinan	515,158	666,003	838,104	948,820	158,666
Others	2,201,805	3,748,818	4,638,729	5,633,313	1,076,653

* Number of households.

Religion	1948	1960	1970
Roman Catholic	15,941,422	22,686,096	31,169,488
Muslim	791,817	1,317,475	1,584,963
Aglipayan	1,456,114	1,414,431	1,434,688
Protestant	444,491	785,399	1,122,999
Iglesia ni Kristo	88,125	270,104	475,407
Buddhist	42,751	39,631	33,639
Others	469,462	574,549*	616,076
None			247,226

* Others and None combined

SINGAPORE

Population

	Total Population	Percentage of Population Urban
1970	2,074,507	100.0
1980	2,413,945	100.0
1988	2,647,100	100.0
1991 (est)	2,756,000	100.0

Population Density (Per Square Kilometer)

1975	1985
3,872	4,274

Ethnic Composition

	1971	1980	1988
Chinese	1,606,600	1,856,237	2,011,300
Malays	317,300	351,508	401,200
Indians	147,500	154,632	171,800
Others	39,000	51,568	62,800

SOUTH KOREA

Population

	Total Population	Percentage of Population Urban
1950	20,357,000	21.4
1955	21,422,000	
1960	24,989,241	
1966	29,207,856	
1970	31,469,132	40.7
1975	35,281,000	48.0
1980	38,124,000	56.9
1985	40,466,577	65.0
1989	42,519,000	72.0
1991 (est)	43,134,000	

Cities

	1949	1962	1970	1980	1985
Seoul	1,446,000	2,983,000	5,536,377	8,364,000	9,645,824
Pusan	474,000	1,271,000	1,880,710	3,160,000	3,516,768
Taegu	314,000	717,000	1,082,750	1,605,000	2,030,649
Inchon	266,000	430,000	646,013	1,084,000	1,387,475
Kwangchu	139,000	313,000	502,753	728,000	905,896
Taejon	127,000	269,000	414,598	652,000	866,303
Ulsan					551,219
Puch'on					456,311
Masan			190,992		449,236
Seongnam					447,832

Population Density (Per Square Kilometer)

1975	1985
352	428

SRI LANKA

Population

	Total Population	Percentage of Population Urban
1946	6,657,339	
1953	8,098,095	
1960	9,896,000	
1971	12,711,143	21.9
1981	14,846,750	21.5
1988	16,600,000	21.4
1991	17,423,000	

SRI LANKA *(Continued)*

Cities

	1971	1981
Colombo	562,160	587,647
Dehiwela-Mt. Lavinia		173,529
Moratuwa		134,826
Jaffna	107,663	118,224
Kotte		101,039
Kandy	93,602	97,872
Galle	72,270	76,863
Negombo		60,762
Trincomalee		44,313
Batticaloa		42,963

Population Density (Per Square Kilometer)

1975	1985
213	256

Ethnic Composition

	1971	1981
Sinhalese	9,147,000	10,980,000
Sri Lanka Tamils	1,416,000	1,887,000
Sri Lanka Moors	824,000	1,047,000
Indian Tamils	1,195,000	819,000
Malays		47,000
Burghers		39,000
Others		28,000

TAIWAN

Population

	Total Population	Percentage of Population Urban
1953	7,591,000	
1960	12,345,000	
1972	15,249,000	
1982	18,271,000	
1988	19,900,000	
1991	20,658,000	

Cities

	1988
Taipei	2,680,000
Kaohsiung	1,300,000

TAIWAN *(Continued)*

Population Density (Per Square Kilometer)
1988

553

Ethnic Composition
	1988
Mainland Chinese	2,000,000
Indigenous	335,827

THAILAND

	Population Total Population	Percentage of Population Urban
1950	19,000,000	
1960	26,257,916	
1971	36,820,000	13.3
1980	46,961,338	
1988	54,465,056	22.5
1991 (est)	56,814,000	22.6

Cities
	1970	**1980**	**1987**
Bangkok metropolitan	2,228,144		5,609,352
Changmai		101,595	
Hat Yai		93,519	
Khon Kaen		85,863	
Phitsanulok		79,942	
Nakhon Rajchasima		78,246	
Udorn Thani		71,142	
Songkhla		67,945	
Nakhon Sawan		63,935	
Nakhon Si Thammaraj		63,162	
Ubon Rajchathani		50,788	

Population Density (Per Square Kilometer)
1975	**1985**
81	99

VIETNAM		

	Population Total Population	Percentage of Population Urban
1960 North	15,916,955	
South	15,917,000*	
1964 North	17,900,000	
South	15,715,000	
1970 North	23,787,000	18.3
South	21,154,000	
1979	52,741,766	19.7
1984	58,310,000	
1989	64,000,000	21.9
1991 (est)	67,568,000	

* Until their reunification in 1976, North and South Vietnam were separate states.

			Cities		
	1955	1960	1970	1973	1979
Ho Chi Minh City (Saigon)			1,763,692	1,825,000	3,419,978
Hanoi		643,576	1,400,000		2,000,000
Da Nang	100,000		427,827	492,000	
Haiphong		369,248			1,279,067
Nha Trang			103,184*	216,000	
Qui Nhon				214,000	
Hué	93,000			209,043	
Can Tho			106,943	182,424	
My Tho			109,967*	120,000	
Cam Ranh				118,000	

* 1969 figure

Population Density (Per Square Kilometer)	
1975	1989
136	181

Ethnic Composition	
	1976
Tay	742,000
Khmer	651,000
Thai	631,000
Muong	618,000
Nung	472,000
Meo	349,000
Dao	294,000

Source: *World Population Prospects: Estimates and Projections as Assessed in 1982* (New York: United Nations), 1982.
UN Demographic Yearbook 1960, 1964, 1974, 1980, 1992.

MAJOR URBAN CONCENTRATIONS IN ASIA

The largest concentration of population in Asia's conurbations (metropolitan areas) is as follows (1992 estimates):

Tokyo	24,000,000
Seoul	15,300,000
Calcutta	11,600,000
Bombay	11,600,000
Jakarta	10,900,000
Manila	10,900,000
Osaka	10,000,000
Shanghai	9,200,000

POPULATION TRENDS IN ASIA

Growth of Population in Asia, 1950–2000

	East Asia[1]	South Asia[2]
1950	671	704
1960	791	877
1970	986	1,116
1980	1,176	1,408
1985	1,250	1,568
1990	1,324	1,734
2000[3]	1,475	2,074

1   China, Japan, Korea

2   India, Pakistan, Bangladesh, Southeast Asia

3   Projected

Life Expectancy at Birth in Asia, 1950–1985

	World	East Asia	South Asia
1950–55	46.0	42.7	39.9
1975–80	58.0	66.6	52.7
1980–85	59.5	68.4	54.9

Infant Mortality in Asia, 1950–1985
(deaths by age 1 year per 1,000 live births)

	World	East Asia	South Asia
1950–55	156	182	180
1975–80	85	39	115
1980–85	78	36	103

Median Age of Population, 1950–1985

	World	East Asia	South Asia
1950	23.4	23.5	20.4
1975	21.9	21.5	19.0
1985	23.5	24.7	20.3

Source: *United Nations World Population Prospects: Estimates and Projections as Assessed in 1984* (New York, 1986).

MAJOR POPULATION AND REFUGEE MOVEMENTS IN ASIA SINCE 1945

1945	Repatriation of approximately three million Japanese from East Asian Co-Prosperity Sphere (Manchuria, Korea and China) to Japan.
1947	At partition of India, over 17 million Hindu and Muslim refugees flee to join coreligionists in the new independent states of India and Pakistan.
1949	Approximately two million Nationalist Chinese under Jiang Kaishek flee to Taiwan after Communist victory in Chinese civil war.
1950–53	Korean War displaces approximately three million Koreans from North to South Korea.
1958	Beginnings of mass immigration to Great Britain from Indian subcontinent.
1959	Dalai Lama heads flight of Tibetan refugees to India after Chinese crush revolt.
1971	Thousands of Bangladeshis flee into India to escape fighting in aftermath of declaration of independence.
1975	Communist victory in Vietnam leads to exodus of "boat people" to other countries of Southeast Asia.
1979	Soviet invasion of Afghanistan leads to an estimated two million Afghan refugees in camps in Pakistan. Thousands of refugees flee Cambodia for Thailand following Vietnamese invasion to end Pol Pot regime; Red Cross estimates two million people in danger inside and outside Cambodia as a result of disruption.

FAMINES AND NATURAL DISASTERS IN ASIA SINCE 1945

1945	Tidal wave in East Pakistan (Bangladesh) kills 4,000.
1948	4,000 killed in earthquake in Japan.
1956	Typhoon in China kills over 2,000.
1958	Typhoon in Japan kills 1,300 people.
1960	3,000 die in East Pakistan floods (October).
1963	10,000 die in East Pakistan hurricane (May).
1964	Burst reservoir kills 1,000 people in India; typhoon kills 7,000 in Ceylon and Madras.
1965	Typhoon kills 10,000 in East Pakistan.

1970   Massive floods in East Pakistan kill between 250,000 and 500,000
       people (November).
1971   5,000 killed by typhoon floods in India.
1974   20,000 feared dead in Chinese earthquake (May); monsoon floods
       in Bangladesh kill 2,000 (August); earthquake in Pakistan kills
       4,000 (December).
1980   UN relief agencies estimate two million facing starvation in Cam-
       bodia.
1981   Floods in Shansi Province, China kill 5,000 people.
1982   Monsoon floods in India kill hundreds and leave millions home-
       less (September).
1984   10,000 killed in typhoon floods in Philippines.
1985   10,000 killed in typhoon floods in Bangladesh (May).
1991   200 killed, 100,000 made homeless by eruption of Mt. Pinatubo
       volcano. Eruption also destroys Clark (U.S.) Air Force Base.
1992   1,500 killed in earthquake on island of Flores in eastern Indonesia.
1993   Worst monsoon floods for 50 years devastate Nepal, northern In-
       dia and Bangladesh (July); thousands killed by earthquake in
       Maharashtra state, India (September).

RICE PRODUCTION IN ASIA, 1962–1985			
(Metric Tons, in Thousands)			
1962	1972	1980	1985

	1962	1972	1980	1985
Bangladesh	15,034	15,134	20,821	21,700
China	86,038	105,197	142,993	172,184
India	52,733	58,868	80,312	90,000
Indonesia	12,393	18,031	29,652	34,300
Japan	16,444	15,319	12,189	12,958
Korea, South	4,809	5,500	5,311	7,608
Korea, North	–	3,783	4,960	5,200
Myanmar (Burma)	7,786	7,361	13,100	14,500
Pakistan	1,824	3,495	4,679	5,210
Philippines	3,957	4,898	7,836	8,150
Thailand	11,267	12,413	17,368	18,535
Vietnam, North	4,600	4,400		
Vietnam, South	6,029	6,348	11,679	14,500

Source: J. Paxton, *The Statesman's Year-Book, 1977–78* (London: Macmillan, 1977), p. xviii; *The Statesman's Year-Book, 1985–86* (London: Macmillan, 1985), p. xviii.

CHAPTER 10

GLOSSARY
OF POLITICAL TERMS,
EVENTS AND PLACES

Adipati (Commander) Title assumed during the Japanese occupation of Burma by Ba Maw, the head of state.

Ajmer Small state in India, merged with Rajasthan in 1956.

Akali Dal A Sikh party in Punjab that seeks greater autonomy for the Sikh community, part of which advocates an independent state of Khalistan.

Alliance of Eight Term used in the Afghan civil war (see p. 000) for the coalition of the eight Shi'ite Mujaheddin groups that were supported by Iran against the Soviet-backed government in Kabul.

Alliance of Seven The Sunni fundamentalist coalition in the Afghan civil war, operating from Peshawar in Pakistan.

Ambon Indonesian island in the Maluku (Moluccas) group. The Ambonese (one of Indonesia's few Christian communities) resisted incorporation into Indonesia in 1950. They have proclaimed a "Republic of the South Moluccas" and perpetrated terrorist acts, especially in the Netherlands.

Amethyst Incident 20 April to 31 July 1949. The British frigate *Amethyst* was shelled on the Yangtze River, previously an international waterway, claimed by Chinese Communists exclusively for China. Seventeen crew members were killed. A failed rescue attempt led to further casualties. *Amethyst* remained moored on the river until successfully breaking out on 30–31 July.

Amritsar City in the Punjab; scene of a massacre in April 1919 when 379 Indians were killed and over 1,200 injured after the British commander, General Dyer, ordered his troops to fire on angry (but unarmed) demonstrators. The Amritsar Massacre left a bitter legacy in Anglo–Indian relations.

Amur River   The river that marks the border of Mongolia and Siberia.

Angkor   The ancient capital of Cambodia, site of the Angkor Wat temple complex and symbol of Cambodian culture and sovereignty.

An Loc   Site of an engagement during the Vietnam War. The siege of An Loc (April–July 1972) by North Vietnamese forces was eventually repulsed with the help of U.S. air support.

Annam   French colonial name for the central Mien Trung region of Vietnam.

Anpo   Japanese name for the U.S.–Japan Security Treaty signed in September 1951 (effective from April 1952) that allowed the United States to retain military bases in Japan. The treaty caused unprecedented popular resentment, generating a wave of mass strikes and violent demonstrations. The Anpo crisis was one of the most severe political crises of postwar Japan. In 1960 the treaty was converted to a more equitable mutual security pact.

April 4th Incident   Term for the rioting that ensued in Beijing following the death of Zhou Enlai on 8 March 1976. Thousands gathered in Tiananmen Square and riots erupted as police removed wreaths and placards.

ASA (Association of Southeast Asian States)   A loose association, formed by the Federation of Malaya, Thailand and the Philippines in 1961, which was superseded by the Association of Southeast Asian Nations. See p. 73.

ASEAN (Association of Southeast Asian Nations)   See p. 73.

Asian and Pacific Council (ASPAC)   A body established in 1966 by Australia, Japan, Malaysia, New Zealand, the Philippines, South Korea, South Vietnam, Taiwan and Thailand to encourage and promote regional cooperation. A defensive anticommunist alliance, its main activity was opposition to the atmospheric testing of nuclear weapons in the area.

Aspri   Acronym in Indonesia for the Council of Assistants to President Suharto.

August Revolution   The successful uprising against the Japanese occupation forces in Vietnam, launched by the VIET MINH in August 1945. The revolt met little resistance from the Japanese in the north, and the Democratic Republic of Vietnam was proclaimed in Hanoi in September. In the south, the returning French regained control in Saigon.

Awami League   A political party proposing independence for East Pakistan, which won 167 seats out of 300 in the Pakistan general election held in December 1970. The Pakistan authorities refused to open the new National Assembly and civil war broke out. The leader of the Awami League, Sheikh Mujibur Rahman, became prime minister of the new nation of Bangladesh, but in January 1975 he abolished all political parties and replaced them with a single party.

Ayodhya   Site in northern India of a Muslim mosque which Hindus believe conceals the birthplace of their own god Rama. Violent attempts by Hindu nationalists to tear down the mosque (inflamed by the revivalist Bharatiya Janata Party) brought about the fall of the Indian government in November 1990. Hindu militants seized the site in December 1992, provoking communal violence throughout India after the destruction of the mosque.

Azad Kashmir (Free Kashmir)   The slogan used by Pakistanis who wish to detach the state of Kashmir from India.

baht   The monetary unit of Thailand.

Bamboo Curtain   Term given to the physical and ideological barrier to movement across the borders of the People's Republic of China. It was lifted after the end of the U.S. embargo on trade with China in 1971, admission of China to the UN, President Nixon's visit to China, and establishment of official relations with the European Community (EC) in 1975. China has been partly isolated again diplomatically since the TIANANMEN SQUARE massacre, although British Prime Minister John Major visited Beijing in September 1991 to discuss Hong Kong.

Bandung Conference   Conference in 1955 organized largely at the initiative of the Colombo Powers and China, to herald a new era of Afro-Asian solidarity. Its guiding principles were the FIVE PRINCIPLES OF PEACEFUL COEXISTENCE that had emerged from the settlement of the Sino–Indian conflict over Tibet (29 April 1954). Despite general agreement, not all countries accepted the neutralist position in world affairs advocated by China. Division and dissent marked the Second Bandung Conference in 1965.

Basic Law   Term for the law that will provide the foundation for the government of Hong Kong after its return to China in 1997.

Beijing Spring   Term coined by the media to describe the student demonstrations in China that culminated in the TIANANMEN SQUARE massacre in Beijing.

Bhopal Disaster   On 3 December 1984, leakage of toxic gas from the Union Carbide pesticide plant near Bhopal, capital of the central Indian state of Madhya Pradesh, due to the buildup of pressure in an underground storage tank, caused 3,500 deaths and 200,000 severe injuries.

Biharis   Minority in Bangladesh who supported the Pakistani side in the Bangladeshi War of Independence (see p. 101). Some 250,000 have been virtually marooned in squalid camps since 1971 awaiting transport to Pakistan. Their repatriation is fiercely opposed by the Sindhi population of Pakistan.

Blue House   Residence in Seoul of the president of South Korea.

boat people   Term used to describe those persons, both Chinese and noncommunist Vietnamese, seeking to escape from Vietnam after 1975, when South Vietnam fell to communist North Vietnam. Many escaped, in overladen small boats, to Malaysia, Hong Kong, and elsewhere. Many fell prey to pirates. The problem became acute in the 1980s as economic hardship in Vietnam provoked further waves of refugees into Hong Kong. Despite an international outcry, Britain began repatriation to Vietnam in December 1989.

Bofors scandal   Political scandal in India surrounding the purchase of arms worth $1.3 billion from the Swedish Bofors Company. On July 18, 1989, a report cited corruption within the Indian government. Although Rajiv Gandhi was not involved, the scandal contributed to his election defeat in November 1989.

Brunei   A British protectorate until 1 January 1984, when it became an independent state under Sultan Muda Hassan al-Bolkiah (qv). It remains (by treaty) under British military protection and has enormous oil wealth.

burakumin   In Japanese, "special hamlet people." An outcast group in Japanese society, often employed to perform unsavory or unpleasant tasks. Burakumin are ethnically Japanese but are still not accepted into mainstream Japanese society.

Burmese Spring   The student demonstrations of March–April 1988 against the Ne Win regime in Burma. The protests escalated into a massive antigovernment clamor, forcing the resignation of Ne Win on 23 July 1988. A provisional government was formed by the veteran U Nu, but on 18 September the armed forces seized power under General Saw Maung. Hundreds of demonstrators were subsequently killed and a vicious and repressive dictatorship established.

bushido   Strict Japanese traditional code of honor of the Samurai, dating from the 12th century and still a strong influence in Japanese society. A military code similar in concept to the knighthood and chivalry of medieval

Europe, it involves the formation of personal honor by pursuit of the principles of courage, honesty, justice and simplicity.

Can Lao   In South Vietnam, an internal security (secret police) agency of Ngo Dinh Diem's government, and very much his personal instrument. Diem used it to control political dissent by infiltrating political, military and trade union organizations. After the overthrow of the regime in November 1963, many of its leaders were executed and the Can Lao disbanded.

Ceylon   The name of the Republic of Sri Lanka prior to 1972. It achieved independence from Britain, which had ruled it since 1796, in 1948.

chaebol   South Korean large industrial conglomerates. The equivalent of the Japanese ZAIBATSU.

Chakma   The largest non-Bengali, non-Muslim tribe living in the Chittagong Hill Tracts of Bangladesh, many of whose members live as refugees across the border in India.

Chenpaodao   An island (also known as Damansky) on the border between China and the former Soviet Union, the scene of armed clashes between the two states in March 1969.

Chollima Movement   The "Flying Horse Movement" in North Korea during the 1957–61 five-year plan that aimed at "uninterrupted innovation" and "continuous advance."

Chongsanri Movement   A policy deriving from the Chongsanri agricultural cooperative in the North Korean province of South Pyongan. Under the policy, North Korean leader Kim Il Sung (qv) in February 1960 called on party leaders to base work in local planning and agricultural mechanization on the strength of the masses.

Chongwadae   See BLUE HOUSE.

Chuche Idea   The philosophy of self-reliance propounded by the North Korean leader Kim Il Sung (qv).

civil disobedience   (satyāgraha) The policy of nonviolent noncooperation with the British in India during the struggle for independence. The policy was promoted by Gandhi with great success.

Cochin China   A French colony in Southeast Asia, established in 1862, in what is now Vietnam.

Colombo Plan   See p. 74.

confrontation   Term applied to the armed conflict between Indonesia and Malaysia in the 1960s. *See* KONFRONTASI.

Congress Party   Indian political party that grew out of the Hindu-dominated nationalist Congress movement of the pre-independence period. It has dominated most of Indian political life since independence. See also INDIAN NATIONAL CONGRESS.

Constructive Engagement   The "soft" policy adopted by Thailand and other Asian countries toward the military regime in Burma after the 1988 coup.

Co-prosperity Sphere   Name given by Japan to eastern and southeastern Asia in the period between World War I and World War II. The area that Japan hoped to control and develop extended from the USSR's Pacific coast to Timor, and from New Guinea to Burma. In World War II Japan did succeed for a time in controlling the whole area except for parts of China and New Guinea and the Soviet territory.

Cripps Mission   Official British mission to India in March 1942 led by Sir Stafford Cripps (1889–1952), Labor MP and leader of the House of Commons, to attempt to win greater support of the INDIAN NATIONAL CONGRESS for the war effort against Japan. The Cripps Plan—devised by Prime Minister Winston Churchill—promised India elections to a constitutional assembly when the war ended, as a preliminary to self-government, and the right of provinces to form separate states outside India. The plan, which did not meet Congress demands for immediate self-government free of British control, was rejected.

Cultural Revolution   The term used to describe the convulsions in Chinese society caused in 1965 by Mao Zedong's movement to purge the country of his opponents and to bring about a revolution in popular ideology.

Curb Loan Scandal   Corruption case in South Korea in 1982 that involved individuals close to President Chun Doo Hwan and in which a number of companies went bankrupt.

Dachenchholing Palace   The royal palace in the capital city of Bhutan, Thimpu.

dacoits   Bands of robbers who harass the rural poor in the Pakistani province of Sind. Since the antigovernment agitation launched in 1983 by the Movement for the Restoration of Democracy, opposed to the martial-law administration of General Zia ul-Haq, they have become a well-armed virtual alternative government, exploiting the corruption of both police and landlords.

Dalai Lama   The spiritual and temporal leader of the Tibetan people. After Chinese troops occupied Tibet in 1951, a major rebellion took place in 1959. The Dalai Lama subsequently fled to India. He was awarded the Nobel Peace Prize in 1989.

Da Nang Location in South Vietnam of first landing of U.S. troops in Vietnam War (on 8 March 1965).

Daqing The biggest oil field in China, producing almost half the country's output. The oilfield, in Heilongjiang province, was discovered in 1956.

Darul Islam Fanatical Muslim sect in Indonesia that proclaimed independence on 26 April 1950. Guerrilla campaigns continued until finally suppressed in 1962.

Dazhai The Chinese commune praised by Chairman Mao (qv).

Dear Leader Term applied (somewhat incongruously) to Kim Chong Il, the son of the North Korean dictator, Kim Il Sung (qv). If Kim Chong Il succeeds to power, North Korea will become the first Communist family "dynasty."

Delkosha Palace In Afghanistan, the headquarters of the former pro-Soviet Revolutionary Council in the capital, Kabul.

Demilitarized Zone Zone that roughly follows the 38th parallel dividing North from South Korea, established in 1953 following the invasion of South Korea by the Communist north in 1950. Acting for the UN, U.S. and British troops helped the south expel the invaders. No military forces of either side are allowed to enter the zone, although in 1974 the first of a series of North Korean tunnels beneath it was discovered.

Democracy Wall Site on Changan Avenue in Beijing, first prominent during the HUNDRED FLOWERS campaign in 1957 when radical students used wall posters to protest their courses. Students again used the wall as a focus for their calls for democracy in 1978–79.

Dengism The modernizing program introduced in China by Deng Xiaoping in 1984 that attempted economic advance through decentralization, individual enterprise, market forces and foreign investment. Agricultural collectivism was weakened to boost production, while in industry managerial authority was strengthened and factories were allowed to retain their profits. The reforms were intensified at the 13th Communist Congress in 1987 but were threatened in late 1988 by inflation and fears of mass unemployment.

Dewan Negra In Malaysia, the upper house of Parliament, consisting of 42 appointed members and 26 elected by state legislatures. See p. 63.

Dewan Rakyat In Malaysia, the lower house of Parliament. See p. 63.

Dien Bien Phu, Battle of The climactic battle of the First Indochina War. In November 1953, the French Commander in Indochina, General Henri Navarre, fortified Dien Bien Phu, a valley 200 miles west of Hanoi, with 15,000 men to cut the supply routes of the VIET MINH guerrillas into Laos and to draw them into a pitched battle. But the French had underestimated the capability of General Giap (qv), the Viet Minh commander, to concentrate men and heavy artillery on the hills overlooking Dien Bien Phu. The vital airfield was rendered unusable, and the French garrison was overwhelmed on 7 May 1954. The defeat ended French power in Indochina, and was confirmed at the peace conference in Geneva.

Diet   The Parliament of Japan, a title first adopted under the Meiji Constitution of 1889. See p. 61.

doi moi   The Vietnamese equivalent of the Soviet *glasnost* and *perestroika*, symbolized in the early 1990s by moves toward a market economy.

domino theory   Premise of early 1960s U.S. foreign policy that if South Vietnam became Communist as a result of a Viet Cong/North Vietnamese victory, other Southeast Asian countries would follow.

doves   Americans opposing or advocating a negotiated end to U.S. military involvement in Vietnam. The term is now applied to politicians taking moderate stances on foreign policy issues. See also HAWKS.

Druk Yal   The name ("Land of the Thunder Dragon") given to the Himalayan kingdom of Bhutan by its people. The ruler of Bhutan is known as Druk Gyalpo—literally the "Precious Ruler of the Dragon People," the "Dragon King."

Durand Line   Border between Afghanistan and present-day Pakistan delineated in 1893 by Sir Mortimer Durand.

East Asian Economic Caucus   An idea for a huge Asian trading bloc first suggested by Malaysian prime minister Mahathir bin Mohamad in 1991. Such a bloc, led by Japan, would rival NAFTA (the North American Free Trade Agreement) and also the European Community. Although unenthusiastically received at first, the plan is now supported by Singapore, Thailand, Indonesia, Brunei and the Philippines.

East Bengal   That part of the former British Raj, the mainly Moslem part of the province of Bengal, which became East Pakistan after PARTITION in 1947.

Easter Rising   The major North Vietnamese offensive of March 1972 during the Vietnam War (see p. 97). It was ultimately repelled by South Vietnamese forces backed by U.S. air strikes.

East Pakistan   The former name of Bangladesh, before it gained independence from Pakistan in 1971.

Emergency, the   Term for the Communist uprising in Malaya in the late

1940s (a formal declaration of the "emergency" was made in February 1948). Under the counterinsurgency campaign of Sir Gerald Templer, and especially the STRATEGIC HAMLETS policy, the Communist guerrillas were effectively defeated by the mid-1950s. The emergency was finally declared over in 1960. See p. 94.

Enola Gay   The aircraft (named after the pilot's mother) that dropped the first atomic bomb on Hiroshima, 6 August 1945.

Farakka Barrage   Construction on the Ganges some 17 kilometers upstream from the Bangladesh–India border, begun by India in 1970 to control the river waters. A continuing source of dispute between the two countries.

Five Principles of Peaceful Coexistence   The key elements of Chinese foreign policy, first put forward at the 1955 BANDUNG CONFERENCE. These five principles were mutual respect for sovereignty and territorial integrity; mutual nonaggression; noninterference in each other's internal affairs; equality and mutual benefit; and peaceful coexistence.

Formosa   Portuguese name for Taiwan. From the Portuguese for "beautiful land."

Four Dragons   Term for the rapidly industrializing and expanding economies of Singapore, Malaysia, Taiwan and Hong Kong.

Four Modernizations   The policy of modernizing Chinese agriculture, industry, science, technology and defense, reemphasized after Mao's death in 1976 and the emergence of Deng Xiaoping. The policy had lapsed during the CULTURAL REVOLUTION.

FRETELIN   The independence movement against colonial rule in the former Portuguese colony of East Timor. Indonesia seized and occupied the territory in 1975 shortly after East Timor declared independence from Portugal, and has savagely put down the nationalist movement in a policy of virtual genocide. See also TIMOR.

Gaimusho   The Ministry of Foreign Affairs in Japan.

Gang of Four   Those Chinese political leaders—Wang Hongwen, Zhang Chungqiao, Yao Wenyuan and Jiang Qing—who were publicly denounced following the triumph of the moderates in 1976. There has been a constant division between moderates and radicals in the Chinese Communist Party. After the moderates regained control of the party, a vicious propaganda campaign against the Gang of Four commenced through the medium of street posters. The Gang were arrested and accused of planning to take control of the army. During 1977, Deng Xiaoping was rehabilitated and given charge of a modernization program. Demands for greater freedom were tolerated for a time, but stopped after violent outbreaks by radicals in Shanghai. To aid industrialization, China strengthened links with the West, and on the 30th anniversary of the foundation of the People's Republic, the Cultural Revolution was denounced as a calamitous mistake. A show trial was held of the Gang of Four, and a death sentence, which was suspended, was passed on Jiang Qing in January 1981.

Geneva Accords The April 1988 agreements signed in Geneva, which helped end the conflict in Afghanistan. Afghanistan and Pakistan pledged not to interfere in each other's internal affairs, and an agreement was made on the mutual return of refugees. There was also agreement on the withdrawal of Russian troops from Afghanistan. Both the United States and the Soviet Union acted as guarantors of the Geneva Accords.

Geneva Agreement Negotiated in a two-month conference by the foreign ministers of the United States, USSR, Britain, France and China and signed on 21 July 1954, it ended the French colonial war in Laos, Cambodia and Vietnam, dividing Vietnam in two along the 17th parallel. The division was meant to be temporary, but the United States, which had been supporting the French, refused to sign the agreement, and set about helping Ngo Dinh Diem create a separate South Vietnamese state. Elections scheduled for 1956, which were to have determined the government of a united Vietnam, were never held.

Gestapu In Indonesia, an acronym for the 30 September Movement, the abortive Communist *coup* attempt in 1965.

Goa Former Portuguese colony on the coast of India. In 1961 it was forcibly incorporated into India as a Union Territory (along with Daman and Diu Island). In May 1987 it became a State of the Union.

Golden Temple The holiest site of the Sikh religion, in Amritsar. It was stormed by the Indian Army in 1984 because of the presence of armed Sikh militants who favored a separate state. The attack provoked the assassination of Indian prime minister Indira Gandhi, which in turn caused communal riots in which thousands were killed.

Golden Triangle Name given to the mountainous border areas of Thailand, Laos and Myanmar (Burma). Inhabited by tribal peoples, it is one of the major opium-growing areas of the world and is controlled by local Chinese and Shan warlords commanding private armies.

Golkar The ruling political party in Indonesia under President Suharto in the 1970s and 1980s.

Gol Khana Palace The residence of the Afghan president in Kabul.

Great Leader Term used to describe the North Korean dictator, Kim Il Sung.

Great Leap Forward Chinese slogan denoting a series of radical changes in social and economic policy between 1958 and 1961 intended to hasten the establishment of a truly communist society. Private consumption was cut and material incentives withdrawn in order to allow diversion of resources to other sectors; massive agricultural communes were set up, with light industry and construction projects established to service them. The effort failed, partly because of natural disasters such as bad harvests, and partly as a result of the withdrawal of technical aid by the USSR. Managerial difficulties also arose, and in 1962 a more regular system of economic planning was restored.

Growth Triangle Term used in Singapore for the southern Malaysian region of Johore, and such Indonesian islands as Batam and Bintan. The intention is that Singaporean investment and expertise, coupled with the abundance of labor, will transform this area into a major economic growth region.

Guam Doctrine The doctrine, propounded by President Richard Nixon, of Vietnamization (i.e., handing over the conduct of the war in Vietnam to the South Vietnamese), made at a press conference on Guam on 23 July 1969. Nixon stated that after 1969, Saigon would increasingly have to rely on its own ground troops as and when U.S. forces were withdrawn.

Guangdong Province of China, the scene of a dramatic increase in prosperity and consumerism, containing the three Special Economic Zones of Shenzhen, Zhuhai and Shantou. It is adjacent to Hong Kong and also contains Guangzhou (formerly Canton). Deng Xiaoping has urged Guangdong to be as economically strong in two decades as Asia's four newly industrializing powers—Hong Kong itself, Singapore, South Korea and Taiwan.

guided democracy Ideological underpinning of President Sukarno's Indonesian regime from July 1959 until his overthrow by an army coup in October 1965. Sympathetic to the left and with Communist support, guided democracy involved strong executive government and an attempt to institute NASAKOM, a union of national, religious and communist forces.

Guomindang See KUOMINTANG.

Gurkhas Term applied to the inhabitants of Nepal (conquered by the Gurkhas in 1768–69) renowned for their military qualities, who have been allies of the British since 1816, and provide a brigade of the British army.

Properly, the name is that of the royal family of the small kingdom of Gurkha and their followers, the Thakurs, Khas, Magars and Gurwngs.

Haiphong   Strategic port in North Vietnam. In response to Communist attacks in the South, areas around Hanoi and Haiphong were bombed after April 1972. Much controversy surrounded the US decision to mine Haiphong harbor in May 1972.

Hang Seng   The shares index of the Hong Kong Stock Exchange.

Harijans   Mahatma Gandhi's term for the lowest caste in Hindu society— the "UNTOUCHABLES." The term is translated "Children of God."

Hartal   Ceylonese (Sri Lankan) general strike organized by Marxists in 1953 in protest against rapid price rises, particularly of rice. Repressive measures were introduced, and there were clashes between government forces and strikers. Prime Minister Senanayake, of the United National Party, was forced to resign, and the opposition Sri Lanka Freedom Party won the 1956 election. The term is used throughout South Asia for a mass strike.

hawks   American politicians who wished to continue, intensify or escalate the Vietnam War (1965–72). The term is now applied generally to politicians taking an aggressive stance on foreign policy issues. See also DOVES.

Heisei   The name ("Achieving Peace") adopted for his reign by the present emperor (Akihito) in Japan. Akihito (qv) succeeded his father, the Showa ("Enlightened Peace") emperor Hirohito (qv), in 1989.

Hermit Kingdom   Name for Korea after its attempted 17th-century isolation from foreign influences. Sometimes used of North Korea today.

Hiroshima   Japanese city with 350,000 inhabitants, selected as the target for the first use of the atomic bomb on 6 August 1945. An estimated 80,000 were killed outright, a similar number injured, and an estimated further 100,000 died within a few years of cancer, radiation sickness and other injuries. Immediate victims and their children continue to die from complaints related to the bombing. See also NAGASAKI.

Hoa Hao   Buddhist religious group in Vietnam, members of which worked for the U.S. Central Intelligence Agency (CIA) as anti-Viet Cong mercenaries during the 1959–75 Vietnam War.

Ho Chi Minh Trail   Elaborate system of routes along the South Vietnam border with Laos and Cambodia used to bring North Vietnamese supplies to VIET CONG forces in the 1959–75 Vietnam War.

Hong Kong   Island ceded to Britain by China by the Treaty of Nanking in 1842. South Kowloon and Stonecutters Island were ceded by the Treaty of Peking in 1860, and the New Territories leased to Britain by China for 99 years in 1898. Occupied by Japan from 1941 to 1945. Preliminary discussions between Great Britain and China on Hong Kong's future began in 1979, and agreement was reached in 1984 on its return to China in 1997.

Huk   The Hukbalahap (*Hukbo nang Bayan Laban sa Hapon*, "People's Army against Japan"). Founded in the Philippines in March 1942 as a Communist-led peasant movement by Luis M. Taruc and Castro Alejandrino, who attempted to transform it into a united front of all classes against the Japanese occupation. It was aided by and came under the influence of Chinese Communists. Disarmed by the U.S. in 1945, the Huk continued to confront landlords and the government, and was outlawed in March 1948. The ban on the weakened movement was revoked in 1950, but in 1957 both the Huk and the Communist Party of the Philippines (CPP) were banned as subversive. In 1969–70 the Huk was reorganized and renamed *Bagong Hukbo nang Bayan* ("New People's Army"). Despite the collapse of the corrupt regime of Ferdinand Marcos in 1986, the Huk remained a source of instability to the new government.

Hundred Flowers   Chinese government-sponsored attempt to attract constructive intellectual criticism in 1956–57 that was so enthusiastically received that the government ended the campaign. Derived from Mao Zedong's "Let a hundred flowers bloom and a hundred schools of criticism compete."

Hwai Hai   The last major battle of the Chinese civil war, fought from November 1948 to January 1949, and resulting in the fall of Beijing on 22 January. Involved an estimated one million combatants, the Communist Central Plains and East China armies routing the Nationalist Second and Seventh Army Groups.

Hyderabad   Large, predominantly Hindu state in southern India whose ruling prince, the Muslim Nizam, did not want to join the Indian Union in 1947. The area was occupied by the Indian army and became part of India. See also JUNAGADH.

Ia Drang   The first major battle between U.S. and North Vietnamese forces in the Vietnam War, fought in October–November 1965 in Ia Drang Valley near the Vietnam–Cambodia border.

Imjin River   A successful defensive battle fought in the Korean War from 22–25 April 1951 by United Nations forces to hold back a Chinese–North Korean spring offensive.

Indian National Congress   The dominant political party in India since independence. Founded in December 1885 as an educational association to prepare Indians for government, initially with the approval of the British. Congress turned against British rule following the unpopular partition of Bengal in 1905. Led after 1915 by the moderate Mohandas Karamchand Gandhi (1869–1948), whose nonviolent strategy of civil disobedience was adopted by Congress in the 1920s and 30s. Congress won control in six of the 11 provincial assemblies given internal self-government by the 1935 India Act. Congress leaders were imprisoned from 1942–45 for their opposition to Britain's unilateral decision to bring India into World War II, but were released to negotiate terms of independence. In 1947 Jawaharlal Nehru (1889–1964), Congress president since 1929, became India's first prime minister.

Indochina   Southeast Asian territories in Annam, Cambodia, Cochin-China, Laos and Tonkin colonized by France from the 1860s and held until the Geneva Agreement of 20 July 1954 recognized the independence of Cambodia, Laos and Vietnam.

Irian Barat   See below, under Irian Jaya.

Irian Jaya   The largest of Indonesia's provinces, covering the western half of the island of New Guinea. Known as Irian Barat from 1963–76. The main town is Jayapura.

Iron Triangle   Term used in Laos in the 1980s to refer to the aging trio of politicians made up of Kaysone Phomvihane (the secretary general of the Lao Revolutionary Party), General Khamtay Siphandon (who succeeded Kaysone as premier in August 1991) and National Assembly president Nouhak Phoumsavan.

Janata   Alliance of opposition groups in India, formed in 1977 to contest the elections against Indira Gandhi's Indian Congress Party. It won the election and Morarji Desai became prime minister, but in July 1979 he found himself unable to control the elements within the coalition. Heavily defeated in the 1980 elections, the Janata Dal rose to prominence again in 1989.

Jars, Plain of   The central part of the Tran Ninh plateau in Laos (named after the prehistoric stone jars discovered there by the French in the 19th century). It was the scene of bitter fighting between the Communist PATHET LAO and government forces in the 1960s.

Jatiya Sangsad   The name of the parliament (national assembly) in Bangladesh.

Jing An   The index of the fledgling Shanghai Stock Market in China. Other stock markets, such as those in Guangzhou and Shenzhen (over the border from Hong Kong), are also opening up as China in the 1990s turns in part to capitalist ventures.

Jogjakarta Former sultanate in Central Java. Center of revolt against Dutch rule from 1825 to 1830 and a leading center of the nationalist fight for independence from 1945 to 1949.

Junagadh Small seaport state on the coast of Gujarat with a predominantly Hindu population but whose Muslim ruler, the Nizam, preferred to join Pakistan rather than the Indian Union in 1947. The area was occupied by the Indian army and became part of India. See also HYDERABAD.

Kabutocho The Japanese name for the Tokyo Stock Market. See also NIKKEI INDEX.

Kachins An ethnic minority in Myanmar (Burma).

Kahuta Site of Pakistan's nuclear testing ground.

Kaifu Doctrine A proposed economic strategic policy under which Japan would become the regional economic superpower in Asia, heading a trading bloc which would rival the United States or the European Community. The proposal was outlined in January 1991 by Japanese Prime Minister Toshiki Kaifu.

kamikaze (divine wind) Japanese aircraft suicide missions of late World War II. Laden with bombs, planes were flown directly into U.S. warships. Attributively, the pilots of such planes.

Karakoram Highway Strategic and commercial land route linking Pakistan and China. Built by Pakistan with Chinese help, the road passes through Azad Kashmir to connect Pakistan with the Chinese province of Xinjiang.

Karens An ethnic minority in Myanmar (Burma) that has never accepted rule by Rangoon. In the 1980s, following central government military repression, their area was declared an autonomous region with its capital in Manerplaw under the presidency of Bo Mya. Many Karens have sought refuge across the border in Thailand.

Kashag The India-based Tibetan government in exile, established following the Chinese occupation in 1951 and the rebellion of 1959.

Kashmir A predominantly Muslim border area between Indian and Pakistan, controlled by India but whose ownership is disputed. Scene of wars between India and Pakistan in 1947, 1965 and 1971 that have not resolved the issue.

Keibatsu ("nepotism") Pre-World War II industrial combines that controlled the Japanese economy. Disbanded by the United States in 1945, they reemerged with the Mitsui, Mitsubishi, Sumitomo, Fuyoh, Sanwa and

Ichi-kan combines as the *shinko-keibatsu* ("new nepotism"). Widely diversified, they account for 15% of Japan's GNP and exercise control through networks of industrialists and politicians, cemented by intermarriage among leading families.

Keidanren   (Keizai Dantai Rengo Kai) The Japanese Federation of Economic Organizations. Formed in 1945 to help rebuild the economy, it is the largest private Japanese industrial and financial organization and includes agricultural, banking and financial, manufacturing and trade sectors.

Kerala   Indian state formed in 1956 from the amalgamation of the Malayalam-speaking state of Travancore-Cochin and the Malabar District of Madras. A Communist Party of India (Marxist) Democratic Front won the 1987 elections.

Khad   Communist secret police in Afghanistan during the period of Soviet intervention.

Khalistan   The name used by Sikhs for the independent homeland which their activists seek.

Khalq   Afghan political party.

Khalsa   (from Arabic, "pure," "sincere," "free") In India, the Sikh Commonwealth in the Punjab, the "brotherhood of the pure"; also a land revenue collected directly by government officials.

Khengyeshuntsog   The Council of Ministers in Bhutan—the country's administrative institution and consultative body on policy matters.

Khe Sanh   U.S. Marine base on the Vietnam–Laos border besieged by North Vietnamese forces from January through April 1968, during the TET offensive. Its abandonment in July following the lifting of the siege in April raised questions about the value of the base and the wisdom of defending it.

Khmer Rouge   Cambodian Communist movement that by 1974 had taken control of the Cambodian countryside, before capturing the capital city of Phnom Penh in 1975. Revolution ensued, and in 1976 a government led by POL POT was installed. The population of the entire country was forced onto the land to increase agrarian productivity, and there were reports of mass political killings. The government was replaced by the Vietnamese-backed Cambodian Liberation Front for National Renewal following the war of 1978–79. By the late 1980s, the Khmer Rouge was again a powerful guerrilla force in Cambodia, although in retreat in 1994.

Khural   The parliament of Mongolia.

Khyber Pass   The most important mountain pass between Pakistan and Afghanistan. About 30 miles long, the pass reaches a height of 3,520 feet. It was of great strategic influence during the British Raj in India. Over three million refugees escaped to Pakistan by this route during the Afghan civil war.

Killing Fields Term for Cambodia (Kampuchea) during the period of the Khmer Rouge government. The Khmer Rouge committed ideologically motivated massacres on an enormous scale during this time. Estimates of the victims vary from 500,000 to as many as two million.

Kōenkai The "personal support group" that plays a major role in the Japanese political system.

Komeito The "Clean Government Party" founded in Japan in 1964, initially as the political wing of the Buddhist lay movement. Komeito favored democratic socialism and attempted to form a center-left coalition in opposition to the ruling Liberal Democratic Party.

Konfrontasi Indonesian term for the "confrontation" with Malaysia between 1963 and 1966. President Sukarno (qv), opposing the formation of Malaysia, launched a guerrilla offensive in SARAWAK and SABAH in April 1963. British, Australian and New Zealand troops assisted Malaysia, while disaffection mounted in the Indonesian armed forces. Suharto (qv), Sukarno's successor, abandoned confrontation in 1966.

Kopkamtib In Indonesia, the domestic security and intelligence agency.

Koreagate Scandal exposed in 1977 in which several members of the U.S. Congress were shown to have accepted bribes from South Korean agents in return for supporting continued large-scale economic and military aid to the politically repressive South Korean government. At the time, President Jimmy Carter was committed to a reduction of aid to the regime, which he publicly criticized. The derivation of the term is by analogy with the more sensational Watergate scandal.

Kuk Hoe The National Assembly in South Korea.

Kuomintang (KMT) Chinese Nationalist party, founded in 1891 by Sun Yat Sen, which participated in the first Chinese revolution of 1911, led the second the following year, and by 1930 dominated southern China. On the death of Sun Yat Sen in 1925 Jiang Kaishek became its leader. From 1928 on it was the effective government of China, and conducted its defense against Japan from 1937 to 1945. The KMT government departed from Sun Yat Sen's principles of democratic republicanism along western lines, and degenerated into a reactionary, repressive and corrupt military oligarchy. After years of unrest and civil war, the regime collapsed in 1949 and was replaced by the Communist Party, leaving Jiang and his followers to rule Taiwan with American aid.

Kure The second city of Hiroshima Province in Japan. From 1945 to 1951, it was the headquarters of the British Commonwealth Occupation Force in Japan.

Kuril Islands See NORTHERN TERRITORIES.

Kwangju Uprising Antigovernment demonstrations in South Korea in which a massacre of demonstrators took place on 18 May 1988.

Labuan A Malaysian island in the South China Sea. It is a rapidly developing offshore financial center.

Laogai The Chinese equivalent of the Soviet Gulag. China, as the largest abuser of human rights in the world, has an estimated 2,000 prison camps with perhaps 10 million prisoners forced to work prison farms, salt mines etc.

Lao Issara The Laotian independence movement ("Free Laos") that set up a government under Prince Phetsarath in 1945 on the withdrawal of Japanese forces. The French returned in 1946 and the leaders of Lao Issara fled to Thailand.

Linggadjati Agreement Accord between Indonesia and the Dutch in November 1946 in which Indonesia conceded the principle of a federal Indonesia.

Lion of Kashmir The popular name of the leader of the Kashmiri struggle for independence, Sheikh Mohammad Abdullah (qv).

Little Boy Name given to the atomic bomb dropped on Hiroshima on 6 August 1945.

"Little Tigers" Term for the fast-expanding, rapidly industrializing new economies of Asia—especially Taiwan, Hong Kong, South Korea, Singapore and now Thailand, Malaysia and the Philippines. Sometimes referred to as NICs—newly industrializing countries.

Lockheed Scandal Financial scandal that surfaced in 1976 involving bribery by the American Lockheed Aircraft Corporation, which had spent $24 million in bribes to win orders in countries as diverse as Italy, the Netherlands and Japan. In Japan, All-Nippon Airways bought Lockheed aircraft in a scandal that led to the arrest of former prime minister Tanaka Kakuei (qv).

Lodai Tsokde The Royal Advisory Council in Bhutan. Established in 1965, it acts as a consultative body on policy matters, overseeing administration and advising the king.

Lok Sabha The lower house (House of the People) in the bicameral Indian parliament. The upper house (Rajya Sabha) is the Council of States.

Long March The 8,000-mile retreat of Communist forces from October 1934 to October 1935 under Kuomintang attack. The march, led by Mao Zedong, Zhu De and Lin Biao, was from the beleaguered Jiangxi Soviet to the more defensible Yenan region in northwest China. Of the 100,000 who set out only 30,000 survived, but the march became an inspiring legend of the Chinese Revolution.

Lop Nor Remote site in the barren empty desert country of Xinjiang Uygur Autonomous Region in China, used as the testing ground for the Chinese nuclear weapons program.

Lost Generation Term for those persons (estimated at over 160 million) who grew up during the chaos and upheaval of the CULTURAL REVOLUTION in China and whose education was very severely disrupted.

Loya Jirga The "Grand Assembly" in Afghanistan.

Macao (alternative spelling Macau) A former Portuguese colony in south China, first occupied by Portugal in 1557. Recognized as a dependency by China in 1887. In 1961 it became an "overseas province" of Portugal and in 1974 an autonomous Chinese territory under Portuguese constitutional law. It has an elected legislative assembly. In 1987 Portugal agreed to return the territory to China in 1999. Formerly best known for its casinos, it is now a developing industrial center based on the exploitation of cheap labor.

Madonna Strategy In the 1989 general election in Japan the JSP (Japanese Socialist Party) fielded a record number of women candidates, presumably in the hope of winning the women's vote at a time of disillusion with the male domination of Japanese politics. The name is taken from the singer (and sex symbol) Madonna.

Mahatma Title (from the Sanskrit "great soul") bestowed on Indian national leader Mohandas Karamchand Gandhi (1869–1948) by his Hindu followers, in recognition of his asceticism, simplicity and saintly qualities.

Malacanang Palace The official residence of the president of the Philippines. Located on the Pasig River in Manila. The first Philippine president to live there was President Manuel Quezon.

Manchukuo The name given to the Chinese province of Manchuria by the Japanese when they occupied it in 1931. They installed a puppet regime under the last Chinese Manchu emperor, Henry Pu Yi, which was overthrown by Chinese Communists and the USSR in 1945. Manchuria subsequently became a Communist stronghold.

Manerplaw Town in Myanmar (Burma) near the Thai border that is the headquarters of the Karen rebels. In 1990, when the ruling State Law and

Order Restoration Council refused to recognize the victory of the antigovernment pro-democracy forces in the 1990 general election, the opposition National Coalition Government of the Union of Burma was established at Manerplaw.

Manila Treaty   On 8 September 1954, Australia, France, Great Britain, New Zealand, Pakistan, Philippines, Thailand and the United States formed the South East Asia Treaty Organization (SEATO), guaranteeing collective action against internal or external aggression together with economic cooperation.

Maoism   The communist system adopted in China under Mao Zedong (1893–1976). Marxism guided the Chinese Communist Party between 1921 and October 1949 (when the People's Republic was proclaimed); but from 1949 onward Mao sought to adapt it to fit Chinese conditions. He had achieved a communist revolution in a peasant, not an industrial economy, and as early as 1926 had maintained that the peasantry was an ally of the proletariat, not an enemy left over from earlier modes of economic production. A rural revolution, in which the feudal classes would be overthrown, could therefore occur, making it possible to bypass the capitalist stage if proletariat and peasantry acted together. Maoism therefore envisaged a more flexible system than Marxism-Leninism in which self-reliance, suited to the peasantry, is more important than state authority. The concept of revolutionary momentum, as expressed in the CULTURAL REVOLUTION, counts for more than the state machine. Continual struggle is necessary if the revolution is to endure; there can be no question of establishing a socialist state and then waiting for it to wither. Rather, pressure must be applied to ensure that both state and party adhere to the broad wishes of the masses.

Maphilindo   A loose federation of the three countries of Malaya, the Philippines and Indonesia, proposed by President Sukarno of Indonesia at Manila in 1963.

Masyumi   Acronym for the Indonesian Muslim Advisory Council; until its banning in 1960 an important political party.

Matsu   Small island off mainland China, under Nationalist Chinese control. See also QUEMOY.

Mayaguez Incident   Incident in May 1975, following the Communist takeover of Cambodia, involving the seizure of an American merchant vessel with 39 crew members. The United States responded with force when the *Mayaguez* was taken to Cambodia. Air strikes were launched against coastal targets and marines were landed, but Cambodia had released the crew members a day earlier.

Mayekawa Report A Japanese government analysis in 1986 that called for a major structural transformation of the economy, involving a reduction in Japan's dependency on exports.

Meli Shura The Afghanistan National Assembly formed in July 1987, consisting of two houses, the Sena and the Wolasi Jirgah.

Merdeka The Malaysian term for independence from colonial rule by Great Britain.

Mohajirs The "old" settlers in Pakistan who came from India at the time of partition in 1947. The mohajirs are in contrast to the new immigrants such as the PATHANS and PUNJABIS.

Montagnards French colonial term for the hill tribes of the uplands of Indochina. Literally "mountain people."

Mountbatten Plan A term sometimes used to describe the British partition of India in 1947. Lord Mountbatten (qv) was the last Viceroy of British India.

Mujaheddin Afghan resistance fighters against Communist rule. They were Islamic fighters committed to a jihad (holy war). The term is more loosely used of any militant Islamic fighters across the Arabic and Islamic world.

Mukden-Chinchow A key battle, fought from 27–30 October 1948, in the Chinese civil war. It resulted in the almost complete destruction of the nationalist Manchurian army by the Communists.

Mukden Incident The pretext under which Japan began its seizure of Manchuria from China. After alleging that China had bombed a Japanese railroad, the Japanese Kwangtung Army seized Mukden on 18–19 September 1931. Japanese forces went on to capture all of Manchuria, renaming it Manchukuo and installing a puppet ruler. Japanese occupation lasted until 1945.

Mukhti Bahini The East Pakistan (qv) irregular forces who fought for freedom from West Pakistan in 1971. Their success led to the establishment of Bangladesh.

Myanmar Name given to Burma by the military junta that seized power in 1988.

My Lai A Vietnamese village whose entire population was massacred by U.S. Army troops on 16 March 1968. At first covered up by the participants and their superiors, the massacre was eventually made public through the efforts of a few outraged soldiers. Ultimately two low-ranking officers were court-martialed; one was acquitted and the other's sentence was commuted by the president of the United States. The My Lai massacre caused serious doubts in the United States about the true nature of the war, the government's policies, and the role of the armed forces.

Nagaland   Area in northeast India bordering Myanmar (Burma). On Indian independence in August 1947 the Nagas refused to become part of India, and a Naga National Council declared independence. The area was nevertheless absorbed into India as part of Assam Province. There was violent guerrilla activity from 1955 until 1975, with a cease-fire from 1964 to 1972. Under the 1975 Shillong Accord, Nagaland became a full state in the Indian Union, but the area has remained unsettled.

Nagasaki   City on Kyushu Island where the second atomic bomb (following HIROSHIMA) was dropped on 9 August 1945. An estimated 40–70,000 were killed outright and an equal number injured. Over 50,000 have died since of injuries and illnesses connected with the bomb.

Nanjing   (Nanking) The Nationalist capital of China from 1928 to 1949.

Nasakom   (*Nas*ionalisme, *A*gama dan *Kom*unisme) A synthesis of nationalism, religion and communism projected in Indonesia by Achmed Sukarno (1901–70). See GUIDED DEMOCRACY.

Nationalist China   The Republic of China from 1926 to 1949; the island of Taiwan following the Nationalists' defeat in the civil war in 1949.

Naxalite Movement   Armed uprisings of landless rural workers in eastern India organized by the Communist Party of India (Marxist-Leninist). The movement began in 1967 and was named after the Himalayan foothill village of Naxalabi. It developed in 1968 into an urban guerrilla movement, particularly in Calcutta, reaching a climax in 1971 with a campaign of strikes, riots and assassinations. Bloodily suppressed in 1977, the Naxalites weakened after a CPI (M-L) split. They killed 47 passengers in a rail ambush in October 1990.

Netherlands East Indies   Dutch name for Indonesia during the period of colonial rule. Occupied by Japan during World War II, Indonesia proclaimed its independence on 17 August 1945, beginning an ultimately successful four-year war of independence.

New People's Army   The Filipino armed Communist guerrilla movement. After the suppression of the HUK movement in the 1950s, Communist agitation continued. The New People's Army was founded in 1969 as the armed forces of the Communist Party of the Philippines (Marxist-Leninist).

New Territories Term applied to that part of Hong Kong acquired by Britain from China under a 100-year lease in 1897.

NICs Newly industrializing countries. The term was first applied in Asia to such countries as Taiwan, South Korea, Hong Kong and Singapore, and now is extended to more recently industrializing countries such as Malaysia, Thailand, Indonesia and the Philippines.

Nikkei Index The principal index of the Japanese Stock Exchange. The Nikkei fell from its 1989 high (known after the collapse as the Japanese Bubble) by more than 60% by mid-1992, but has since stabilized.

Nordpolitik Policy pursued by South Korea, particularly in the late 1980s under President Roh Tae Woo (qv), of improving relations with North Korea by courting the friendship and support of China and the former Soviet Union. One fruit of the policy was the entry of both North Korea and South Korea into the United Nations in 1991. The term is borrowed from German, by analogy with *Ostpolitik*, the *rapprochement* sought by West Germany with East Germany.

Northern Territories Japanese term for the four islands (Habomai, Shikotan, Etorofu and Kunashiri) off Japan's north coast that were incorporated into the former Soviet Union in 1945. They are now part of Russia's Kuril Island chain. Russia has so far resisted Japanese demands for their return, and the issue remains a major source of contention between Moscow and Tokyo. Japan has refused economic aid to Russia ("no islands, no money") until the dispute is settled.

Northwest Frontier Border area of Afghanistan and British India in the northwest of the PUNJAB, inhabited by mostly Muslim PATHAN tribes. The KHYBER PASS is in this area and was of great strategic importance to the defense of India. Britain annexed the region in 1849 and made it a separate Indian province in 1901. It has been part of Pakistan since 1947.

Okinawa One of the Ryukyu Islands between Japan and Taiwan, commanding the southern approaches to Japan. Stubbornly defended by 120,000 Japanese troops, it was captured following an American assault from April to June 1945. Occupied by the United States until 1972, when it was returned to Japan.

One Country, Two Systems The formula whereby a capitalist Hong Kong (and maybe even Taiwan) can be accommodated in a communist China.

"Open Door" economic policy American policy toward China from 1899 on, seeking to maintain equal trading access to China by the United States and its European rivals and the guarantee that China would not be divided by foreign states. See also UNEQUAL TREATIES.

Opening to China   Visit to China by U.S. President Richard Nixon in February 1972 that ended the diplomatic estrangement between the two countries that began with the Communist victory in 1949 and intensified in the Korean War.

OSGAP   Office of the United Nations Secretary General in Afghanistan and Pakistan, responsible for monitoring complaints by the two states against violations of the Geneva Accords (qv).

Outer China   Term used to refer to Nei Monggol (Inner Mongolia), Xinjiang Uygur (Sinkiang Uighur), Heilongjiang (Heilungkiang), Jilin (Kirin), Liaoning and Taiwan. The remaining provinces and regions constitute China proper.

Pagan   The former capital of Myanmar (Burma) before the British established Rangoon (Yangon).

Pancasila   "Five Principles," the ideology composed for Indonesia's constitution in 1945 by the first president, Achmed Sukarno (1901–70). The principles were one god, legal justice, national unity, consultative democracy and social justice.

Panjshir Valley   Valley region in Afghanistan, 60 miles northeast of the capital, Kabul. The scene of intense mujaheddin resistance following the Soviet invasion of 1979. Heavy Soviet bombing led to a massive civilian exodus to Kabul.

Panmunjon   Village next to the DMZ (demilitarized zone) between North Korea and South Korea where armistice talks were moved following their opening at Laesong on 8 July 1951. Following early tension, agreement was reached at Panmunjon on the division of Korea on 27 July 1953.

Parcham   The "Flag" political party in Afghanistan.

Partition   Term for the division of British India under the Partition Plan of 1947. The outcome was the creation of two newly independent states, India and Pakistan, the latter made up of West Pakistan and East Pakistan (later to become Bangladesh). Partition was accompanied by much communal violence, massacres and massive refugee movements across the border in both directions.

Pathans   A Muslim people of Pakistan and Afghanistan, concentrated in the mountainous northwest frontier region of Pakistan. In 1947 the British North-West Frontier Province voted to become part of Pakistan, but the "Red Shirt" supporters of Ghaffar Khan continued to demand a Pathan homeland of Pathanistan or PUKHTUNISTAN, a demand that became entangled with the 1979–89 Aghanistan civil war.

Pathet Lao   Laotian rebel movement established in 1949 and led by Prince Souphanouvong (qv). It collaborated with the VIET MINH in the 1953 invasion of Laos. During the civil war the Pathet Lao fought against Royal Lao government troops and joined the coalition government formed in 1974. It effectively took control of Laos in 1975, and in December of that year Prince Souphanouvong became president of the Lao People's Democratic Republic.

Pearl Harbor   Major U.S. Navy base in Hawaii attacked by Japanese aircraft on 7 December 1941. The aircraft were transported on carriers as part of a larger fleet that left the Kuril Islands on 25 November, moving secretly for a surprise attack on the Americans. No official declaration of war preceded the attack, which took place while diplomatic negotiations were continuing between the two powers in Washington. There have been suggestions that U.S. intelligence, having broken Japanese diplomatic codes, was aware that the attack would take place. In less than two hours, five U.S. battleships, 14 smaller vessels, and 120 aircraft were destroyed; 2,000 U.S. seamen and 400 civilians were killed. The Japanese lost only 29 of their 353 aircraft. But U.S. aircraft carriers, which later proved invaluable in the battles of the Pacific, were not in port when the attack occurred, and three damaged battleships were repaired. Congress declared war on Japan the following day. Japan's allies, Germany and Italy, declared war on the United States on 11 December. The attack failed in its main objective of gaining decisive sea superiority for Japan in the Pacific, and the initial advantage won by the Japanese proved transitory.

Pentagon Papers   Official study undertaken in 1967 of U.S. policy in Southeast Asia, sections of which were leaked to the *New York Times* by former government employee Daniel Ellsberg in 1971. They exposed a history of deceit, inefficiency and intragovernment disagreement. Publication of the full 47 volumes intensified opposition to U.S. involvement in the Vietnam War and led to demands for less government secrecy.

People's Liberation Army   Title adopted on 1 May 1946 by the army of the Chinese Communist Party, which went on to fight and win a three-year civil war against the Nationalist forces.

Pergau   Site of proposed dam in northern Malaysia. Claims that British aid for this dam was linked to arms sales, and that high-ranking Malaysians were involved in bribery, led to a worsening of British relations with Malaysia in early 1994.

Permesta   From Perjuangan *Semesta*, "universal struggle," an expression used to describe the 1957 Sulawesi revolt in Indonesia.

Philippine election of 7 February 1986   Presidental election in which the incumbent Ferdinand Marcos, dictator for 21 years, faced Corazon Aquino, widow of the opposition leader Benigno Aquino, assassinated by Marcos's forces in 1983. Fraudulent government figures gave the election to Marcos, but Aquino's insistence on her victory triggered two weeks of mass demonstrations that brought the Philippines to the brink of civil war. Both Marcos and Aquino held inauguration ceremonies on 25 February. See also PHILIPPINE REVOLUTION.

Philippine Revolution   Following the Philippine election of 7 February 1986 in which both candidates—Ferdinand Marcos and Corazon Aquino—claimed victory, the Philippines appeared on the edge of civil war. U.S. representatives pressed Marcos to stand down, and support for Aquino grew in the United States and the Philippines. On 22 February, Marcos's leading backers, Army Chief of Staff Lieutenant General Fidel Ramos and Defense Minister Juan Ponce Enrile, announced their support for Aquino, followed by the bulk of the armed forces. Mass demonstrations continued. Marcos fled to Hawaii on 25 February; Aquino became president, and attempted to restore constitutional government after the 21-year Marcos dictatorship.

Pingfang   Village in the puppet state of Manchukuo in north China where a secret research center conducting experimentation on live human beings was operated by the Japanese army's Unit 731 from 1936 until August 1945. At least 3,000 Chinese, Russians, Mongols and Koreans were injected with viruses, exposed to poison gases, frozen, or dissected alive. On Japan's surrender, attempts were made to destroy the center. The United States released the 3,000 officers and men involved at the center without trial or punishment in exchange for the research data.

Ping-pong Diplomacy   An American table-tennis team was warmly welcomed in China in 1971 by Zhou Enlai, who said the visit "opened a new page" in Chinese–U.S. relations. The United States acknowledged the signal, and Secretary of State Henry Kissinger visited China in July, preparing for a later visit by President Nixon.

Pokharan   Site of India's nuclear testing ground. Located in the Rajasthan desert.

Pondicherry   Formerly the main French trading base in India, this was the collective name for the French territories (Pondicherry, Karaikal, Mahe and Yanam) whose administration was taken over by India by treaty in 1954 and which were ceded by France in 1962.

Potala Palace   The former residence of the Dalai Lama in Lhasa, Tibet.

Princely States   The 570 mostly small states in British India that were ruled by princes, rather than directly by Britain.

PRRI   The Revolutionary Government of the Republic of Indonesia (Pemerintah Revolusioner Republik Indonesia), the rebel government in Sumatra in 1957–58.

Pueblo Incident   On 21 January 1968, the USS *Pueblo*, an electronic intelligence-gathering ship, was captured in international waters by North Korean patrol boats, following earlier border incidents between North and South Korea. In captivity, the 83 crew members allegedly confessed to entering North Korean territorial waters. The U.S. government decided against retaliatory action, instead entering into negotiations that led to the release of the crew following a humiliating U.S. apology (which was later withdrawn).

Pukthunistan   Pakistani territory on the Afghanistan border. On Pakistan's independence from Great Britain in 1947, Afghanistan insisted that it become a separate state for the Pukhtuns (PATHANS) within Pakistan. Afghanistan opposed Pakistan's entry into the United Nations over this issue, and the dispute was a source of friction in relations between the two states. In 1961 Afghanistan backed tribal unrest in Pakistan.

Punjab   Northwestern province of British India until 1947, when the eastern section became the Indian state of Punjab and the western a province of Pakistan. Despite the 1960 Indus Waters Treaty settling disputes over irrigation canals, the area was the scene of fighting between India and Pakistan in 1965 and 1971. In 1966, Indian Punjab was divided to create a Sikh-majority state of Punjab and a Hindi-speaking state of Haryana. Militant Sikhs are campaigning for an independent homeland ("Khalistan"); direct presidential rule was imposed in May 1987. See also SIKHS.

Pushtun   The dominant ethnic group in Afghanistan. Sometimes rendered as "Pukhtun". See PUKHTUNISTAN.

Quaid-e-Azam   The Great Leader, a title given to the Pakistani leader Mohammed Ali Jinnah (1876–1948) by the Constitutional Assembly on 12 August 1947.

Quang Tri   Site of a battle in March–April 1972 in which a North Vietnamese division crossed the border into South Vietnam's Quang Tri province, capturing Quang Tri city and taking many prisoners. South Vietnamese forces recaptured the city in September.

Quemoy   A Chinese Nationalist-controlled island six miles from the mainland, used by Nationalist forces as a base for raids on Communist China from 1953. The Communists bombarded and threatened it with invasion in August–September 1958. The US then deployed a fleet in the Taiwan Straits and pledged to defend the island. See also MATSU.

Quit India Movement   Movement formed by the INDIAN NATIONAL CONGRESS in 1942 to agitate for a British withdrawal from India by refusing to cooperate with the authorities.

Radcliffe Award   The decision of two boundary commissions chaired by Sir Cyril Radcliffe on the borders between India and Pakistan on independence in 1947. The two Muslim and two Hindu judges were unable to agree, and the final decision was made by Radcliffe, though not announced until two days after independence for fear of the response to the decision.

Raj   The British government in India from 1858 to independence in 1947.

Rajasthan   An Indian state formed by the merger of four large and 18 smaller PRINCELY STATES in 1947, and enlarged in 1956.

Rakkhi Bahini   Paramilitary security force formed in 1972 by the Awami League in Bangladesh for "public order" duties in rural areas. Thirty thousand strong by 1975, the force was denounced by opponents as Sheikh Mujib's "private army" and there were criticisms of its violent tactics.

Rann of Kutch   Disputed territory in India, part of which is claimed by Pakistan. Pakistan and India fought a major tank battle in the region during the 1965 war.

Rathbanklang   The name of the central government in Thailand.

Razakars   Irregular troops recruited from among the Biharis by Pakistan and used in the massacre of Pakistan's opponents in the war for Bangladesh independence in 1971.

Recruit Scandal   Political scandal in Japan in 1988 in which the information and property company Recruit Cosmos offered cheap shares of its stock as bribes to politicians and civil servants. It caused the downfall of the finance and justice ministers. The prime minister, Noboru Takeshita, also eventually resigned, on 25 April 1989.

Red China   The People's Republic of China, proclaimed in Peking (Beijing) on 1 October 1949 after the Communists ("Reds") seized power.

Red Flags   See WHITE FLAGS.

Red Guards   Young members of the People's Liberation Army of China, authorized to travel the country helping to further the revolution. They came to prominence during the CULTURAL REVOLUTION, for which their fanatical enthusiasm was notorious, with attacks on "revisionism," "bourgeois decay" and Western diplomats. With the end of the Cultural Revolution, attempts were made to bring them to order, but by then they had firmly supplanted the Communist Youth League.

Red Purge   Term used for attacks on Socialists in Japan in the 1950s.

Rengo   The name of the Japanese trade union movement.

Rhee Line   The unilaterally declared limit of South Korean territorial waters, announced in 1952 by President Syngman Rhee. The declaration hindered attempts to resume normal relations with Japan. During the 1950s, South Korea detained hundreds of Japanese ships. After the fall of Syngman Rhee, relations with Japan improved, and the boundary dispute was settled by the fishing agreement of December 1965.

Rising Sun   The emblem of Japan—hence, by association, Japan or Japanese policies.

Rizal Reef   Disputed area in the South China Sea. A rich fishing ground, it is claimed by both Malaysia and the Philippines.

Rohingyas   The minority Muslim population of Myanmar (Burma). Many thousands have fled to such Bangladeshi border areas as Cox's Bazaar and Bandarban to escape persecution at the hands of the ruling military junta that seized power in 1988. Myanmar, in return, claims that Bangladesh is harboring Burmese antigovernment insurgents. The most active group fighting for the rights of the Rohingyas is Arif (the Arakan Rohingya Islamic Front). Rohingyas currently constitute 70% of the total population of four million of the province of Arakan. Similar Burmese oppression forced 300,000 Rohingyas to flee to Bangladesh in 1978; most were sent back a year later after talks between Bangladesh and Burma.

Sabah   Formerly British North Borneo. It was united with Labuan in 1946 to become a Crown colony. In 1963, adopting the name Sabah, it became part of the Federation of Malaysia.

Saemaul Movement   The "new community" movement launched in 1971 in North Korea to provide for village development and to attempt to reduce the urban–rural gap in living standards.

Sagaing Massacre   The killing in Myanmar (Burma) in 1988 of 300 pro-democracy demonstrators by the military regime.

Salang Highway   Vital strategic route north from Kabul, leading to the former Soviet Union. The important Salang Tunnel lies 100 km (62 miles) north of Kabul and was opened in 1964.

Santa Cruz Massacre   At the Santa Cruz cemetery in Dili, capital of East Timor, the Indonesian authorities (who had seized control of this former

Portuguese colony) committed a massacre of protesters in November 1991 that outraged world opinion.

Saphaphutan   The Thai name for the House of Representatives, the lower chamber in Parliament. Under the 1974 constitution, the Saphaphutan consisted of 269 elected members. The upper chamber, or Senate, is the Wuthisapha, consisting of 100 appointed members.

Sarawak   A state of Malaysia, on the island of Borneo. Ruled by the Brooke family, the "WHITE RAJAHS," after it was ceded in 1841 by the Sultan of Brunei. A British Crown Colony after 1946, it joined the Federation of Malaysia in 1963 (after a guerrilla war in 1962–63).

Satyāgraha   The practice of passive political resistance associated with Gandhi.

Saur Revolution   The April 1978 revolution in Afghanistan that overthrew President Daud, who was killed, together with several members of his family. The revolution took its name from the month of the Afghan calendar.

Senkaku Islands   Uninhabited group of islands in the East China Sea between Okinawa and Taiwan, which are claimed by both Japan and China (they are known to the Chinese as the Diaoyutai Archipelago). The waters around the islands are believed to contain rich oil and natural gas reserves. The dispute last erupted in October 1990, when Japanese patrol boats prevented two Taiwanese vessels from putting men ashore to claim sovereignty.

Seventeenth Parallel   Dividing line at latitude 17° north between northern and southern Vietnam set by the terms of the GENEVA AGREEMENT in July 1954.

Shan   Ethnic minority in Myanmar (Burma). They are Thai-speaking Buddhists, living mainly in the valley regions. The Shan State Army, based in the eastern Shan state, is the main guerrilla group fighting for autonomy.

Shanghai Communiqué   The declaration of February 1972 that announced the intention of reestablishing normal diplomatic relations between Communist China and the United States.

Shanti Bahini   Outlawed separatists in Bangladesh seeking a separate homeland for the 600,000 tribesmen of the Chittagong Hill Tracts. The tribesmen (variously Buddhists, Hindus and Christians) differ from the Muslim Bengalis. By 1994, violence had lasted for 20 years.

Shawhi Dibosh   The Bangladeshi Martyrs' Day. It commemorates the massacre of 21 February 1952, when 26 people died after police opened fire on students protesting against the imposition of Urdu as the official language of Pakistan.

Shenzhen   A previously unimportant Chinese village until it was designated by Deng Xiaoping in 1980 as China's first Special Economic Zone. Rioting erupted in a stampede to buy shares at the newly opened stock exchange there in August 1992.

Showa   Title of the Japanese imperial era under Emperor Hirohito (1926–89). The name means "enlightened peace."

Showa Constitution   The constitution adopted by Japan in 1947.

Siachen Glacier   Disputed area in Kashmir, the scene of conflict between India and Pakistan—for example, in 1984. Talks are currently (1994) being held to try to resolve the dispute.

Sikhs   (Hindu, derived from Sanskrit "disciple") Sect founded by Nanak (1469–1538) with aim of uniting Muslims and Hindus. The Moghul Emperor Akbar (1542–1605) allowed them to build a center at Amritsar (the Golden Temple). In the 17th century a fanatical Muslim became emperor, and under their leader Govind Singh (1666–1708) the Sikhs became warriors to protect themselves. Govind Singh instituted a number of conventions: admission to the sect was by special rite; caste distinctions were abolished; hair was worn long; and the word Singh ("lion") was added to Sikhs' original names. They were organized into 12 misls (confederacies), but divisions soon appeared. A single powerful kingdom was established by Ranjit Singh (1780–1839), but following wars with Britain in 1845–46 and 1848–49, the Sikh commonwealth of the PUNJAB was annexed by Britain. During the 1980s, demands by Sikhs for a homeland ("Khalistan") independent from India brought violence to the Punjab.

Simla Agreement   Treaty signed in 1972 between India and Pakistan following the end of the 1971 war that resulted in the independence of Bangladesh.

SLORC   State Law and Order Restoration Council, formed in Burma (Myanmar) in September 1988 by the military following their coup. SLORC refused to allow the National League for Democracy to take power following the NLD's 80% vote in the May 1990 elections, and continued the repression that had preceded the elections.

SOHYO   The General Council of Trade Unions of Japan, the largest labor federation in the country with 11 large unions as participants.

Spratley Islands   A small archipelago in the South China Sea, believed to lie over a massive underdeveloped oil field. The islands also straddle the vital sea route along which Japan receives oil from the Middle East. They are claimed by China, the Philippines and Vietnam, as well as Malaysia, Brunei and Thailand. In April 1992, China extended its territorial waters to cover both the Spratley and Paracel Islands.

Storay Palace   The building in the Afghan capital, Kabul, that houses the Ministry of Foreign Affairs.

strategic hamlets   Policy adopted by the British in Malaya to counter the Communist guerrilla threat of the 1950s. It was particularly successful under the British army commander Sir Gerald Templar after January 1952, and the practice was later attempted by the United States in Vietnam. See also EMERGENCY.

Subic Bay   Major U.S. Navy base in the Philippines since the Spanish-American War. In the absence of the Soviet threat, and in the face of Philippine opposition, the United States did not renew its lease on the facilities, transferring such activities elsewhere in Southeast Asia.

Suchow   Site of the decisive battle of the Chinese civil war, fought from December 1948 to January 1949. Communist forces, advancing on Guangzhou (Canton), inflicted an estimated 250,000 casualties on the defending Nationalist armies, effectively destroying the morale of Jiang Kaishek's remaining forces.

Swaraj   (Sanskrit, "self-government") The agitation movement against the RAJ in pre-independence India, led by Mahatma Gandhi (1869–1948).

Swarajya   Self-government Party, founded in 1922 in India to reassert CONGRESS PARTY influence in the Indian legislature following the failure of a tactic of noncooperation with the British authorities. Its leaders, C. R. Dois, Motilal Nehru and Vithalbhai Patel, hoped to force concessions from the colonial power by obstructing parliament.

Tajiks   Second largest ethnic group in Afghanistan.

Tamil Nadu   Formerly the Indian state of Madras, renamed in 1968 and including a large Tamil-speaking population. Placed under direct presidential rule in January 1988, and again in January 1991. See also TAMILS.

Tamils   A Hindu grouping originating in southern India and concentrated in the Indian state of TAMIL NADU. Descendants of Tamils imported as manual labor into Sri Lanka in the 19th century have cooperated with Sri Lankan Tamils against the majority Sinhalese on the island, demanding autonomy for the Tamil eastern and northern provinces. Some have joined the militant guerrilla Tamil Tigers.

Tangshan   Coal-mining city in China, 150 km east of Beijing. The scene in 1976 of the most devastating earthquake in Asia since World War II. Measuring 7.8 on the Richter scale, the earthquake killed an estimated 500,000 people.

Tashkent Agreement   Agreement between India and Pakistan reached at the conference held in Tashkent (former USSR) from 3–10 January 1966, convened by Alexei Kosygin, chairman of the Council of Ministers of the USSR. Indian prime minister Lal Bahadur Shastri and Pakistan's president Ayub Khan agreed to end the war on the Kashmir border and to restore normal relations.

Tatmadaw   The armed forces of Myanmar (Burma).

Teen Murti House   Home of the first Indian prime minister, Jawaharlal Nehru (1889–1964), from 1948 until his death; now the Nehru Memorial Museum and Library.

Tet   Period during which the Buddhist lunar new year is celebrated. In Vietnam from 29 January to 25 February 1968, Viet Cong and North Vietnamese troops mounted the major "Tet offensive" against Saigon (now Ho Chi Minh City), Hué and 140 other population centers. Both sides sustained heavy casualties, and although the Communists, whose gains were insubstantial, were forced to withdraw, South Vietnamese and American forces were psychologically undermined by the offensive.

Thakins   Masters, the title given to leaders of the Burma National Army and nationalist movement in the 1940s.

Thirty Comrades   The original members of the Burma Independence Army, also known as the "Thirty Heroes," organized by Aung San in 1941 to campaign for independence from Great Britain. They went to Japan, returning to Burma with the invading Japanese armies.

thirty-eighth parallel   Latitude 38° north, the demarcation line between North and South Korea, established at the 1945 Yalta Conference as a preliminary to unification and the holding of democratic elections. The north's invasion of the south and the subsequent Korean War from 1950 to 1953 ended hopes of immediate peaceful unity.

Thirty Heroes   See THIRTY COMRADES.

Tho Cho   Disputed island claimed by both Cambodia and Vietnam. Under Vietnamese control in 1993, but Khmer Rouge guerrillas were insisting on its return.

Three Principles of the People   The aims of the 1911 Chinese Revolution popularized by Sun Yat-sen (1867–1925) in the 1920s on the reestablishment of the Kuomintang. The principles, which were accepted by both the Nationalists and the Communists, were the rights of the Chinese people to national self-determination, democratic government and social reform.

Three Villages Dispute　Dispute between Laos and Thailand over the control of three villages—Ban Mai, Ban Klang and Ban Sawang. The dispute began in March 1984 and derives from differing interpretations of the 1907 Franco–Siamese Treaty.

Tiananmen Square　The main square in Beijing, the scene on 4 June 1989 of a massacre of predominantly student prodemocracy demonstrators by hard-line elements of the Chinese armed forces. The massacre was followed by widespread arrests of reform supporters.

Tibet (Xizang)　An autonomous region under British control following the collapse of the Chinese Empire in 1911, Tibet retained its autonomy until 1950–51, when Communist Chinese troops reoccupied the country. Following a failed rebellion in 1959, the Dalai Lama and many of his supporters fled. Tibet was administered as a province of China until 1965, when it became an autonomous region of the People's Republic. A further revolt in 1987 met with heavy repression.

Timor　East Indies island formerly divided between Portugal (eastern half) and the Netherlands (western half). Occupied by Japan in World War II, Dutch Timor became part of Indonesia in 1949. The left-wing FRETELIN movement declared Portuguese Timor independent in 1975. Indonesian occupation of East Timor in 1976 was met by Fretelin resistance, which continues.

Tin Bigha Corridor　Territory in dispute between India and Bangladesh.

Tokyo Trials　Trials of 27 Japanese leaders held between May 1946 and November 1947 on war crimes charges, including the charge of causing the war. Seven were sentenced to death (among them former prime minister Tojo Hideki) and 16 to life imprisonment. Emperor Hirohito did not face trial, General Douglas MacArthur arguing that this would threaten postwar Japanese stability.

Tonkin Gulf Resolution　Passed by both houses of the U.S. Congress on 7 August 1964, authorizing President Lyndon B. Johnson to "take all necessary steps, including the use of armed force" to assist in the defense of SEATO members. The resolution followed alleged North Vietnamese attacks on two U.S. Navy ships, the destroyers *Maddox* and *Turner Joy*, in the Gulf of Tonkin in August 1964. Retaliatory raids on North Vietnamese naval installations and oil refineries were mounted. President Johnson used the resolution as general authority to escalate American involvement in Vietnam.

totalitarian capitalism   Term used to describe China's market-oriented capitalist economy within the framework of a communist one-party state.

Triads   Originally, the organizations making up an underground resistance movement among Chinese peasants, founded in the 17th century to overthrow the Manchurian Ching dynasty. Over the past century the Triads have developed into a kind of Mafia. After the 1949 Communist victory in the civil war, many fled to Hong Kong, Macao and Taiwan, and now constitute a sophisticated international organized crime network.

Tsogdu   The National Assembly in Bhutan.

Twenty-One Demands   Demands made by the Japanese government on 18 January 1915, backed by military threats, in an attempt to transform China into a protectorate. Japan demanded the right to appoint political, financial and military advisers. Persuaded by Great Britain not to force the issue, Japan did gain important mineral concessions and influence in Manchuria and Shantung. The demands caused alarm in the United States over Japanese territorial ambitions.

Uighurs   A Turkic-speaking Muslim people living in East Turkestan in the People's Republic of China. An independent East Turkestan Republic was established with Soviet backing in 1944, but in 1949 the state was absorbed by China. Its leaders died in suspicious circumstances in August 1949 after being invited to negotiations in Beijing.

Unequal Treaties   Used by the Chinese to describe the conditions imposed on them by Belgium, Britain, France, Italy, Japan, the Netherlands and the United States at the 1921 Washington Conference, particularly the agreement on an OPEN DOOR policy in China.

UNGOMAP   Acronym for the United Nations Good Offices Mission in Afghanistan and Pakistan, established in 1988 to monitor the withdrawal of Soviet and other forces.

UNTAC   Acronym for the United Nations Transitional Authority in Cambodia.

Untouchables   The HARIJANS, people considered unclean by "caste Hindus" because of the ritually unclean nature of their menial occupations. Harijans began organizing against their status in the late 19th century; the 1950 constitution of India abolished untouchability, and discrimination against Harijans became an imprisonable offense in 1955. The legislation was not totally effective, and Harijans continued to organize against discrimination.

USOM   The United States Operation Mission in Thailand, formed in

1952 to channel financial and technical aid. Aid has reached up to $25 million a year and includes assistance in rural development, national security and education.

Uttar Pradesh   Indian state made up of the former United Provinces and a number of PRINCELY STATES.

Viet Cong   "Vietnamese Communists." Forces fighting a guerrilla war against the South Vietnamese government, and their political arm, the Front for the Liberation of South Vietnam, established in 1960. Active in the 1965–73 Vietnam War, they were so called by the South Vietnamese government to distinguish them from the VIET MINH, an organization that included noncommunists.

Viet Front   See VIET MINH.

Viet Minh   Vietnam Doc-Lap Dong-Minh, the Vietnam Independence League, founded in May 1941 to resist the Japanese occupation. It included other nationalists but was dominated by Communists, including Ho Chi Minh (1892–1969) and Vo Nguyen Giap (1912–86). On the Japanese surrender in 1945, the Viet Minh declared a Democratic Republic of Vietnam and fought against France for Vietnamese independence. It was renamed the Viet Front in 1951.

Vietnamization   U.S. policy in Vietnam of transferring military responsibility to the South Vietnamese forces as U.S. troops were gradually withdrawn. The first major action undertaken after this policy began was the invasion of Cambodia in March 1971 by the South Vietnamese with American support. The weak performance of South Vietnamese troops against the North Vietnamese Army in attacks on the HO CHI MINH TRAIL in Laos called the effectiveness of the policy into question.

warlords   Provincial Chinese leaders, powerful between 1916 and 1928, who maintained private armies to dominate their localities.

Watan   The "Homeland" Party of former President Najibullah of Afghanistan.

WHAM   Acronym for "winning hearts and minds," a propaganda exercise carried out by U.S. forces in the 1965–73 Vietnam War to persuade the people of South Vietnam of the value of Western democracy and friendship with the United States. The campaign combined coercion with expenditure in the interests of the Vietnamese.

White Flags   The pro-Soviet wing of the Burma Communist Party, led in the 1940s by Than Tun. It was opposed by the Trotskyist Red Flags led by Thakin Soe.

White Rajahs   Term used for the ruling Brooke family in SARAWAK until 1946, when the territory became a Crown colony. Sarawak had been ceded to the Brooke family by the sultan of Brunei in 1841.

Wuthisapha   The Senate or Upper House in Thailand. Under the 1974 constitution it consisted of 100 members appointed by the chairman of the Privy Council.

Xinhua   The New China News Agency. Its staff of 600 in Hong Kong is reputed to be China's government-in-waiting in anticipation of the transfer of sovereignty from Great Britain to China in 1997, and an important source of intelligence for the Chinese.

Xinjiang   The vast northwest province of China bordering Mongolia and three newly independent (formerly Soviet) central Asian republics. The area is also important to China's economy as a source of agricultural and mineral resources, particularly oil, and acts as a buffer against Middle Eastern and Central Asian political instability.

Xizang   The Chinese name for TIBET.

Yakuza   The Japanese equivalent of the Italian Mafia. Organized gangs making huge amounts of money from drugs, gambling, extortion and prostitution. The largest Yakuza organization is the Yamaguchi-gumi.

Yan'an   (Formerly Yen'an) The headquarters, in Shanxi Province, of the Chinese Communist Party, established there after the LONG MARCH. It was here that their basic revolutionary policies and style were developed (the "Yan'an spirit"). It remained the Communist headquarters throughout the Japanese war until falling to the Nationalists in 1947. It was recaptured by the Communists under Peng Dehuai in 1948.

Yasukuni Shrine   The memorial to the Japanese war dead of World War II. In Japan, visits to the shrine by government leaders, right-wingers and nationalists have led to protests within Japan as well as in other Asian countries. It is widely seen outside Japan as a symbol of Japanese militarism.

year zero   The first year of the Communist KHMER ROUGE regime in Cambodia (Kampuchea) under Pol Pot (qv).

yen   The monetary unit of Japan. When introduced in 1871 it was exactly at par with the dollar. From 1945 to 1970, it remained at approximately 360 to the dollar. By March 1994 it was trading at 105 to the U.S. dollar.

Yongbyong   Site in North Korea of suspected nuclear facility. North Korea's refusal to open this to international inspection has escalated tension on the Korean peninsula.

Youyighuan   "Friendship Pass." Popular name for the crossing point on the Chinese–Vietnamese border. Now a less-than-appropriate name, given the recent hostilities between the two countries.

Yuan   Term for parliament in both China and Taiwan.

Yushin Program   The name of the South Korean program (from 1972 to 1979) of revitalization. It was marked by the replacement of the constitution, the proclamation of martial law, and curtailment of rights of freedom of speech and assembly.

Zaibatsu   Large family-run business corporations that dominated the Japanese economy prior to World War II. The word means "wealth and family."

Zunyi Conference   The 1935 Conference at Zunyi in Guizhou at which Mao Zedong was elected leader of the Chinese Communist Party.

CHAPTER 11

BIOGRAPHIES

Abdullah, Muhammad (1905–82)   Indian politician. Chief minister of Jammu and Kashmir, supported by Muslim and non-Muslim Kashmiris. Entered politics in 1931, campaigning to overthrow Kashmir's Hindu maharajah. Opposed Kashmir joining Pakistan, favoring an independent state, though once arrested for alleged Pakistan sympathies.

Abdul Rahman   See RAHMAN, TUNKU ABDUL.

Abdul Razak (1922–76)   Prime minister of Malaysia, 1970–76. Served with British-led resistance during World War II. Appointed head of the United Malays National Organization (UMNO) Youth in 1950, and UMNO deputy president in 1951. Deputy prime minister on independence in 1957, succeeding TUNKU ABDUL RAHMAN as UMNO president and Malaysian prime minister in 1970. As prime minister he drew a number of opposition groups into a coalition government and introduced the Second Malaysian Plan for economic and political restructuring.

Agus Salim Haji (1884–1954)   Indonesian nationalist. Founder of the Barisan Panjedar PSII. Helped to formulate the 1945 Jakarta Charter. Served as vice-minister from 1946–49 and subsequently as minister of foreign affairs.

Aidit, Dipa Nusantra (1923–65)   Indonesian Communist leader. Member of the Politburo, 1948. Party secretary, 1951. Captured and shot after the Gestapu rising in 1965.

Akihito (1933–   )   Eldest son of Emperor HIROHITO of Japan, succeeding him in 1989. His title was Prince Tsugu until his inauguration as crown prince in 1952. Married a commoner, Shōda Michiko, a businessman's daughter, in 1959.

Ali Sastroamidjojo (1903–75)   Indonesian nationalist politician. Twice headed cabinets (1953–54, 1956–57). Played major part in Indonesia's role in the nonaligned movement.

Ambedkar, Bhimrao Ramji (1893–1956)   Indian politician. Born into an Untouchable, or low-caste Hindu family. Founded the Scheduled Castes Federation, which opposed the Indian National Congress. Joined Congress after Indian independence and was law minister from 1947–51, playing a prominent part in drafting the Indian constitution.

Amin, Hafizullah (1928–79)   Afghan politician. Joined the People's Democratic Party of Afghanistan in 1965 and was elected to parliament in 1969. Responsible for organizing party supporters in the armed forces. Following intraparty disputes after the April 1978 coup, Amin became president of Afghanistan in September 1979. Overthrown and killed following the December 1979 Soviet invasion.

Aquino, Benigno (1932–83)   Prominent opposition leader during the MARCOS regime in the Philippines. Imprisoned 1972–80. Assassinated on 21 August 1983 on his return from exile.

Aquino, Corazon Cojuangco (Cory) (1933–   )   President of the Philippines from February 1986 to July 1992, surviving a number of attempted coups. Widow of BENIGNO AQUINO, became politically active following his assassination in 1983. Stood as a compromise candidate against MARCOS in the 1986 presidential election and took office following his forced resignation.

Asanuma Inejiro (1898–1960)   Japanese politician. Member of the Diet and of Tokyo City Council. Involved in radical farming politics in the 1920s. One of the founders of the Japan Socialist Party (JSP) in 1945; chief secretary of the JSP in 1948. Protested against the revision of the U.S. Security Treaty in 1960 and was assassinated by a right-wing militant.

Aung San (1915–47)   Leader of the Burmese independence movement. Organized a student strike in 1936, becoming secretary-general of Dobama Asiayon, a nationalist organization, and of the Communists. Commanded an anti-British Burma Independence Army that moved into Burma with the Japanese invasion force in January 1942, becoming minister of defense in the Ba Maw puppet government. Turned against the Japanese and led the underground Anti-Fascist Organization with the Communist and People's Revolution movements. In 1945 was prominent in the Anti-Fascist People's Freedom League (AFPFL), becoming its president. Became prime minister in the Governor's Executive Council in 1946, and in 1947 negotiated Burmese independence from Great Britain. Assassinated by a political opponent on 19 July 1947.

Aung San Suu Kyi (1945–) Opposition leader in Myanmar (Burma). Under house arrest since 1989. Winner of Nobel Peace Prize, 1991, for her opposition to the military junta. Daughter of AUNG SAN.

Ayub Khan, Mohammed (1907–74) President of Pakistan from 1958 to 1969. Commissioned in British Indian army in 1928, chief of the Pakistan army in 1951, and defense minister in 1954–55. Head of state on declaration of martial law in 1958, winning presidential elections in 1960 and 1965. Resigned in 1969 following riots against repressive rule.

Bandaranaike, Sirimavo (1916–) Prime minister of Ceylon (the world's first female prime minister), 1960–65, 1970–77. Succeeded her husband SOLOMON BANDARANAIKE as leader of the Sri Lanka Freedom Party. Defeated in 1965, she was returned with an increased majority in 1970. A new constitution in 1972 renamed Ceylon the Republic of Sri Lanka. Defeated in the 1977 election, she was barred from parliament in 1980 for alleged unconstitutional actions. Failed in attempt to win presidency in December 1988.

Bandaranaike, Solomon (1899–1959) Prime minister of Ceylon (renamed Sri Lanka in 1972), 1956–59. Led the Ceylon National Congress movement in the 1930s. Minister of health from 1948–51, he founded the Sinhalese Sri Lanka Socialist Freedom Party in 1952. Became prime minister at head of a "People's United Front" in April 1956. Pursuing a policy of neutrality, he closed British military bases, began nationalization and attempted to make Sinhalese the official language, alienating the Tamil community. Assassinated by a Buddhist monk in 1959.

Bao Dai (1913–) Last emperor of Vietnam, from 1925 to 1945, when he abdicated under Communist pressure. With the return of French administration he became prime minister and "puppet emperor" in 1949, but was deposed following a referendum in South Vietnam in 1955. Lived in exile in France.

Bhave, Vinoba (1896–1982) Indian leader. Born into a high-caste Brahmin family, became a follower of MAHATMA GANDHI in 1916. Interned in the 1920s and 1930s for opposing British rule, and imprisoned 1940–44. Founded movement to assist Indian refugees in 1948, and in 1958 formed the Bhoodan movement to acquire land for landless low-caste members. Led the Shantri Sèna movement for economic and social reform.

Bhumibol Adulyadej (1927–) Reigning monarch of Thailand from 1946. A figurehead as constitutional head of state and commander-in-chief, but his long experience enabled him to act as moderating influence.

Bhutto, Benazir (1953–) Pakistani politician. Prime minister, 1988–

90. American-educated daughter of ZULFIKAR ALI BHUTTO, she returned from Great Britain in 1986 and became prime minister following the Pakistan People's Party election success in November 1988. She was dismissed by the president for alleged corruption and nepotism in August 1990. After the 1993 elections she formed a coalition government and became prime minister once again.

Bhutto, Zulfiqar Ali (1928–79)   President of Pakistan from 1971–73; prime minister, 1973–77. Foreign minister from 1963 to 1966, when he resigned over the Indo–Pakistan truce. Founded the People's Party, which won a majority in the assembly in 1970. Took Pakistan out of the Commonwealth in 1972. Accusations of ballot-rigging in 1977 led to riots, his overthrow in a military coup and his execution in 1979.

Binh, Nguyen Thi (1927–   )   Vietnamese politician. Imprisoned 1951–54 for militant anticolonial activities. Joined the National Liberation Front in 1961, becoming member of its central command in 1962. Participated in Paris peace talks 1968–73. Foreign minister in Provisional Revolutionary Government of South Vietnam, minister of education and councillor of state in Socialist Republic of Vietnam, 1976–87.

Birla, Ghanshyam Das (1890–1975)   Indian industrialist and financier. A member of one of India's most influential industrial families. The main financial supporter of MAHATMA GANDHI, he funded the Untouchables organization, the national language movement and many welfare projects.

Boun Oum (1911–80)   Premier of Laos 1949–50, December 1960; rightwing and U.S.-supported. From 1962 a member of the National Union government led by SOUVANNA PHOUMA.

Bui Diem (*fl.* 1960s)   South Vietnam's ambassador to the United States 1966–72, later an international representative of President NGUYEN VAN THIEU. Born in North Vietnam, fled to the south, where he was a newspaper publisher before entering the government.

Bui Tin (*fl.* 1970s)   North Vietnam Communist army officer and deputy editor of the Hanoi official military newspaper *Quan Doi Nhan Dan*. Accepted the surrender of South Vietnam, 30 April 1975.

Chang Myun (John M. Chang) (1899–1966)   Prime minister of the Republic of Korea in 1950–1952 and 1960. Korea's first ambassador to the United States in 1949. Prime minister 1950–52. Joined the opposition Democratic Party in 1952. Narrowly elected prime minister in 1960, he presided over Korea's only fully democratic government but was overthrown in a military coup in May 1961.

Chen Boda (1904–89)   A leading theoretician, a promoter of the Great Leap Forward and of the 1966–69 Cultural Revolution. A member of the Communist underground, he emerged as a leading Maoist ideologue in 1937 and acted as Mao's personal and political secretary. Sentenced to 18 years' imprisonment as a "Gang of Four" member in 1977 but released on health grounds in 1981.

Ch'en Li (1901–72)   Chinese general. Member of Chinese Communist Party in 1921. Joined Mao Zedong's force in 1928 and became leading guerrilla fighter, organizing underground groups in central and south China during the Long March. Commanded Fourth Army against the Japanese, and prominent in the civil war. Mayor of Shanghai, foreign minister from 1958–66. Disgraced in the Cultural Revolution.

Chiang Ching   See JIANG QING.

Chiang Kai-shek   See JIANG KAISHEK.

Chin Peng (1922–   )   Malaysian Communist guerrilla leader, beginning operations against the British in Malaya in 1948—forcing a 10-year state of emergency—and later against the Thais. Negotiated a truce with Thailand in 1989.

Chou En-lai   See ZHOU ENLAI.

Chun Doo Hwan (1931–   )   President of South Korea. Led the military coup following the crushing of the Kwangju uprising (qv).

Datuk Hussein Onn (1922–90)   Prime minister of Malaysia, 1976–81. Served with British Liberation Forces, joining the Malay Administration Service in 1945. Became youth leader and national secretary of the United Malay National Organization (UMNO). Politically inactive after independence in 1957, he later became minister of education and deputy prime minister, then prime minister.

Daoud Khan, Sardar Mohammed (?–1978)   Afghan leader. Cousin of King Zahir, prime minister from 1953–63. Prominent figure in coup that overthrew the monarchy in July 1973. Head of state from 1973–78, killed in 1978 in the revolution.

Deng Xiaoping (1904–   )   Secretary General of the Chinese Communist Party in the 1950s and 1960s, playing a major part in ideological disputes with the Soviet Union. Purged in the 1966–69 Cultural Revolution, he reemerged in 1973 and was appointed deputy prime minister and effectively head of government. He fell from power in 1976 when HUA GUOFENG became prime minister but was reinstated in 1977, led the attack on the

"Gang of Four" and successfully promoted better relations with the United States. He has turned China towards a market-oriented economy.

Desai, Morarji (1896–   )   Indian prime minister, 1977–79. A civil disobedience movement activist in the 1930s, he emerged as a leading Congress Party figure after independence. Conflicts with INDIRA GANDHI led to his imprisonment from 1975–77. Led the Janata Party alliance to victory against Mrs. Gandhi in 1977, becoming prime minister, but he lost power when the alliance split.

Diem, Ngo Dinh   See NGO DINH DIEM.

Dinh Nguyen Thi (1920–   )   Vietnamese revolutionary. Joined revolutionaries at age of 11. Imprisoned 1940–43. Active against NGO DINH DIEM regime, leading an uprising at Ben Tre on 17 January 1960 that effectively began the second Vietnam War. Became member of the National Liberation Front Presidium and chair of the South Vietnam Liberation Association. Elected to Central Committee of the Communist Party in 1976.

Do Muoi (1917–   )   Vietnamese politician. Joined Communist Party in the 1920s and held government office in North Vietnam. Had prominent role in socialization of the south from 1976. Elected prime minister in 1988 and subsequently president.

Duong Van Minh (1916–   )   South Vietnamese military leader. Military adviser to President NGO DINH DIEM from 1962 to 1963, when he led a military coup against Diem. Chairman of the Revolutionary Military Committee government from November 1963 to January 1964, head of state, January–October 1964. Served as last president of South Vietnam for two days in April 1975 to surrender to Communist forces.

Enrile, Juan Ponce (1924–   )   Philippine businessman, lawyer and politician. Minister of defense under President MARCOS, against whom he mounted an army mutiny in February 1986. President CORAZON AQUINO appointed him defense secretary but dismissed him for questioning her power. Elected to the Philippine Senate in 1987.

Ershad, Hussain Mohammed (1930–   )   Bangladeshi politician. Leader of the Jatiya Dal. Seized power in a bloodless coup on 24 March 1982, becoming president in December 1983. Overthrown by popular opposition in December 1990. Imprisoned in June 1991 for illegal arms possession.

Fukuda Takeo (1905–   )   Japanese politician. Finance minister, 1965–66, 1968–70, 1973–74; foreign minister, 1971–72; deputy prime minister, 1974–76; prime minister, 1976–78. An official in the Ministry of Finance until accused of corruption in 1948 (exonerated in 1958). Elected to House of Representatives in 1952, supporting the Kishi faction of the Liberal Democratic Party.

Gandhi, Indira (1917–84)   Indian prime minister from 1966–77 and from 1980–84. Daughter of JAWAHARLAL NEHRU, she joined the Congress Party in 1939. Minister for broadcasting and information, 1964–66. Assumed dictatorial powers following declaration of state of emergency in 1975, leading to electoral defeat in 1977. Reelected in 1980, promising firm government, but was assassinated by Sikh extremists in 1984.

Gandhi, Mohandas Karamchand ("Mahatma") (1869–1948)   Indian national leader. Led passive resistance campaigns in South Africa against Transvaal government discrimination against Indians from 1907–14. Returned to India to lead the Congress Party and to become an influential figure in the campaign for Indian independence, advocating nonviolent civil disobedience. Collaborated with the last viceroys of India to plan independence and partition. Assassinated in 1948.

Gandhi, Rajiv (1944–91)   Indian prime minister 1984–89. Entered politics in 1981, holding various ministerial offices under his mother INDIRA GANDHI, succeeding her as prime minister on her assassination. His period in office was marked by growing scandal over his alleged corruption, and he was defeated in the 1989 elections. Assassinated while campaigning in the 1991 elections.

Gao Gang (1902–55)   Chinese Communist political leader. Appointed viceroy to Manchuria by MAO ZEDONG, he was dismissed in 1954 after accusations of treachery on behalf of the Soviet Union. Committed suicide.

Giap Vo Nguyen See VO NGUYEN GIAP.

Goh Chok Tong (1941–)   Singapore politician. An economist, he entered parliament in 1976 as member of the ruling People's Action Party. Appointed first deputy prime minister in 1985, succeeding LEE KUAN YEW as premier in November 1990.

Hatoyama Ichiro (1883–1959)   Prime minister of Japan, 1954–56. Founding president of the Liberal Party in 1945, he was politically inactive until 1951 and then went on to establish the Democratic Party in 1954. Became prime minister with Socialist support but then merged his party with the Liberals to form the Liberal Democratic Party. Reestablished relations with the Soviet Union in 1956.

He Long (1896–1969)   Chinese revolutionary. Joined the Communist Party in 1926, participating in the Long March (qv), the war against Japan and the Chinese civil war. Appointed a marshal in 1955. Denounced during the Cultural Revolution, he died in hospital after accusing the authorities of planning his death.

Heng Samrin (1934–) Cambodian politician. Installed by the Vietnamese as state president in 1979, becoming party leader in 1981. He had earlier fled to Vietnam after serving as a Khmer Rouge military commander to escape POL POT's purge of the eastern provinces. Generally regarded as a Vietnamese "puppet" president.

Hieu Nguyen Van (1918–) Vietnamese politician. Journalist, participated in Viet Minh risings in 1946. Joined the National Liberation Front in 1960. Acted as NLF spokesman and propagandist in the West. Appointed minister of culture in Socialist Republic of Vietnam in 1976.

Hiratsuka Raicho (1886–1971) Leader of the Japanese women's movement, campaigning from 1920 on for female suffrage and education. President of the Federation of Japanese Women's Organizations in 1953. In 1954 called on women to help outlaw the hydrogen bomb.

Hirohito (1901–89) Emperor of Japan, succeeding to the throne in 1926 after acting as regent since 1921. Accepted military demands for war against the United States in 1941 but supported moves toward peace in 1945. Renounced divine status in January 1946, becoming a constitutional monarch.

Hoang Duc Nha (*fl.* 1960s) Special adviser to President NGUYEN VAN THIEU, his cousin; particularly influential after 1972. Later left Vietnam and settled in the United States.

Ho Chi Minh (1892–1969) Vietnamese Communist, president of North Vietnam from 1954–69. A founding member of the French Communist Party, he lived outside Vietnam from 1908 to 1945, forming the Indochina Communist Party in 1930 and the Viet Minh nationalist movement in 1941. Proclaimed the Democratic Republic of Vietnam in September 1945 and led an anticolonialist struggle against France from 1946–54. After the Geneva agreement recognized his presidency in the north, Ho encouraged Viet Cong resistance against the U.S.-backed Republic of (South) Vietnam, but died before its success in 1975.

Ho Dam (1929–91) North Korean diplomat and politician. Foreign minister, 1970–83; vice-premier, 1973. Became a Politburo member in 1983 and head of the Committee for the Peaceful Reunification of the Fatherland and was also involved in North Korea's growing diplomatic friendliness towards Japan.

Honasan, Gregorio "Gringo" (1947–) Philippine army officer active in the 1986 rising against President MARCOS. Mounted a failed coup against CORAZON AQUINO in 1987 and escaped while under arrest.

Hua Guofeng (1912–) Chinese Communist Party chairman from 1976–81, prime minister from 1976–80. Elected to Central Committee in 1969, becoming a Politburo member in 1975. A critic of the Cultural Revolution, Hua won control of the party following the death of MAO in 1976, and moved against the radical "Gang of Four" led by Mao's widow JIANG QING.

Hun Sen (1951–) Cambodian prime minister, 1985–93. After fleeing to Vietnam to escape POL POT's purges, returned to Cambodia in 1979 as foreign minister in the pro-Hanoi government. A skilled diplomat and negotiator, but distrusted by hard-liners for his liberal attitudes.

Huynh Tan Phat (1913–) Vietnamese politician. Anti-French student militant in the 1930s. Became secretary general of the Vietnam Democratic Party, joining the Viet Minh as a noncommunist. Joined the National Liberation Front in 1960 and served as its general secretary 1964–66. President of the Provisional Revolutionary Government in 1969 and, though remaining a noncommunist, held government offices after 1975.

Ieng Sary (1930–) Foreign minister in the POL POT regime. The most powerful Khmer Rouge leader in Cambodia after Pol Pot.

Ikeda Hayato (1899–1965) Prime minister of Japan, 1960–64. Deputy finance minister, 1947–48; finance minister, 1949–52, 1956–57; international trade and industry minister, 1959–60. As prime minister, continued emphasis on rapid development of Japan's economy.

Ishibashi Tanzan (1884–1973) Prime minister of Japan. December 1956–February 1957. Served briefly as finance minister in 1946 but was banned from political activity from 1947–51. Involved in formation of Democratic Party in 1954, later becoming international trade and industry minister and then prime minister, an office he held for only three months.

Jiang Kaishek (1887–1975) President of China from 1928–49, having declared himself president of the Kuomintang in 1928. His dictatorship was challenged by the Communists, by sections of the army, and by the Japanese, who occupied Manchuria in 1931 and attacked China in 1937. Despite support from the United States, Jiang's forces were defeated by the Communists in a civil war that ended in 1949. Jiang withdrew to Taiwan.

Jiang Qing (1914–91) An actress who became the wife of MAO ZEDONG. Became Mao's "first lady" in 1949 and was active behind the scenes in the party's use of culture as a political weapon. A leading pro-Mao activist as cultural adviser to the army in the Cultural Revolution, with great influence as a member of a "shadow" Politburo. On Mao's death in 1976, arrested as a member of the radical "Gang of Four," expelled from the Communist Party in 1977, and sentenced to death in 1981 (commuted to life imprisonment in 1983).

Jiang Zemin (1926–   )   Chinese Communist leader. As the party leader in Shanghai he was appointed party secretary by DENG XIAOPING following the ousting of ZHAO ZIYANG after the Tiananmen Square massacre (qv). Now state president of China.

Jinnah, Mohammed Ali (1876–1948)   First governor-general of independent Pakistan in 1948. A lawyer, he joined the All-India Muslim League in 1913 and attempted to work with Congress in the independence struggle. But as differences increased with Congress leader MAHATMA GANDHI, Jinnah's Muslim League sought separate nationhood for the majority Muslim areas of India, leading to partition and the creation of Pakistan in 1947. Assassinated after a year in office.

Kaifu Toshiki (1931–   )   Japanese politician. Prime minister 1989–91 in succession to the disgraced SOSUKE UNO. Almost unknown outside Japan and with no power base in the ruling Liberal Democratic Party, he was seen as an interim leader but was able to hold his position until factional disputes forced his removal.

Kanemaru Shin (1914–   )   Leading member of Japan's Liberal Democratic Party (LDP), known as "the godfather of Japanese politics." Resigned as a member of the Diet's Lower House in 1992 after admitting receiving over $2 million in illegal donations from businesses and being involved with criminal leaders. As the leader of the largest faction in the LDP, he dominated intraparty affairs.

Kang Sheng (*c.* 1900–75)   Creator and head of Communist Chinese security services. Founded the Ministry of Public Security in 1949 to combat the regime's opponents, but purged the ministry in the 1966–69 Cultural Revolution. Formed a network of security agencies, including the Investigation Department of the Central Committee, the Military Commission, the People's Armed Police and the Ministry of State Security.

Karmal, Babrak (1929–   )   Afghan Communist leader. President of Afghanistan from 1980–86. Leader of the Parcham faction of the People's Democratic Party of Afghanistan (PDPA). Installed as president following the December 1979 Soviet invasion. Resigned from PDPA politburo and as president of the Revolutionary Council in 1986.

Katayama Tetsu (1887–1978)   Japanese prime minister, 1948. Active in campaigning for workers' and farmers' rights, he helped found the Japan

Socialist Party (JSP) in 1945. His brief government coalition collapsed after disputes over wage and price controls. President of the National League for the Protection of the Constitution, 1953. Adviser to a breakaway group of the JSP, the Democratic Socialist Party, in 1960.

Kaysone Phomvihane (1920–92)   Laotian politician. Fought with Viet Minh against Japanese, 1944–45. Joined the Free Laos Front in 1945 and the Lao Dong (Vietnam) Communist Party in 1949. Assisted in formation of the Pathet Lao (qv), becoming commander of its forces in 1954. Formed and became general secretary of the Communist People's Revolutionary Army of Laos in 1955. Chairman of the Council of Ministers of Laos (premier) in 1975. Held post until August 1991, then president until November 1992.

Khieu Samphan (1932–   )   Cambodian politician. Commander of Khmer Rouge (qv) troops in the Cambodian civil war from 1973. Deputy premier and defense minister in Prince SIHANOUK's government-in-exile, 1970. Head of state following Sihanouk's resignation in April 1976.

Khuang Aphaiwong (1902–74)   Thai politician. Prime minister for three short periods. Held a number of cabinet appointments. Vice president of the Thai House of Representatives, 1943–44. Leader of the Prachatiphat (Democrat) party from 1955 until his death.

Kim Il Sung (1912–   )   Prime minister of the Democratic People's Republic of Korea (North Korea) 1948–72. President since 1972. Joined the Communist Party in 1931, fought with Korean contingent in Red Army in World War II. Installed by USSR as North Korean leader in 1948. Following the Korean War (1950–53), Kim attempted to remain neutral in the Sino–Soviet ideological conflict, building a personality cult in North Korea.

Kim Young-Sam (1927–   )   President of South Korea since February 1993. Elected in December 1992 as the first civilian president for 32 years. Kim has had a long political career as a dissident, gaining world attention for his hunger strike in 1983 against CHUN DOO HWAN's authoritarian rule. A presidential candidate in 1987, he split the opposition vote. In 1990 Kim merged his party, the Reunification Democratic Party, with ROH's ruling Democratic Justice Party to form South Korea's dominant party, the Democratic Liberal Party.

Kishi Nobusuke (1896–1987)   Prime minister of Japan, 1957–60. Involved as a civil servant in putting Japan's economy on a war footing and in industrial development in Manchuria. Imprisoned in 1945, but released without trial. Elected to the House of Representatives in 1953, becoming leader of the new Liberal Democratic Party in 1955. Minister of foreign affairs before becoming prime minister in 1957. Promoted policy of easing relations with Asian neighbors and cementing U.S.–Japanese links. Resigned following riot over the revised Japan–US Security Treaty, which he had negotiated.

Kong Le (1924–)   Laotian military leader. Led the neutralist forces, 1960–62. Took control of Vientiane in August 1960.

Kongsompong Sunthorn (*fl.* 1990)   Thai general. Supreme commander of the Thai forces who led the bloodless coup on 23 February 1991 to overthrow the government of Chatichai Choonhavan for alleged corruption. After the coup, the Thai constitution was suspended, provoking a suspension of American economic and military aid.

Lattre de Tassigny, Jean de (1889–1952)   World War II commander of the French First Army; commander-in-chief in Indochina from 1950–51.

Le Duan (1908–)   Vietnamese politician. Founding member of the Indochinese Communist Party, 1930; Central Committee member, 1945. Led Communist insurgency against South Vietnam government from 1954, forming the National Liberation Front in 1960. First Secretary, Vietnam Workers Party (Lao Dong) in 1959, succeeded HO CHI MINH and became party secretary general in 1976.

Le Duc Tho (born **Phan Dinh Khai**) (1911–1990)   Vietnamese politician. Founding member of the Indochinese Communist Party, 1930, and of the Viet Minh, 1941. Led North Vietnamese negotiating team at Paris peace talks, 1968–73. Awarded, and rejected, Nobel Peace Prize with Henry Kissinger following cease-fire agreement, 1973.

Lee Kuan Yew (1923–)   Prime minister of Singapore, 1959–90. Founder and secretary general of the People's Action Party, 1954. Elected prime minister when Singapore achieved internal self-government. Member of the federal parliament between 1963 and 1965, when Singapore was part of the Federation of Malaysia.

Liaquat, Ali Khan (1896–1951)   First prime minister of Pakistan, 1947–51. Leading member of the Muslim League in the 1920s and 1930s. As prime minister he was criticized for efforts to improve relations with India and his refusal to declare Pakistan an Islamic state. Assassinated in 1951.

Lin Biao (1908–71)   Chinese Communist leader. Commanded an army on the Long March (qv), 1934–35. Defeated Kuomintang armies in 1948, leading the advance into central China in 1949. Commanded Chinese volunteers in Korean War, 1950–52. Appointed a marshal in 1955; minister of defense in 1959. Active in organization of 1966–69 Cultural Revolution.

Designated as successor to MAO ZEDONG at Ninth Party Congress in 1966. Killed in an air crash in 1971 while escaping following an unsuccessful coup attempt.

Li Peng (1928–)   Hard-line Chinese politician. Adopted son of former premier ZHOU ENLAI. Elected to Central Committee, 1982. In 1985 became head of State Education Commission. In 1987, succeeded ZHAO ZIYANG as premier. A close political ally of Chen Yun, DENG XIAOPING's chief rival. Took hard-line stance in 1989, crushing pro-democracy demonstrations in Tiananmen Square (qv).

Liu Shao-Chi See LIU SHAOQI.

Liu Shaoqi (1898–1974)   Chairman of the People's Republic of China (head of state), 1959–69. Elected to Communist Party Central Committee, 1927. Political commissar during the Long March (qv). Principal party vice-chairman on establishment of People's Republic in 1949, he succeeded MAO ZEDONG as chairman in 1959 (a post he held until 1969), but was deprived of position as heir apparent in 1966. Criticized for seeing industrial workers rather than peasants as spearhead of the revolution, he was stripped of all party offices in 1968.

Li Xiannian (1909–92)   Chinese politician. Former carpenter, joined the Communist Party in 1927. Leader of anti-Japanese guerrilla forces in central China, 1944; deputy commander of Fourth Field Army in the civil war. Appointed vice-premier in 1954, minister of finance in 1957, director of the State Council's Financial and Economic Affairs Bureau in 1959, and vice-chairman of the State Planning Commission in 1962. Pro-economic reform vice-chairman of the Financial and Economic Commission in 1979. President, 1983–88, traveling widely abroad. Retired in 1988 but remained influential as one of the veteran Communist "eight elders."

Lon Nol (1913–)   Cambodian military and political leader. President of Khmer Republic (Cambodia), 1972–75. Held various ministerial offices under Prince SIHANOUK, including that of armed forces commander. Prime minister from 1966–67, 1969–71. Headed government after Sihanouk was deposed in 1970, establishing close ties with the United States and South Vietnam. Assumed total power as president and armed forces commander in 1972, but fled the country in 1975 as Communist Khmer Rouge approached the capital.

Macapagal, Diosdado (1910–)   President of the Philippines, 1961–65, when he attempted land reform and clashed with the U.S. over his pro-Indonesian policy. Member of the House of Representatives, 1949–56; leader of delegation to the United Nations, 1950–51; vice president, 1957–61.

MacArthur, Douglas (1880–1964)   United States general. U.S. Army chief of staff, 1930–35. Commander in the Philippines, 1936 until their capture in 1942. Supreme Allied Commander, Southwest Pacific, he led a combined operations strategy against Japan and accepted her surrender in 1945. Commander of occupation forces, he demilitarized and democratized Japan. As commander of UN forces in Korean War, he advocated attacking China and was dismissed by President Truman in 1951.

Magsaysay, Ramon (1907–57)   President of the Philippines, 1953–57. A prominent guerrilla leader in World War II. A congressman, 1946–49, then secretary of national defense after 1950. His popularity in leading the campaign against the Huk (qv) guerrillas won him the presidency in 1953. Killed in an air crash, 1957, at height of his popularity.

Mahendra Bir Vikram Shah Deva (1920–72)   King of Nepal, 1956–72. His 1959 constitution introduced democracy to Nepal, but in 1960 the constitution was withdrawn, all political parties were outlawed and their leaders jailed. Continuing to rule as an absolute monarch, he appointed nonpolitical assemblies in 1962.

Mao Zedong (1893–1976)   Chairman of the People's Republic of China, 1949–76. A founding member of the Chinese Communist Party in 1921, he saw the peasantry rather than the industrial working class as the main revolutionary force. When the Communists were pushed out of central China by JIANG KAISHEK he led the 1934–35 Long March to northwest China. His armies (in alliance with Jiang) defeated the Japanese occupying forces and then Jiang in the civil war, proclaiming a People's Republic in 1949. Mao first led China on a pragmatic program of land reform and state socialism. But he became increasingly radical, initiating the 1958–59 Great Leap Forward, in which millions died, and the equally disastrous 1966–69 Cultural Revolution. For the last five years of his life he was a figurehead, with ZHOU ENLAI managing an unexpected rapprochement with the West.

Marcos, Ferdinand E. (1917–90)   President of the Philippines, 1965–86. Served in the armed forces during World War II. Special assistant to President ROXAS, 1946–47; member of the House of Representatives, 1949–59; Senate, 1959–66. An authoritarian president, acting harshly against any opposition, he declared martial law in 1972. Growing international concern at his corruption, despite his anticommunist alliance with the United States, led to presidential elections in 1986 and, although he claimed victory, Marcos was forced into exile.

Massoud, Ahmad Shah (1953–   )   Afghan guerrilla leader. Leader of the Jamiat-i-Islami Party, the largest of the mujaheddin rebel groups following the 1979 Soviet invasion. Successfully resisted seven Soviet attacks on his Panjshir Valley bases and negotiated a year-long peace with Soviet forces in 1983. Spread control over northern Afghanistan after Soviet withdrawal in 1989. His advance on Kabul in 1992 prompted the fall of President Najibullah.

Menon, Vengalil Krishnan Krishna (1897–1974) Indian politician, teacher and lawyer. Became secretary of the India League in London in 1929 and a lobbyist for independence. High commissioner in London, 1947–52; India's representative at the United Nations, 1953–62, helping negotiate peace in Korea and Indochina. Minister of Defense, 1957–62, but resigned following India's defeat in war with China. Left Congress Party but remained in parliament until his death.

Miki Takeo (1907–88) Prime minister of Japan, 1974–76. Tried to weaken big business influence in politics but was forced to resign when the Liberal Democratic Party (LDP) became increasingly unpopular through his deflationary economic policies. Elected to Diet as youngest member in 1937; secretary of LDP in 1956; minister of international trade and industry, 1965–66; foreign minister, 1966–68; deputy prime minister, 1972–74.

Miyazawa Kiichi (1919–) Japanese politician. Resigned as finance minister in December 1988 because of involvement in corruption scandal. Became prime minister in November 1991 promising to clean up Japanese politics. Lost power in the July 1993 election.

Mountbatten, Louis (Earl) (1900–79) British admiral. Chief of combined operations, 1942; Supreme Allied Commander Southeast Asia, 1943. Appointed last viceroy of India in 1947, he sped the transition to independence and became India's first governor-general, 1947–48. First sea lord, 1955–59: chief of defense staff, 1959–65. Assassinated by Irish terrorists in 1979.

Nakasone Yasuhiro (1917–) Prime minister of Japan, 1982–87. Minister of transport, 1967–68; minister of state and director-general, defense agency, 1970–71; chairman of the executive council, Liberal Democratic Party (LDP), 1971–72; minister of international trade and industry, 1972–74; LDP secretary general, 1974–76, and chairman, 1977–80; minister of state, 1980–82.

Navarre, Henri (1898–1983) Commander-in-chief of the French forces in Indochina in 1953–54. Made the fatal decision to fight at Dien Bien Phu (qv).

Nehru, Jawaharlal (1889–1964) Indian prime minister, 1947–64. Active in the Indian Congress movement following the 1919 Amritsar massacre.

General secretary of the All-India Congress Movement in 1929, he was chief tactician of the independence campaign and spent nine years in prison. Became prime minister and foreign minister on independence in 1947. Under his leadership India made technical, industrial and social advances, and assumed moral leadership of the Third World, playing a mediating role in various international crises. Died in office.

Ne Win, U (1911–)   Burmese political leader. Member of anti-British "We Burmans Association" in 1930s. Chief of staff of collaborationist army in Japanese-occupied Burma, 1942–44. Led guerrilla force supporting Allies against Japan, 1944. General and second in command of army on Burmese independence, 1948. Caretaker prime minister, 1958–60. Seized power in coup, 1962, leading the Burmese Socialist Program Party (BSPP) to create a one-party state. President, 1974–81. Faced increasing resistance from Communist and minority groups. Resigned as BSPP chairman following violently suppressed antigovernment demonstrations, 1988.

Ngo Dinh Diem (1901–63)   First prime minister and president of South Vietnam, 1954–63. A civil servant and nationalist leader from 1931, he refused office as minister of the interior under HO CHI MINH and lived abroad until 1954. Prime minister under BAO DAI. U.S.-backed head of state when South Vietnam was declared a republic in 1955. His rule was increasingly repressive and he was overthrown in a military coup and murdered in 1963.

Ngo Dinh Nhu (1910–63)   Brother and principal adviser of NGO DINH DIEM; organizer of the Can Lao (qv), an effective private army supporting Diem's regime. Assassinated with Diem in 1963.

Ngo Dinh Nhu, Madame (1924–)   Wife of NGO DINH NHU, unpopular "dragon lady" of the South Vietnamese regime of bachelor president NGO DINH DIEM. Retired to Rome in 1964.

Ngo Dinh Thuc (*fl.* 1960s)   Archbishop of Hué and brother of South Vietnam President NGO DINH DIEM. Excommunicated from Roman Catholic church for his extremism.

Nguyen Cao Ky (1930–)   Prime minister of South Vietnam, 1965–67; vice-president, 1967–71. Former member of French forces; commander of South Vietnamese Air Force from 1963; leader of coup against Phan Huy Quat, 1965. Fled to United States in 1975.

Nguyen Co Thach (1925–)   Vietnamese foreign minister after unification in 1975; a deputy to LE DUC THO at the 1968–73 Paris peace negotiations. His attempts to improve relations with the United States after 1977 failed.

Nguyen Huu Tho (1910–)   Vice president, Socialist Republic of Vietnam, 1976. Lawyer and Vietnamese nationalist leader against France and the United States. Imprisoned, 1954–61; president of the National Liberation Front for South Vietnam, although not a Communist, 1961–69.

Nguyen Khanh (1927–)   South Vietnamese general, chief of staff to General DUONG VAN MINH, whom he supported in a successful coup against NGO DINH DIEM in 1963. Overthrew Minh in 1964 and was prime minister for a year.

Nguyen Van Thieu (1923–)   President of South Vietnam, 1967–75. Armed forces chief of staff, 1963–64; deputy premier and minister of defense, 1964–65; chairman of the National Leadership Committee and U.S.-backed head of state, 1965–67. He was president until the fall of Saigon in 1975.

Nie Rongzhen (1899–)   Chinese Communist leader. Born into a wealthy family, he joined the Communist Party in 1923. Active in the Long March (qv), he became the First Front Army chief of staff. Appointed a marshal of the army in 1955, with responsibility for the nuclear weapons project as head of the Academy of Science. Stripped of offices in the Cultural Revolution, he was involved in the coup against the Gang of Four that followed the death of MAO ZEDONG.

Norodom Sihanouk (1922–)   Cambodian prince and political leader. King of Cambodia, 1941–55, when he abdicated to become prime minister, holding this office until elected president in 1960. Deposed by the American-backed LON NOL in 1970, Sihanouk formed a government in exile in Beijing, campaigning in association with his former opponents, the Communist Khmer Rouge (qv). Restored as head of state in 1975, he resigned in 1976 after being arrested by POL POT. Headed government-in-exile from 1982 in territory held by Khmer Rouge soldiers on Thai border. Returned to Cambodia in 1990 to work with government for national unity, becoming titular president in 1991. In 1993 he became king for the second time.

Nosaka Sanzo (1892–1993)   Japanese Communist. After Communist activity abroad, joined the Japanese Communist Party and was imprisoned from 1923–28. In USSR and China, 1931–46. Elected to the Diet in Japan in 1946 but removed on orders of General MACARTHUR in 1950. Leader of the party in Upper House of Diet, 1956–77; chairman of the Central Committee, 1958–82.

Nu, U (1907–)   Burmese politician. Prime minister 1948–58, 1960–62. Joined Dobama Adi-ayone nationalist movement in 1937, imprisoned by British for sedition in 1940. Served in puppet BA MAW government under

Japanese occupation, but after breaking with it helped form the Anti-Fascist People's Freedom League, which negotiated Burmese independence. Became premier following assassination of AUNG SAN. Attempted to build a neutralist welfare state but fell in 1962 because of economic problems and Communist and ethnic opposition. Imprisoned from 1962–66; in exile 1969–80.

Ochirbat, Gombojavyn (1929–   )   Mongolian politician. Chairman of the Central Council of Mongolian Trade Unions from 1972–82. Joined politburo of Mongolian People's Revolutionary Party (MPRP) in 1990 and became party leader. Advocate of slow move towards a market economy.

Ochirbat, Punsalmaagiyn (1942–   )   Mongolian politician. Appointed deputy fuel and power minister in 1972, becoming minister in 1976. Led the presidium of the People's Great Hural (upper house) and elected president and ex officio armed forces leader in September 1990.

Ohira Masayoshi (1910–80)   Prime minister of Japan, 1978–80. Civil servant until entering politics in 1952, when he was elected to the Diet for the Liberal Democratic Party. Foreign minister, 1962–64, when he worked toward the China–Japan Peace and Friendship Treaty and improved relations with South Korea; minister of international trade and industry, 1968–70; finance minister, 1974–76. Died in the 1980 election campaign.

Pak Chong Hui (Park Chung Hee) (1917–79)   South Korean leader. Led a military coup against the government in 1961, becoming president in 1963. He was assassinated in 1979.

Patel, Sardar (1875–1950)   Indian politician. A lawyer, organized civil disobedience campaigns in the 1920s and was frequently imprisoned. President of the Indian National Congress in 1931 and involved in India partition negotiations. Deputy prime minister, 1947–50. As home affairs minister attempted to harmonize relations between Hindus and Muslims.

Peng Dehuai (1898–1974)   Chinese soldier. Became member of Communist Party in 1927 and led guerrilla Workers' and Peasants' Army against the Nationalists, later joining MAO ZEDONG on the Long March (qv). Commanded Chinese army in Korean War, signing Panmunjom (qv) armistice in 1953. Minister of defense and member of Politburo in 1954. Removed from office in 1959 for attacking the Great Leap Forward policy but rehabilitated in 1968.

Penn Nouth, Samdech (1906–   )   Prime minister of Prince SIHANOUK's Royal Government of National Union for Cambodia (GRUNC) in exile in Beijing. Continued as prime minister until 1976, when he resigned following Sihanouk's resignation. Succeeded by POL POT, but remained high counselor of the State Presidium.

Pham Van Dong (1906–)   Prime minister of North Vietnam from 1955; first prime minister of the Socialist Republic of Vietnam in July 1976. Involved in nationalist politics, fled to China, where he was one of founders of the Indochinese Communist Party with HO CHI MINH. Cofounder of the Viet Minh (qv), 1941, leading its delegation to the 1954 Geneva Conference.

Phibun Songkhram See PIBUL SONGGRAM.

Phizo, Angami Zapu (1907–90)   Nagaland nationalist leader. Founded the Naga National Council in 1947, demanding independence from India and organizing armed resistance. Fled to Great Britain in 1960 after being condemned to death in absentia. Nagaland was officially inaugurated as a separate state of the Indian Union in 1963, but dissent continued.

Phoumi Nosavan (*fl.* 1960s)   Laotian army officer. Commander of the Royal Laotian Army; defense minister, 1958. Overthrew SOUVANNA PHOUMA in 1960 but went into exile following failure of a coup in 1965.

Pibul Songgram (or Phibun Songkhram) (1897–1964)   Thai general and politician. Prime minister 1938–44, 1948–57. Participated in bloodless coup in 1932, becoming defense minister and army commander-in-chief. Professed admirer of Hitler. Ousted government in 1938 and ruled as autocrat until overthrown in 1944, during which period he collaborated with Japan and declared war on the United States and Britain in 1942. Returned to office as an anticommunist in 1948, taking Thailand into SEATO. Overthrown for corruption in 1957. Became a Buddhist monk in exile in Japan.

Pol Pot (1925–)   Communist prime minister of Democratic Kampuchea (Cambodia), 1976–79. Member of anti-French resistance under HO CHI MINH in 1940s. Leader of Khmer Rouge, 1963. Became prime minister following Khmer Rouge victory in civil war. Led a ruthless regime responsible for deaths of up to two million. Overthrown in 1979 after Vietnam invaded Kampuchea, sentenced to death in absentia for genocide. Led guerrilla forces from 1979–85.

Prasad, Rajendra (1884–1963)   Indian politician. President of India 1950–62. Associated with MAHATMA GANDHI from 1917, imprisoned many times for civil disobedience. President of Indian National Congress 1934, 1939 and 1947. Minister of food and agriculture in 1946 interim government; president of 1946–49 Constituent Assembly that formulated the constitution. Became president on declaration of Republic of India.

Premadasa, Ranasinghe (1924–93)   Sri Lankan politician. Entered Parliament, 1960. Prime minister after 1977 of UNP government. Sub-sequently president. Assassinated May 1993.

Prem Tinsulanonda (1920–   )   Thai soldier and politician. Army com-mander, appointed prime minister in 1980, a post he held until the 1987 coup. Appointed to the privy council by the Thai king following the coup.

Qian Qichen (1928–   )   Chinese foreign minister. Special envoy in 1983–87 Sino–Soviet consultations. Has improved China's world image since the 1989 Tiananmen Square massacre (qv).

Qiao Shi (1924–   )   Chinese politician. Member of the standing commit-tee of the Communist Party Politburo. Specialist in party discipline, organi-zation and security. Appointed by DENG XIAOPING as head of the party's Discipline Inspection Committee.

Quezón, Manuel Luis (1874–1944)   Philippine politician. President, 1935–42. Elected to the Philippines Assembly, served as Resident Commis-sioner for the Philippines in Washington, 1909–16. Member of Philippine Senate until 1935, when he was elected the first president of the Common-wealth of the Philippines. In Australia from 1942 following Japanese occu-pation.

Radhakrishnan, Sarvepalli (1888–1975)   Indian academic and politician. President of India, 1962–67. Professor of eastern religion and ethics at Oxford University, 1936–52. Ambassador to the Soviet Union, 1949–52; vice president, 1952–62.

Rahman, Sheikh Mujib ur- (1920–75)   Prime minister of Bangladesh, 1972–75. Leader of the Awami League in 1954, he campaigned for East Bengal's independence from Pakistan. Charged with treason in 1971, he was released following Indian military intervention. Became prime minister on the establishment of Bangladesh as an independent republic. Assumed dictatorial powers in 1975 and was murdered in an army coup.

Rahman, Tunku Abdul (1903–90)   First prime minister of independent Malaya, 1957–63, and of Malaysia, 1963–70. Leader of United Malays National Organization (UMNO) and chief minister, 1952–57. Played a major part in the creation of the Federation of Malaysia between Malaya, Singapore, Sarawak and Sabah, but ethnic riots in 1969 (following which he suspended the constitution) and 1970 led to his resignation.

Rajagoplachariar, Chakravarti (1878–1972)   Indian politician. Joined Indian National Congress in 1919, becoming close associate of MAHATMA GANDHI. Regularly imprisoned by the British. Premier of Madras, 1937–39. Governor-general of India, 1948–50; chief minister for Madras, 1952–54. Left the Congress Party in 1959 and helped found the Swatantra Party.

Ramos, Fidel (1928–)   President of the Philippines since July 1992, when he succeeded CORAZON AQUINO. Previously defense secretary and deputy commander-in-chief of the armed forces. A second cousin of FERDINAND MARCOS, he nonetheless joined with JUAN PONCE ENRILE in the popular revolt that followed the rigged elections of 1986.

Rao, P. (Pamulaparti) V. (Venkata) Narasimha (1921–)   Indian politician. Prime minister, 1991. Holder of almost every senior office in government and the Congress Party, he was a highly successful foreign minister under both INDIRA and RAJIV GANDHI. As prime minister, he faces mounting problems of communal violence accompanying an upsurge of Hindu nationalism.

Rhee Syngman (1875–1965)   President of South Korea, 1948–60. In exile in United States from 1912–45, acting as a spokesman for Korean independence. Returned to Korea in 1945 with U.S. support and was elected first president of the south following the division of Korea. His authoritarian military rule provoked continuous unrest, including the riots that led to his resignation in 1960. Died in exile in Hawaii.

Roh Tae Woo (1932–)   President of South Korea, 1988–93. Army general, became head of the ruling Democratic Justice Party (DJP) in 1985. Chosen by President CHUN DOO HWAN as his successor in 1988. Merged his DJP with the two major opposition parties in 1990, creating the Democratic Liberal Party. Developed "nordpolitik" (qv) and cultivated a populist image.

Romulo, Carlos Pena (1899–1985)   Philippine politician. Newspaper publisher in 1930s. Accompanied General DOUGLAS MACARTHUR to Australia in 1942 and was appointed a U.S. Army general. Philippines representative at the United Nations; president of the General Assembly, 1949–50, and of the Security Council, 1956. Active in 1955 Bandung Conference. Held various offices under President FERDINAND MARCOS, including foreign minister 1968–1984. Supported imposition of martial law in 1974.

Roxas, Manuel (1892–1948)   Philippine politician. President, 1946–48. A lawyer, he entered local politics in 1917, later becoming Speaker of the House of Representatives. Led Independence Mission to Washington in 1932 that led to the 1935 constitution. Served in pro-Japanese government under occupation but was not tried as a collaborator. Backed by General DOUGLAS MACARTHUR, he became president in 1946 but his period in office was marked by corruption.

Sarit Thanarat (1908–63)   Prime minister of Thailand, 1958–63. After serving as minister of defense and armed forces commander-in-chief, he emerged as prime minister following a coup. Initiated educational and economic development.

Sato Eisaku (1901–75)   Prime minister of Japan, 1964–72. Civil servant before entering politics in 1948. Minister of postal services, 1951–52; minister of construction, 1952–53. Forced from the cabinet following corruption allegations in 1954, he returned as minister of finance from 1958–60; minister of international trade and industry, 1961–62. As premier, negotiated the return of Okinawa and other Ryukyu islands in 1972. Was awarded the Nobel Peace Prize for his efforts to preserve Japan as a nuclear-free zone, 1974.

Savang Vatthana (1907–81)   King of Laos, 1959–75. Failure to gain international guarantees for Laos following Vietnam War prompted his abdication in 1975.

Saw Maung (1929–   )   Burmese general. Led the military coup in September 1988 that abolished all state institutions and established the State Law and Order Restoration Council (SLORC), which he chaired.

Sayem, Abusadat Mohammed (1916–   )   President of Bangladesh, 1975–77, following service as chief justice.

Senanayake, Don Stephen (1884–1952)   Sri Lanka politician. Rubber planter, elected to the Ceylon Legislative Council in 1922, becoming vice president of the State Council in 1936. Minister of agriculture and land, 1931–47. Negotiated independence from Britain in 1947 as leader of the United National Party.

Seni Pramoj (*fl.* 1940s)   Prime minister of Thailand, 1945–46. Ambassador to the United States during World War II and active in the "Free Thai" movement. Leader of the Prachatiphat (Democrat) Party, 1975.

Sharif, Nawaz (1948–   )   Pakistani politician. Prime minister after October 1990 when his Islamic Democratic Alliance swept to victory in the general election, inflicting a crushing defeat on BENAZIR BHUTTO. A lawyer, he was chief minister of the Punjab, 1985–90. He lost office in 1993.

Shastri, Lal Bahadur (1904–66)   Prime minister of India, 1964–66. Joined Congress Party, 1920. Minister for railways and transport, 1952–58, later minister for commerce and minister for home affairs. Left office to work in party organization in 1963 but returned in 1964 to succeed JAWAHARLAL NEHRU as prime minister. Collapsed and died at end of Soviet-sponsored talks at Tashkent to secure peace between India and Pakistan following 1965 war.

Shintaro Abe (1924–   )   Japanese politician. Elected to parliament in

1958. Minister of agriculture, forestry and fisheries, 1974; chief cabinet secretary, 1977; chairman of Liberal Democratic Party (LDP) policy research, 1979; minister of international trade and industry, 1981; foreign minister, 1982; chairman of LDP general council, 1986; LDP secretary-general, 1987. He returned to the back benches in 1989.

Sihanouk, Norodom. See NORODOM SIHANOUK.

Singh, Vishwanath Pratap (1931–)   Prime minister of India, 1989–90. A former Congress (I) member, he held various posts including that of defense minister under INDIRA GANDHI. He broke with Congress in 1987. President of the Janata Dal coalition that defeated RAJIV GANDHI in the November 1989 election. His minority government was weakened by growing Hindu nationalism, and increasing violence led to the fall of his government in November 1990.

Son Sen (1930–)   Cambodian politician. Teacher who became a Khmer Rouge leader and was responsible in 1975 for driving the population from Phnom Penh, beginning a three-year reign of terror in which as many as two million Cambodians died. Returned to Cambodia in 1991 as member of coalition Supreme National Council to restore peace.

Souphanouvong (1909–)   Laotian politician and prince. President of Lao People's Democratic Republic since 1975. Founding member of Communist Pathet Lao (qv), 1950; became vice premier but was imprisoned and escaped to lead procommunist military group; chairman, Joint National Political Council, 1974–75. In recent years, a figurehead only. Half-brother of SOUVANNA PHOUMA.

Souvanna Phouma (1901–)   Laotian politician and prince. Leader of Laos on independence in 1949; headed a royalist-neutralist government during the civil war, 1962–75. Counselor to Government of Laos, 1976.

Suharto, Raden (1921–)   Indonesian military and political leader. President sinced 1968. Member of Japanese-organized Java Defense Force, 1942. Guerrilla fighter against the Dutch, 1946–49. Army chief of staff, 1965–68, he took emergency powers in 1966, replaced SUKARNO in 1967, and was elected president in 1968. A right-wing dictator, he severed links with China, ended the confrontation against Malaysia, attempted to work with the United States and Great Britain, and restored domestic stability. His regime has faced increasing opposition from Islamic fundamentalists.

Sukarno, Ahmed (1901–70)   Indonesian politician, known as Bung Karno ("The Leader"). President, 1949–68. Founding member of movement for Indonesian independence, the PNI, 1927. In prison or in exile, 1929–44, he welcomed Japanese occupation in 1942. Declared Indonesia independent from the Dutch in August 1945, beginning a four-year struggle that culminated in his appointment as president in 1949 on independence. Despite the success of the Bandung Conference in 1955, his authoritarian rule aroused resistance from 1956 on. Confrontation with Malaysia coincided with economic stagnation from 1963–65 and he lost executive power to General SUHARTO in 1966, though he retained the title of president until 1968.

Suzuki Kantaro (1867–1948)   Japanese naval officer. Prime minister, 1945. Promoted to admiral in 1923 and appointed a privy councilor; wounded in the February 1936 military rising. Appointed by HIROHITO in April 1945 to head the government that negotiated Japan's surrender.

Suzuki Zenko (1911–   )   Japanese politician. Prime minister, 1980–82. Owner of a fishing business, entered politics as a socialist in 1947 but joined the Liberal Democratic Party in 1959. Became premier to promote the "politics of harmony."

Tanaka Kakuei (1918–93)   Japanese politician. Prime minister, 1972–74. Elected to the Diet in 1947 and survived corruption allegations. Secretary general of the Liberal Democratic Party (LDP), 1966; minister of postal services and minister of finance, before becoming minister of international trade and industry in 1971. Removed as premier after allegations of involvement in the Lockheed scandal that led to his arrest in 1976. Found guilty but continued to wield political influence until suffering a stroke in 1985.

Taruc, Luis (1913–   )   Philippine political leader. Joined the Socialist Party and the Philippines Anti-Fascist Front in 1935. Formed the Hukbalahap (qv) on Luzon and became its commander in 1942; controlled the rural areas of the island by 1945. Elected to the House of Representatives in 1946, but political pressure from the United States prevented him taking his seat. Led underground Huk movement until his arrest and imprisonment in 1954. Released in 1968.

Teng Hsiao-p'ing   See DENG XIAOPING.

Thanom Khittikachorn (1911–   )   Prime minister of Thailand, 1958, 1963–73. Army officer, became head of government after a coup. Lost power following a student revolt in 1973.

Thant, U (1909–74)   United Nations secretary general, 1962–71. A Burmese diplomat, he joined the UN in 1957. Acting secretary general, 1961. As secretary general he established a UN peacekeeping force in Cyprus, made cease-fire arrangements after the 1967 Six-Day War, and eased acceptance of Communist China as a UN member with a seat on the Security Council.

Ton Duc Thang (1888–   )   President of North Vietnam on the death of

HO CHI MINH, 1969. Became the first president of the Socialist Republic of Vietnam, July 1976.

Tran Do (*fl.* 1960s)   Vietnamese Communist military leader. Deputy commander of forces in South Vietnam, prominent in the 1968 Tet offensive.

Tran Kim Tuyen (*fl.* 1950s)   Head of South Vietnamese intelligence. Left North Vietnam in 1954 to organize security for NGO DIN NHU with CIA backing. Involved in plot to overthrow South Vietnam regime but exiled by Nhu before the coup.

Tran Thien Khiem (1925–   )   South Vietnamese politician. A leading member of the coup against DUONG VAN MINH, 1964; defense minister and armed forces commander in chief, 1964; ambassador to the United States, 1964–65; ambassador to Republic of China (Taiwan), 1965–68; deputy prime minister, 1969; prime minister, 1969–75. Fled to Taiwan, April 1975.

Tran Van Don (1917–   )   South Vietnamese army officer. Born in France. Fought with the French against the Viet Minh (qv), becoming a senior officer under NGO DINH DIEM. Involved in the coup against Diem. Fled to United States in 1975.

Tran Van Huong (1903–   )   President of South Vietnam, 21–28 April 1975. Fought with Viet Minh (qv) against French. Mayor of Saigon, 1954; prime minister, 1964–65, 1968–69; vice president, 1971–75.

Tran Van Tra (1918–   )   Vietnamese military leader. Viet Minh (qv) activist. Deputy commander of Communist forces in South Vietnam. Led attack on Saigon during Tet offensive, 1968. Purged for criticizing party leadership after his history of the 1975 offensive was banned.

Truong Chinh (1908–   )   North Vietnamese Communist theoretician. A founding member of the Indochinese Communist Party, 1930. Demoted for failure of land reform program, 1955, but retained political influence.

Tsedenbal Yumzhagiyn (1916–91)   Mongolian People's Republic leader, 1952–84. Entered government in 1939. Prime minister, 1952, combining post with leadership of the Communist Party. Became head of state in 1974. Supported Soviet Union in Sino–Soviet conflict. Removed from office in 1974 under Soviet pressure, expelled from Communist Party and stripped of all titles in 1990.

Uno Sosuke (1922–   )   Japanese politician. After serving as foreign minister he became prime minister in 1989, but was forced to resign after 69 days in office following revelations of extramarital affairs in the 1960s.

U Thant   See THANT, U

Van Tien Dung (1917–)   North Vietnamese political leader. Directed logistics at battle of Dien Bien Phu in 1954 and under VO NGUYEN GIAP in the 1975 attack on Saigon. Defense minister in Socialist Republic of Vietnam after 1975.

Vo Nguyen Giap (1912–86)   Foremost Vietnamese military leader. Joined Communist Party in 1933 and was involved in anti-French uprisings. Cofounder of the Viet Minh (qv), 1941; Viet Minh commander-in-chief, 1946–54, defeating the French at Dien Bien Phu (qv), which led to the collapse of French rule. Deputy prime minister, minister of defense, and commander-in-chief, Democratic Republic of Vietnam until 1976. Vice-premier and minister of national defense, Socialist Republic of Vietnam, from July 1976. Retired in 1982.

Wang Hongwen (1934–92)   Chinese politician, member of the Gang of Four (qv). A cotton mill worker, formed the Shanghai Workers' Revolutionary Rebel General Headquarters in 1967 during the Cultural Revolution (qv) and led a general strike, ousting the authorities and becoming vice chairman of the Shanghai Revolutionary Committee. Rapidly becoming a powerful figure, he was elected to the Communist Party Central Committee in 1969; appointed vice chairman of the party in 1973, and of the influential Central Military Commission in 1975. Arrested in October 1976 following the death of MAO ZEDONG with the other Gang of Four members. Tried in December 1980 and sentenced to life imprisonment.

Wang Ming (1907–)   Chinese Communist leader. Followed Russian line in ideological disputes between China and the Soviet Union.

Westmoreland, William Childs (1914–)   U.S. Army general. Served in World War II and Korea. Commander of U.S. combat forces in Vietnam in August 1964 after the Tonkin Gulf Resolution (qv). Left Vietnam in 1968 to become U.S. Army chief of staff.

Xuan Thuy (1912–)   North Vietnamese politician. Foreign minister, 1963–65; led delegation at Paris peace talks, 1968. Negotiated with Kissinger as deputy to LE DUC THO.

Yahya, Aga Mohammad Khan (1917–80)   President of Pakistan, 1969–71. Commander of the Pakistan army, 1966; appointed martial law administrator by AYUB KHAN, 1969. Assumed presidency, 1969. His refusal to accept the results of the East Pakistan elections in 1970–71, in which the Awami League triumphed, led to civil war over Bangladesh independence, war with India, and his resignation. Under house arrest, 1972–74.

Yang Shangkun (1908–)   Chinese Communist leader. Born into a wealthy family, joined the Communist Party in 1926. Originally a member of the pro-Soviet faction, he emerged as a leading supporter of MAO ZEDONG and participated in the Long March (qv). Denounced by Mao in the Cultural Revolution, (qv) he spent 13 years in prison before becoming president of China with the backing of DENG XIAOPING.

Yan Jiangan (1905–   )   Nationalist Chinese politician. A banker, served in post-World War II Nationalist government and moved to Taiwan in 1949. Chairman of the Bank of Taiwan and involved in management of economy. Prime minister, 1963–72; vice president, 1966–75; president, 1975–78.

Ye Jianying (1897–1989)   Chinese Communist military leader. Born into a wealthy family, he joined the Communist Party in 1924 and was a long-term ally of ZHOU ENLAI. Became an army marshal. Survived the purges of the Cultural Revolution (qv) and headed the military-party conspiracy against the Gang of Four (qv) following the death of MAO ZEDONG.

Yon Hyong Muk (1925–   )   Premier of North Korea, 1988–92. A reformist technocrat, married to a cousin of Kim Il Sung, he began a series of historic dialogues with the South Korean prime minister, Kang Young Hoon, in September 1990.

Yoshida Shigeru (1878–1967)   Prime minister of Japan, 1946–54. Pre-World War II ambassador to Italy and Great Britain. Leader of Liberal Party, 1946. Advocated alliance with the U.S. and limited rearmament. Resigned in 1954 because of dissatisfaction with his style of leadership.

Zahir (1914–   )   Muhammad Zahir Shah, the last king of Afghanistan, reigning from 1933 until his overthrow by a military coup in 1973, when he went into exile in Europe.

Zhao Ziyang (1918–   )   Former general secretary of Chinese Communist Party. Denounced as an agent of LIU SHAOQI, 1967. Pioneered agricultural and industrial reforms in Sichuan after 1976. Joined politburo, 1977. Prime minister in 1980. Implemented modernization program of DENG XIAOPING, becoming Communist Party general secretary in 1987. Criticized for his reform, he lost the premiership to LI PENG in 1988. Stripped of all posts in June 1989 for "counterrevolutionary rebellion."

Zhou Enlai (1898–1976)   Prime minister of China, 1949–76. Organizer of Communist revolt in Shanghai, 1927. MAO's leading adviser on urban revolutionary activities, 1931. Represented Communists in talks with U.S. mission to mediate in Chinese civil war, 1945–47. Combined premiership with office of foreign minister, 1949–58. Represented China at Geneva

Conference, 1954, and led détente with the United States from 1969 to 1974.

Zhou Nan (1927–)   Chinese diplomat. Assistant foreign minister, 1984–90. Head of Hong Kong branch of Xinhua News Agency (qv)—i.e., virtual Chinese ambassador to Hong Kong.

Zia, Khaleda (1945–)   Bangladeshi politician. First woman prime minister of Bangladesh, March 1991. The widow of President Zia ur-Rahman, who was assassinated in a 1981 coup. Leader of Bangladesh National Party, which won the 1991 elections—the first free elections in Bangladeshi history. Her victory followed the downfall in December 1990 of the military dictator General HUSSAIN MOHAMMAD ERSHAD.

Zia ul-Haq, Mohammed (1924–88)   President of Pakistan, 1978–88. An army general, leader of the coup that ousted ZULFIKAR BHUTTO in 1977, following disturbances over allegations of electoral corruption. Ruled by martial law and instituted an Islamic state. Confirmed as president in a referendum, 1984. Elected to office for five years in 1985, he ended martial law shortly after. Killed in August 1988 when a plane in which he was traveling exploded.

NEW NATIONS OF ASIA 1945–1994

Bangladesh	Prior to 1947 part of British India; 1947–71 known as East Pakistan.
Bhutan	Formerly semiautonomous kingdom linked to British India.
Brunei	Formerly protectorate in British Borneo.
Cambodia	Formerly part of French Indochina.
India	Formerly part of British India, which then included present-day Pakistan, Bangladesh and Myanmar (Burma).
Indonesia	Formerly Dutch East Indies.
Laos	Formerly part of French Indochina.
Malaysia	Formerly the Federation of Malaya (to 1963), previously known as the Straits Settlements and the Federated Malay States.
Mongolia	Prior to 1924 Outer Mongolia.
Myanmar	(Burma until 1989). Formerly part of British India.
North Korea	Formerly part of Japanese-controlled Korea (1910–45); created separate state in 1948.
Pakistan	Prior to 1947 part of British India.
Philippines	American colony from 1898 until independence in 1946.
Singapore	British Crown colony, then part of Malaysia, 1963–65.
Sri Lanka	(Ceylon until 1972). Formerly British colony.
Taiwan	Ceded to Japan by China in 1895, returned to China in 1945. From 1949 has been base for Nationalist Chinese state.
Vietnam	Part of French Indochina to 1954 when separated into North and South; reunited as a single state in 1975.

Note: Thailand has never been a possession of a foreign empire.

APPENDIX II

RECENT PLACE NAME CHANGES AND CHANGES IN ENGLISH TRANSLITERATION

Old Name/Spelling	New Name/Alternative Spelling
Aksai Chin	Aksayqin
Amoy	Xianen
Benares	Varanasi
Borneo	Kalimantan
Burma	Myanmar
Canton	Guangzhou
Cape Cormorin	Kanya Kumari
Celebes	Sulawesi
Central Provinces	Madhya Pradesh
Ceylon	Sri Lanka
Chungking	Chongqing
Dacca	Dhaka
Dutch East Indies	Indonesia
East Pakistan	Bangladesh
Foochow	Fuzhou
Formosa	Taiwan
Hankow	Hankou
Indochina	Vietnam, Laos, Cambodia
Inner Mongolia	Nei Mongol
Jehol	Chengde

Jesselton	Kota Kinabulu
Kampuchea	Cambodia
Kianghsi	Jiangxi
Macassar	Ujung Pandang
Madras (state of)	Tamil Nadu
Mukden	Shenyang
Mysore	Karnataka
Nanking	Nanjing
North East Frontier Agency	Arunachal Pradesh
North Borneo	Sabah
Peking	Beijing
Port Swettenham	Port Kelang
Rangoon	Yangon
Saigon	Ho Chi Minh City
Shensi	Shaanxi
Siam	Thailand
Soochow	Suzhou
Szechwan	Sichuan
Tachai	Dazhai
Taipei	Taibei
Tibet	Xizang
Tientsin	Tianjin
Trichinopoly	Tiruchirappalli
Tsing-tao	Quingdao
United Provinces	Uttar Pradesh
Whampoa	Huangpu

BIBLIOGRAPHICAL NOTE

This volume on Asia since 1945 has been closely modeled on Chris Cook, ed., *Facts On File World Political Almanac* (New York: Facts On File, 2d edition 1992; 3d edition forthcoming). As with that book, this one could not have been compiled without constant reference to newspapers. The *Facts On File News Digest*, published weekly, and its compilation volume, *The Facts On File Yearbook* (New York: Facts On File), published annually since 1941, provide a convenient, well-indexed pathway into this wealth of material. Other annual publications, such as the *Statesman's Year-Book* (London: Macmillan and New York: St. Martin's), the *Annual Register* (London and New York: Longman), the excellent *Political Handbook of the World* (Binghamton, New York: CSA Publications, State University of New York) and the numerous official yearbooks produced by individual governments, provide a wealth of supplementary statistical material. In Britain, the annual editions of *Pears Cyclopedia* (London: Pelham Books) provide a convenient source of chronological information.

Population and urbanization figures can be extracted from the UN's *Demographic Yearbook* (New York: Department of Economic and Social Affairs, Statistical Office, United Nations). For lists of events the Facts On File chronologies by decade, *Day by Day: The 1940s, Day by Day: The 1950s* and so forth are of particular help (New York: Facts On File; the 1980s volume is forthcoming), as is D. J. Sagar, *Major Political Events in Indo-China, 1945–1990* (New York: Facts on File, 1991). An immensely useful publication is Thomas T. Mackie and Richard Rose, eds., *International Almanac of Electoral History*, 3d edition (London: Macmillan, 1991).

For reliable bibliographic guidance for individual countries, the books cited in George Kurian, *Encyclopedia of the Third World*, 3d edition (New York: Facts On File, 1987) should be consulted.

It is hoped that the *Asian Political Almanac* will stimulate readers to take a further interest in these countries. The following titles will help give historical background for the nations of contemporary Asia.

For the Indian subcontinent see Stanley Wolpert, *A New History of India*, 4th edition (New York: Oxford University Press, 1993) and Judith M. Brown, *Modern India: The Origins of an Asian Democracy* (Delhi and New York: Oxford University Press, 1985); see also Judith M. Brown, *Gandhi: Prisoner of Hope* (New Haven: Yale University Press, 1990). On partition, see Anita I. Singh, *The Origins of the Partition of India, 1936–1947* (New York: Oxford University Press, 1987). Post-partition India is discussed in S. Gopal, *Jawaharlal Nehru* (London: Jonathan Cape, 3 vols., 1975–84). India's relations with other states after 1947 are considered in Charles H. Heimsath and Surjit Mansingh, *A Diplomatic History of Modern India* (Bombay: Allied Publishers, 1972) and W. J. Barnds, *India, Pakistan and the Great Powers* (New York: Council on Foreign Relations/Praeger, 1972). See also W. Norman Brown, *The United States and India, Pakistan, Bangladesh*, 3d edition (Cambridge: Harvard University Press, 1972). India's agricultural development is considered in B. M. Bhatia, *Famines in India, 1860–1965*, 2d edition (Bombay and New York: Asia Publishing House, 1967) and Francine R. Frankel, *India's Green Revolution: Economic Gains and Costs* (Princeton, New Jersey: Princeton University Press, 1971). See also B. R. Tomlinson, *The Economy of Modern India, 1860–1970* (New York: Cambridge University Press, 1993).

For background on the emergence of Pakistan, see S. F. Mahmud, *A Concise History of Indo-Pakistan* (New York: Oxford University Press, 1989) and Stanley Wolpert, *Jinnah of Pakistan* (New York: Oxford University Press, 1984). The breakup of Pakistan and the emergence of Bangladesh is considered in Kalim Siddiqui, *Conflict, Crisis and War in Pakistan* (London: Macmillan, 1972); Rounaq Jahan, *Pakistan: Failure in National Integration* (New York: Columbia University Press, 1972); Brig J. Singh, *The Dismemberment of Pakistan: The 1971 Indo-Pak War* (New York and Bombay: South Asia Books, 1988); Richard Siddon, *War and Secession: Pakistan, India and the Creation of Bangladesh* (Berkeley: University of California Press, 1991); and Wayne A. Wilcox, *The Emergence of Bangladesh* (Washington, D.C.: American Enterprise Institute, 1973). See also Craig Baxter, *Historical Dictionary of Bangladesh* (Metuchen, New Jersey: Scarecrow Press, 1989). Foreign policy is examined in S. M. Burke, *Pakistan's Foreign Policy: An Historical Analysis* (London: Oxford University Press, 1973). The Bhutto years are considered in S. J. Burki, *Pakistan Under Bhutto, 1971–1977*, 2d edition (Basingstoke: Macmillan, 1988). On Sri Lanka see A. J. Wilson, *Politics in Sri Lanka, 1947–1979*, 2d edition (London: Macmillan, 1979); also useful is Francis Robinson, ed., *The Cambridge Encyclopedia of India, Pakistan, Bang-*

ladesh, Sri Lanka, Nepal, Bhutan and the Maldives (Cambridge and New York: Cambridge University Press, 1989).

On Afghanistan see Louis Dupree, *Afghanistan* (Princeton: Princeton University Press, 1973), and Ludwig W. Adamec, *Historical Dictionary of Afghanistan* (Metuchen, New Jersey: Scarecrow Press, 1991). On the civil war and Soviet intervention see Mark Urban, *War in Afghanistan*, 2d ed. (New York: St. Martin's Press, 1991); Hafizullah Emadi, *State, Revolution and Superpowers in Afghanistan* (Westport, Connecticut: Greenwood Press, 1990); and Riaz M. Khan, *Untying the Afghan Knot* (Durham, North Carolina: Duke University Press, 1991).

For Southeast Asia, see D. G. Hall, *A History of South-East Asia*, 4th edition (London: Macmillan and New York: St. Martin's Press, 1981) and J. M. Pluvier, *South-East Asia from Colonialism to Independence* (Kuala Lumpur: Oxford University Press, 1974). For the histories of individual countries see J. F. Cady, *A History of Modern Burma* (Ithaca, New York: Cornell University Press, 1958); David K. Wyatt, *Thailand: a Short History* (New Haven: Yale University Press, 1984); Martin Stuart-Fox, *Historical Dictionary of Laos* (Metuchen, New Jersey: Scarecrow Press, 1992); Sisouk Na Champassak, *Storm Over Laos: A Contemporary History* (New York: Praeger, 1961); Jane Hamilton-Merritt, *Tragic Mountains: The Hmong, the Americans and the Secret Wars for Laos* (Bloomington: Indiana University Press, 1993); and Joseph J. Zasloff, *Laos: Beyond the Revolution* (New York: St. Martin's Press, 1991).

On Cambodia, see David P. Chandler, *A History of Cambodia* (Boulder, Colorado: Westview Press, 1992) and *The Tragedy of Cambodian History: Politics, War and Revolution since 1945* (New Haven: Yale University Press, 1992); Craig Etcheson, *The Rise and Demise of Democratic Kampuchea* (Boulder, Colorado: Westview Press, 1984); Karl D. Jackson, ed., *Cambodia 1975–1978: Rendezvous with Death* (Princeton: Princeton University Press, 1992); Milton E. Osborne, *Before Kampuchea: Preludes to Tragedy* (London and Boston: Allen & Unwin, 1979); and William Shawcross, *Sideshow: Kissinger, Nixon and the Destruction of Cambodia* (New York: Simon and Schuster, 1979).

A good introduction to the history of Vietnam is Frances FitzGerald, *Fire in the Lake* (New York: Vintage Books 1973); Stanley Karnow, *Vietnam: A History* (New York: Viking, 1983) has become a standard work. See also Joseph Buttinger, *Vietnam: A Dragon Defiant: A Short History of Vietnam* (New York: Praeger, 1972), and Neil L. Jamieson, *Understanding Vietnam* (Berkeley: University of California Press, 1993). Ralph B. Smith, *An International History of the Vietnam War:* Volume I, *Revolution versus Containment*, and Volume II, *The Struggle for South East Asia, 1961–65* (London: Macmillan, 1983 and 1985) are the first two of four volumes placing the war in an international context. Other good recent works on the war are James P. Harrison, *The Endless War* (New York: Free Press, 1982), and George M. Kahin, *Intervention: How America Became Involved in Vietnam* (New York: Alfred A. Knopf, 1986). A good single-volume account of the French and American Vietnam wars is Marilyn B. Young, *The Vietnam Wars, 1945–1990* (New York: HarperCollins, 1991). For a crucial episode, see James Cable, *The Geneva Conference of 1954 on Indochina* (Basingstoke: Macmillan, 1986). Anthony Short, *The Origins of the Vietnam War* (London and New York: Longman, 1989) is a useful modern summary; see also the Vietnam chapter in John M. Dunn, *Modern Revolutions*, 2d edition (Cambridge: Cambridge University Press, 1988).

For an overview of Indonesian history, see M. C. Ricklefs, *A History of Modern Indonesia, c. 1300 to the Present* (Bloomington: Indiana University Press, 1981), and Wilfred T. Neill, *Twentieth-Century Indonesia* (New York: Columbia University Press, 1973). The Indonesian nationalist movement is considered in Bernhard Dahm, *History of Indonesia in the Twentieth Century* (London: Pall Mall Books, 1971).

For an introduction to Malaysia and Singapore, see Barbara W. Andaya and Leonard Y. Andaya, *A History of Malaysia* (London: Macmillan, 1982 and New York: St. Martin's Press, 1984), or N. J. Ryan, *A History of Malaysia and Singapore* (Kuala Lumpur and New York: Oxford University Press, 1976); Amarjit Kaur, *Historical Dictionary of Malaysia* (Metuchen, New Jersey: Scarecrow Press, 1993); K. Mulliner, *Historical Dictionary of Singapore* (Metuchen, New Jersey: Scarecrow Press, 1991); and Ernest C. T. Chew and Edwin Lee, eds., *A History of Singapore* (Singapore and New York: Oxford University Press, 1991). See also Anthony Short, *The Communist Insurrection in Malaya, 1948–1960* (London: Muller, 1975).

For the Philippines, see Teodoro A. Agoncillo, *A Short History of the Philippines* (Quezon City: University of the Philippines, 1965); Milton E. Osborn, *Region of Revolt: Focus on Southeast Asia* (Ringwood, Victoria: Penguin, 1971); Daniel B. Schirmer, ed., *The Philippines Reader* (Boston: South End Press, 1987); and Leon Wolff, *Little Brown Brother* (New York: Oxford University Press, 1992). On Marcos see Sterling Seagrave, *The Marcos Dynasty* (New York: Fawcett, 1990).

On Korea see Robert T. Oliver, *A History of the Korean People in Modern Times: 1800 to the Present* (Newark: University of Delaware Press, 1993). On the war see Bruce Cumings, *The Origins of the Korean War* (Princeton: Princeton University Press, 2 vols., 1983 and 1990); Jon Halliday and Bruce Cumings, *Korea: The Unknown War* (London: Viking and New York: Viking Penguin, 1988), a concise and well-illustrated volume; Max Hastings, *The Korean War* (New York: Simon and Schuster, 1987); and Richard Whelan, *Drawing the Line: The Korean War, 1950–1953* (Boston: Little, Brown,

1990). For a glimpse of the charismatic Supreme Commander, see *Mac-Arthur in Korea: The Naked Emperor* (New York: Simon and Schuster, 1982).

The two giants of Asia are China and Japan. For an introduction to Japan see Mikiso Hane, *Modern Japan: A Historical Survey* (Boulder, Colorado: Westview Press, 1992), or W. G. Beasley, *The Modern History of Japan*, 2d edition (London: Weidenfeld & Nicolson, 1973), or Peter Duus, ed., *The Cambridge History of Japan*, Vol. 6: *The Twentieth Century* (New York: Cambridge University Press, 1989). Martin E. Weinstein, *Japan's Postwar Defense Policy, 1947–1968* (New York: Columbia University Press, 1971) examines the peaceful role of Japan in the postwar world, while Edwin O. Reischauer, *Japan: The Story of a Nation*, 4th ed. (New York: Alfred A. Knopf, 1991) and Akira Iriye and Warren I. Cohen, eds., *The United States and Japan in the Postwar World* (Lexington: University Press of Kentucky, 1989) deal with the character of Japanese-American postwar relations. Karel Van Wolferen, *The Enigma of Japanese Power* (London: Macmillan and New York: Alfred A. Knopf, 1989) poses questions about Japan's role as an economic superpower with little military power.

A good general history of China is John King Fairbank, *China: A New History* (Cambridge: Belknap Press of Harvard University Press, 1992). For China since the Communist revolution, see Colin Mackerras, *The Cambridge Handbook of Contemporary China* (New York: Cambridge University Press, 1992); Ross Terrill, *China in Our Time* (New York: Simon and Schuster, 1992); and Roderick MacFarquhar, ed., *The Cambridge History of China*, Vol. 15: *The People's Republic, Part 2: Revolutions Within the Chinese Revolution, 1966–1982* (New York: Cambridge University Press, 1991). Jurgen Domes, *The Internal Politics of China, 1949–72* (New York: Praeger, 1973) and J. M. H. Lindbeck, ed., *China: Management of a Revolutionary Society* (Seattle: University of Washington Press, 1971) give some insight into the dynamics of party leadership. Jan Myrdal and Gun Kossle, *China: The Revolution Continued* (New York: Pantheon, 1970) deals with the Cultural Revolution. For China's foreign relations, see Marius B. Jansen, *Japan and China: From War to Peace, 1894–1972* (Chicago: Rand McNally, 1975); Wang Gungwu, *China and the World Since 1949* (London: Macmillan, 1977); and John Gittings, *The World and China, 1922–1972* (London: Eyre Methuen, 1974). For relations with the United States, see J. K. Fairbank, *The United States and China* (Cambridge: Harvard University Press, 1971).

INDEX

Page numbers followed by b indicate biography; page numbers followed by g indicate glossary.

A

Abdul Halim Maudzam Shah, Sultan 43
Abdullah, Muhammad 188, 209b
Abdul Rahman *See* Rahman, Tunku Abdul
Abdul Razak 209b
Abeygoonasekera, Ossie 148
Achariya, Tanka 45
Adipati (Commander) 171g
Afghanistan: basic data 1; border conflicts 178, 193, 197; chronology 31–32; civil war 104, 171, 180, 186–187, 191; constitution 56–57; coups 56, 108; defense and armed forces 112; heads of state and government 34–35; international organizations 75, 79; landmarks and historic sites 177, 180, 202; legislature 56–57, 189, 191; political parties 56, 104, 114–115, 186, 194, 206; population and ethnic composition 151–152, 194, 197, 202; provinces and regions 194; refugees 169, 186; Saur Revolution 200; terrorism 106, 191; transportation and travel 199; treaties, alliances and agreements 80–82, 86, 91, 111; UN peacekeeping operations 194, 205
AFPFL *See* Anti-Fascist People's Freedom League (AFPFL) (Myanmar)
Agrarian Law (China) 14

Agrarian Party (South Korea) 145
agreements, diplomatic 79–89
Agus Salim Haji 209b
Ahle Sunnat 141
Ahmad Shah, Sultan 43
Ahmad Tajuddin 36
Ahmed, Fakhruddin Ali 40
Ahmed, Kazi Zafar 36
Ahmed, Khandakar Mushtaq 24, 35
Ahmed, Moudoud 36
Ahmed, Shehabuddin 35
Ahmed, Tajuddin 35
Aidit, Dipa Nusantra 109, 209b
air piracy 105–107
Ajmer 171g
Akali Dal 119, 134, 171g
Akbar, Emperor 201
Akihito 17, 30, 41, 182, 209b
Algeria 113
Ali, Chaudri Mohammed 47
Ali, M. Mansoor 36
Ali, Mohammed 47
Ali Sastroamidjojo 209–210b
Alliance of Eight 171g
Alliance of Nationalist, Democratic and Peace Forces (Vietnam) 131
Alliance of Seven 171g
Alliance Party (Malaysia) 122, 138
All-Nippon Airways 188
Amaral, Francisco do 39
Ambedkar, Bhimrao Ramji 210b
Ambon 171g
Amethyst Incident 171g
Amin, Hafizullah 34–34n, 35, 109, 210b
Amin, Nurul 47
Amirthalingam, Appapillai 109
Amritsar 171–172g, 201
Amur River 172g
Ananda Mahidol (Rama VIII) 12, 51
Anand Panyarachun 52
Angkor 172g
Angola 85
An Loc 172g
Annam 172g
Anpo (U.S.-Japan Security Treaty) 172g

Antarctic Treaty 111
Anti-Fascist People's Freedom League (AFPFL) (Myanmar) 123, 139
Anyaoku, Emeka 76
April 4th Incident 172g
Aquino, Benigno 23, 25–27, 109, 196, 210b
Aquino, Corazon Cojuangco (Cory) 210b; Communist/Muslim insurgency 101; elections 28, 32, 143, 196; Enrile and 214; as head of state 48; Honasan and 217; political parties 125; revolution 196; Romulo and 229
Arakan League for Democracy 140
Arakan Rohingya Islamic Front (ARIF) (Myanmar) 199
Araujo, Arnaldo 39
area, land 1–9
Argentina 113
armed forces 112
arms control agreements 111
ASA *See* Association of Southeast Asia (ASA)
Asanuma Inejiro 108, 210b
ASEAN *See* Association of South East Asian Nations (ASEAN)
Ashida Hitoshi 41
Asian and Pacific Council (ASPAC) 83–84, 87–88, 172g
ASPAC *See* Asian and Pacific Council (ASPAC)
Aspri 172g
assassinations 108–110 *See also names of specific leaders*
Association of Southeast Asia (ASA) 86–87, 172g
Association of South East Asian Nations (ASEAN) 73–74, 83–84, 87
atomic bombs *See* nuclear weapons and tests
Atomic Energy Commission (India) 13
August Revolution 172g
Aung San 45, 108, 203, 210b, 211, 226
Aung San Suu Kyi 211b
Australia: international organizations 75–77, 172, 190; trea-

245